והגדת לבנך
THE OHR
SOMAYACH
HAGGADAH

Based on the lectures of
RABBI UZIEL MILEVSKY
Edited by Moshe Schapiro

OHR SOMAYACH INSTITUTIONS
TARGUM/FELDHEIM

First published 1998

ISBN 1-56871-137-9

Translation of the Haggadah text taken from *The Yeinah Shel Torah Haggadah* with permission of Feldheim Publishers

Published by:
Targum Press Inc.
22700 West Eleven Mile Rd.
Southfield MI 48034

Distrbuted by:
Feldheim Publishers
200 Airport Executive Park
Nanuet NY 10954

Distributed in Israel by:
Targum Press Ltd.
POB 43170
Jerusalem 91430

Printed in Israel

Dedicated in memory of
my teacher, Rebbi, and friend

Rabbi Y. Uziel Milevsky, *zt"l.*

May this Hagaddah transmit his
wisdom, Torah, and novel interpretations
to future generations, as he himself did
throughout his life.
As he changed the lives of all of his students,
may he continue to do so
through the depth of his writings.

S. Richard Gordon & Family
Toronto, Canada

Dedicated to the memory of

Rabbeinu Harav Hagaon
Yeruchem Uziel Milevsky, *zt"l*

As have the great Sages of our history,
so too will the enduring influence and enormity of
Rav Uziel's Torah scholarship and teaching
pervade the generations of
Klal Yisrael.

Gerald and Madelaine Greenberg
Nathaniel, Michaella, Elisha, Rahma & Immanuel
Toronto, Canada

Dedicated to our revered teacher
of Torah and *midot*

Rabbi Uziel Milevsky, *zt"l*

Yechezkel & Batsheva Mink
Old City Jerusalem

Dedicated to the memory of our loving parents

יעקב בן שמואל ע״ה
נפטר כ״ב טבת תשל״א
Jacob Glasenberg

and

יהודית בת יעקב ע״ה
נפטרה כ״ו תשרי תשכ״ז
Iren Judith Kolman

and

ברוך בן זלמן ע״ה
נפטר ל׳ כסלו תשמ״ב
Benjamin Sunness

By their children
Alex and Resa Glasenberg
and grandchildren
Zahava, Akiva, Michal & Yonatan

סֵדֶר בְּדִיקַת חָמֵץ

Before starting to search, wash your hands so they will be clean for the *berachah*.

בָּרוּךְ אַתָּה יְיָ אֱלֹהֵינוּ מֶלֶךְ הָעוֹלָם אֲשֶׁר קִדְּשָׁנוּ בְּמִצְוֹתָיו וְצִוָּנוּ עַל בִּעוּר חָמֵץ:

When saying this *berachah* be sure to have in mind that it also covers burning the *chametz* in the morning and its nullification tonight and tomorrow morning.

After the search, say the following:

כָּל חֲמִירָא וַחֲמִיעָא דְּאִכָּא בִרְשׁוּתִי, דְּלָא חֲמִתֵּהּ וּדְלָא בִעַרְתֵּהּ וּדְלָא יְדַעְנָא לֵיהּ, לִבְטִיל וְלֶהֱוֵי הֶפְקֵר כְּעַפְרָא דְאַרְעָא.

סֵדֶר שְׂרֵפַת חָמֵץ

On the morning of the 14th of Nissan we burn the *chametz*. As soon as it is completely burned we nullify it by saying this formula (some say it three times):

כָּל חֲמִירָא וַחֲמִיעָא דְּאִכָּא בִרְשׁוּתִי, דַּחֲזִיתֵּהּ וּדְלָא חֲזִיתֵּהּ, דַּחֲמִיתֵּהּ וּדְלָא חֲמִתֵּהּ, דְּבִעַרְתֵּהּ וּדְלָא בִעַרְתֵּהּ, לִבָּטֵל וְלֶהֱוֵי הֶפְקֵר כְּעַפְרָא דְאַרְעָא.

עֵרוּב תַּבְשִׁילִין

When *Erev Pesach* falls on Wednesday, take a matzah and some cooked dish, both of which are intended for eating on the coming Shabbos, and say this:

בָּרוּךְ אַתָּה יְיָ אֱלֹהֵינוּ מֶלֶךְ הָעוֹלָם אֲשֶׁר קִדְּשָׁנוּ בְּמִצְוֹתָיו וְצִוָּנוּ עַל מִצְוַת עֵרוּב.

בַּהֲדֵין עֵרוּבָא יְהֵא שָׁרֵי לָנָא לְמֵיפָא וּלְבַשָּׁלָא וּלְאַטְמָנָא וּלְאַדְלָקָא שְׁרָגָא, וּלְמֶעֱבַד כָּל צָרְכָנָא, מִיּוֹמָא טָבָא לְשַׁבַּתָּא, לָנוּ וּלְכָל יִשְׂרָאֵל הַדָּרִים בָּעִיר הַזֹּאת:

SEARCHING FOR *CHAMETZ*

Before starting to search, wash your hands so they will be clean for the *berachah.*

BLESSED are You, Hashem our God, King of the world, Who has made us holy with His mitzvos and commanded us about the eradication of *chametz.*

When saying this *berachah* be sure to have in mind that it also covers burning the *chametz* in the morning and its nullification tonight and tomorrow morning.

After the search, say the following:

ALL sourdough and *chametz* in my possession, that I have not seen and have not eradicated and do not know about, is hereby nullified and made like the dust of the earth.

ERADICATING THE *CHAMETZ*

On the morning of the 14th of Nissan we burn the *chametz.* As soon as it is completely burned we nullify it by saying this formula (some say it three times):

All sourdough and *chametz* in my possession, whether I have seen it or I have not seen it, whether I have eradicated it or I have not eradicated it, is hereby nullified and made like the dust of the earth.

ERUV TAVSHILIN

When *Erev Pesach* falls on Wednesday, take a matzah and some cooked dish, both of which are intended for eating on the coming Shabbos, and say this:

BLESSED are You, Hashem our God, King of the world, Who has made us holy with His mitzvos and commanded us about the mitzvah of Eruv.

WITH this *eruv,* may we and all the Jews of this town be permitted to bake, cook, put food on the fire, light candles, and do all that we need to, on this Yom Tov for [the following] Shabbos.

סִימָנֵי הַסֵּדֶר

קַדֵּשׁ, וּרְחַץ, כַּרְפַּס, יַחַץ;

מַגִּיד, רָחְצָה, מוֹצִיא, מַצָּה;

מָרוֹר, כּוֹרֵךְ, שֻׁלְחָן ,עוֹרֵךְ;

צָפוּן, בָּרֵךְ, הַלֵּל, נִרְצָה.

Longing for Redemption

On the night of Passover, we have an obligation to delve into the details of the Exodus. This is the difference between the general obligation of *lizkor yetzias Mitzrayim* (to remember the Exodus) and *lesaper yetzias Mitzrayim* (to relate the story of the Exodus.) It is for this reason that the Haggadah was written: although we mention the Exodus in the morning and evening prayers every single day of the year, on the night of Passover we are obligated to describe the miracles that God performed on our behalf in even greater detail.

The Seder opens with a poem that lists the fifteen steps of the Seder; it begins with the words *Kadesh, Ur'chatz, Karpas, Yachatz....* The number fifteen is by no means coincidental — the Sages intentionally incorporated fifteen steps in the Seder so that they should correspond with the fifteen steps in the Holy Temple that led from the outer courtyard up to the inner courtyard. These steps of the Temple in turn correspond with the fifteen Songs of Ascent that appear in the Book of Psalms. Each chapter opens with the words *shir hama'alos,* which literally mean, "a song of steps" (see Psalms 120–134). The Talmud tells us that the Levites would stand along the fifteen steps of the Temple and sing these fifteen Songs of Ascent while the worshipers climbed toward the inner recesses of the Temple (*Sukkah* 51b).

Evidently, there is a deeper correlation linking the fifteen steps of the Temple, the fifteen Songs of Ascent and the fifteen steps of the Seder. What is it?

The idea of fifteen is very closely connected with the first half of the Tetragrammaton, the four-letter Name of God. The

The Traditional Order of the Seder

KADESH, U'rechatz, Karpas, Yachatz;

Maggid, Rachtzah, Motzi-Matzah;

Maror, Korech, Shulchan Orech;

Tzafun, Barech, Hallel, Nirtzah

---

first two letters of this divine Name are *yod* and *heh*; they themselves combine to comprise a Name of God. The Kabbalists point out that the numerical value of these two letters is fifteen. Hence, this two-letter name which has a numerical value of fifteen is, in a sense, the gateway leading to the complete four-letter Name of God. Based on this correlation, the Maharal of Prague explains that man's connection to God is represented by the number fifteen — the ascent to the Temple via the fifteen steps symbolizes the connection between our current spiritual level and our pursuit of higher spiritual achievements.

This, too, is the essential purpose of the fifteen steps of the Seder — to elevate and intensify our relationship with God. We express our newly attained closeness with God at the conclusion of the Seder by reciting *Hallel*, a song of praise.

Kadesh

The first of the fifteen steps is *Kadesh*, the recitation of *Kiddush*. At first glance, the *Kiddush* of the Seder follows the same format as the one we recite on Shabbos and on all other Festivals. This resemblance could lead one to conclude that the *Kiddush* recited on Passover is not an essential part of the Haggadah, but merely a technical requirement. At first glance it would seem that it has been included in the Haggadah merely because it must be recited on Passover (as on all Three Festivals), but not because it is an essential component of the Seder night. However, this would be an erroneous conclusion, for the *Kiddush* recited on the night of Passover is indeed an integral part of the Haggadah.

קַדֵּשׁ

Fill all of the cups with wine.

If the Seder falls on Shabbos, start here:

וַיְהִי עֶרֶב וַיְהִי בֹקֶר

יוֹם הַשִּׁשִּׁי וַיְכֻלּוּ הַשָּׁמַיִם וְהָאָרֶץ וְכָל צְבָאָם: וַיְכַל אֱלֹהִים בַּיּוֹם הַשְּׁבִיעִי מְלַאכְתּוֹ אֲשֶׁר עָשָׂה וַיִּשְׁבֹּת בַּיּוֹם הַשְּׁבִיעִי מִכָּל מְלַאכְתּוֹ אֲשֶׁר עָשָׂה: וַיְבָרֶךְ אֱלֹהִים אֶת יוֹם הַשְּׁבִיעִי וַיְקַדֵּשׁ אֹתוֹ כִּי בוֹ שָׁבַת מִכָּל מְלַאכְתּוֹ אֲשֶׁר בָּרָא אֱלֹהִים לַעֲשׂוֹת:

When the Seder falls on a weekday, start here:

סַבְרִי מָרָנָן וְרַבָּנָן וְרַבּוֹתַי

בָּרוּךְ אַתָּה יְיָ אֱלֹהֵינוּ מֶלֶךְ הָעוֹלָם בּוֹרֵא פְּרִי הַגָּפֶן:

One sign of the unique characteristic of the *Kiddush* that is recited on the night of Passover is the dual role of the cup of wine — it is at once the *Kiddush* cup and the first of the Four Cups of wine that are to be drunk during the Seder. Obviously, if the *Kiddush* were unrelated to the Seder, one would have to drink the cup of *Kiddush* first, and then an additional Four Cups. The very fact that the cup of wine drunk with *Kiddush* is counted as one of the Four Cups proves that the *Kiddush* of Passover is an essential component of the Seder.

Further proof of the special quality of the Passover *Kiddush* is that, on all other occasions, the prevalent custom is that one person recites *Kiddush*, and then each person drinks a sip of wine from the *Kiddush* cup. This is *not* the custom followed on the Seder night — at this time, each person has a full cup of wine in front of him. Why? Because, as we have mentioned earlier, on Passover night the *Kiddush* is not just a technical requirement of the Festival, but an integral component of the Four Cups that each participant is obligated to drink. But why is the *Kiddush* of the Seder so unique? The text is almost identical to the standard *Kiddush* recited on most other festive occasions.

KADESH

Fill all of the cups with wine.

If the Seder falls on Shabbos, start here:

Whispered: It was evening, and It was morning

THE sixth day: Heaven and earth were finished with all their legions. On the seventh day God finished His work that He had been doing, and He desisted on the seventh day from His work that He had been doing. God blessed the seventh day and made it holy, for on it He desisted from all His work that He had created and made.

When the Seder falls on a weekday, start here:

Your attention, gentleman!

BLESSED are You, Hashem our God, King of the world, Who creates the fruit of the vine.

The Jerusalem Talmud explains that the Four Cups that are to be drunk on the night of Passover represent the four expressions of redemption mentioned in the Torah, as it is written, "Say to the Children of Israel: I am God, and I shall *take you out* from the burdens of Egypt; I shall *rescue you* from their service; I shall *redeem you* with an outstretched arm and with great judgments. I shall *take you* to Me for a people..." (Exodus 6:6–7). Each of the Four Cups represents one of these four expressions, and each expression in turn represents a more advanced level of redemption.

The first two expressions — "I will take you out" and "I will rescue you" — are very difficult to understand. Logically, we would say that the cessation of work ("I will rescue you") preceded the Exodus from Egypt ("I will take you out"). Yet for some reason, the verses appear in inverted order — "I will take you out" precedes "I will rescue you." This problem is compounded when we consider that the Oral Tradition itself explicitly states that the Jews stopped working a full six months prior to the Exodus. The Talmud tells us that from Rosh Hashanah (that is, six months before Passover), Pharaoh stopped forcing the Jews to

בָּרוּךְ אַתָּה יְיָ אֱלֹהֵינוּ מֶלֶךְ הָעוֹלָם אֲשֶׁר בָּחַר בָּנוּ מִכָּל עָם וְרֹמְמָנוּ
מִכָּל לָשׁוֹן וְקִדְּשָׁנוּ בְּמִצְוֹתָיו וַתִּתֶּן לָנוּ יְיָ אֱלֹהֵינוּ בְּאַהֲבָה (שַׁבָּתוֹת
לִמְנוּחָה וּ) מוֹעֲדִים לְשִׂמְחָה חַגִּים וּזְמַנִּים לְשָׂשׂוֹן אֶת יוֹם (הַשַּׁבָּת
הַזֶּה וְאֶת יוֹם) חַג הַמַּצּוֹת הַזֶּה זְמַן חֵרוּתֵנוּ (בְּאַהֲבָה) מִקְרָא קֹדֶשׁ
זֵכֶר לִיצִיאַת מִצְרָיִם כִּי בָנוּ בָחַרְתָּ וְאוֹתָנוּ קִדַּשְׁתָּ מִכָּל הָעַמִּים
(וְשַׁבָּת) וּמוֹעֲדֵי קָדְשֶׁךָ (בְּאַהֲבָה) וּבְרָצוֹן בְּשִׂמְחָה וּבְשָׂשׂוֹן
הִנְחַלְתָּנוּ. בָּרוּךְ אַתָּה יְיָ מְקַדֵּשׁ (הַשַּׁבָּת) וְיִשְׂרָאֵל וְהַזְּמַנִּים:

---

work even though he had not yet agreed to release them (*Rosh Hashanah* 11b). In other words, during their last six months in Egypt, the Jews were not free to leave, but they were exempted from having to perform hard labor. Hence, the only form of "slavery" that the Jews experienced during their last six months in Egypt was their lack of freedom — they could not leave the country, but they were no longer forced to work. The Oral Tradition explains that at that time the Jews were supported by government food distribution, just as they were when they had been working.

Ironically, during their wanderings in the desert, the Jews remembered with nostalgia the free food they had eaten in Egypt — meaning, the food they were given by the government despite the fact that they no longer worked to earn it (see Numbers 11:5). Strangely enough, throughout the Jewish people's odyssey in the desert, they conveniently forgot about the 210 years of brutal enslavement and fondly reminisced over this idyllic six-month period of free benefits.

To return to our question, why does the Torah state, "I will take you out of Egypt" before "I will rescue you from their service"? As we have proven, the order of these two statements seems to run contrary to the chronological sequence of events, for the Jews were released from their labor a full six months before the Exodus.

The Maharal of Prague answers the question by explaining that the expression "I will take you out" does not refer to the

BLESSED are You, Hashem our God, King of the world, Who chose us out of all peoples and exalted us more than any tongue, and made us holy with His mitzvos. Hashem our God, You gave us with love (Sabbaths for rest and) Festivals for happiness, celebrations and times for joy: this (Shabbos day and this) day of the Festival of Matzos, the time of our liberation, a hallowed day (with love) in memory of the Exodus. For You chose us and sanctified us from among all peoples, and gave us Your holy (Shabbos and) Festivals (with love and with favor) with happiness and joy, to be our inheritance. Blessed are You, Hashem, Who sanctifies (Shabbos and) the Jewish People and the Festivals.

---

physical Exodus, but rather, to the spiritual and intellectual redemption of the Jewish people. This spiritual Exodus was much more crucial to the continuing existence of the Jewish people than was their physical Exodus. By writing "I will take you out" before "I will rescue you," the Torah is teaching us that only after the Jewish people had been redeemed from their intellectual exile were they worthy to be saved.

What exactly do we mean by an "intellectual exile"? We find in the Oral Tradition a great deal of emphasis placed on the fact that the Jewish people in Egypt retained their identity as Jews. The Talmud states that all Jews taught Hebrew to their children — certainly not an easy task for an enslaved nation. In addition, every single Israelite child had been given a Jewish name even though the Jewish people were living in the midst of an intensely pagan society which looked down on Jews (*Midrash Rabbah*, Leviticus 32:5). Furthermore, all Jews wore characteristically Jewish garments — evidently, they were proud to be identified as Jews.

On the other hand, other statements in our Holy Writings seem to contradict this idea. For instance, one discussion in the Midrash informs us that the reason we are obligated to eat matzah on Passover is because the Jews were forced to rush out of Egypt in such haste that they did not have an opportunity to bake bread. Instead, they quickly mixed flour and water and threw it in the oven without waiting for the dough to rise, and matzah was the result. The Midrash goes on to explain *why* we must remember that God rushed us out of Egypt — if we would have stayed there

If the Seder falls on *Motza'ei Shabbos,* add these two *berachos* before *Shehecheyanu.*

בָּרוּךְ אַתָּה יְיָ אֱלֹהֵינוּ מֶלֶךְ הָעוֹלָם בּוֹרֵא מְאוֹרֵי הָאֵשׁ:

---

one moment longer, we would have completely assimilated and faded into extinction.

As is readily apparent, the Sages' statements seem to be irreconcilable — on the one hand they describe a committed Jewish people who are tremendously proud of their ancestry and identity, and on the other, they portray a nation on the verge of complete assimilation!

We should point out that the words of the Sages are to be understood on the symbolic level. They do not mean that, had the Jews stayed two more minutes, or even two more days or two more months, they would have disappeared from the face of the earth. After all, they benefitted by that time from the leadership of Moshe and Aharon. Their statement is rather to be taken metaphorically — the Jewish people stood, as it were, at the edge of the abyss. It is not necessary to dwell upon the precise moment when the point of no return would have commenced; what is significant is to always remember that we were in danger of disappearing. In future generations, when a Jew asks why he should eat matzah, the answer he will hear is that we were rushed out of Egypt because we were in danger of disappearing, and God saved us. The matzah is thus a tangible reminder to us that God is dedicated to Jewish continuity.

Let us now reconcile the Sages' apparently contradictory statements. In truth, there are many living examples of people who live in such a state of dichotomy — on the one hand they show strong external signs of identification with Judaism, and on the other, they intentionally pace along the very edge of the abyss of assimilation. They can at once behave as completely assimilated Jews and feel a strong Jewish identity. For instance, many Jews strongly identify with the Jewish people and with the Land of Israel, speak Hebrew fluently, and show many external signs of commitment to Judaism; however, these signs will not necessarily stop them from marrying out of the faith.

How is this possible? Evidently, there is a dangerous psychological mechanism that tries to put the conscience at ease. We

If the Seder falls on *Motza'ei Shabbos,* add these two *berachos* before *Shehecheyanu.*

BLESSED are You, Hashem our God, King of the world, Who creates lights of fire.

---

tend to believe that a Jew's conscience will give him no rest when he abandons his Judaism. However, the external signs of commitment to Judaism that he retains quell his conscience sufficiently to allow him to proceed down the path of full assimilation. He may think (perhaps subconsciously) that there is nothing wrong with marrying a gentile because, after all, he still identifies with Judaism — he donates money to Jewish charities and supports Jewish causes. It seems that when a Jew engages in activities which *he* thinks guarantee his commitment to the Jewish people, then he tends to belittle the dangers of assimilation and intermarriage. He is simply under the illusion that his continuity will be assured by the outer trappings of Judaism. Unfortunately, he mistakenly thinks that the spark of Judaism within can be satisfied through these external signs of commitment. Being part of a Jewish golf club, for instance, can become a justification for not attending synagogue. Peripheral commitments become justifications for not fulfilling genuine commitments.

Such was the situation of the Jews in Egypt. Their token external signs of dedication to their heritage did not guarantee them continuity. The lesson remains just as true today — the ability to speak Hebrew simply does not ensure Jewish continuity. A survey was recently conducted in public schools all over Israel. The students were asked if they thought of themselves as Jews or Israelis. The vast majority answered that they considered themselves Israelis, not Jews. These students' psychological defense mechanisms tell them that once they are Israelis, there is no need to be Jews anymore. Likewise, many Jews who immigrated to Israel thought, "Now that we are part of the Jewish nation, we don't have to put on *tefillin* anymore." It is clear then that there is no contradiction at all between the two views of the Jews of Egypt which are expressed by our Sages. Their clothing, language, and names proved that they had a strong Jewish identity and were proud of their heritage, yet we see that they were on the verge of complete assimilation.

The Maharal explains that the Jewish people were convinced

בָּרוּךְ אַתָּה יְיָ אֱלֹהֵינוּ מֶלֶךְ הָעוֹלָם הַמַּבְדִּיל בֵּין קֹדֶשׁ לְחֹל בֵּין אוֹר לְחֹשֶׁךְ בֵּין יִשְׂרָאֵל לָעַמִּים בֵּין יוֹם הַשְּׁבִיעִי לְשֵׁשֶׁת יְמֵי הַמַּעֲשֶׂה. בֵּין קְדֻשַּׁת שַׁבָּת לִקְדֻשַּׁת יוֹם טוֹב הִבְדַּלְתָּ וְאֶת יוֹם הַשְּׁבִיעִי מִשֵּׁשֶׁת יְמֵי הַמַּעֲשֶׂה קִדַּשְׁתָּ. הִבְדַּלְתָּ וְקִדַּשְׁתָּ אֶת עַמְּךָ יִשְׂרָאֵל בִּקְדֻשָּׁתֶךָ. בָּרוּךְ אַתָּה יְיָ הַמַּבְדִּיל בֵּין קֹדֶשׁ לְקֹדֶשׁ:

When reciting *Shehecheyanu,* have in mind that it covers the Yom Tov itself and all the mitzvos of this night. Women (and men too) who recited this *berachah* when lighting the candles should not say it again during Kiddush.

---

that they were in Egypt to stay. They believed that they would never get out of Egypt. It is not difficult to imagine their state of mind. They lived under the rule of the tyrant Pharaoh, who was in complete control of every aspect of Egyptian life. He decreed that no one could leave Egypt without his permission, and he never gave that permission to anyone. How *could* the Jews have hoped that the entire nation would ever manage to leave Egypt? Such an eventuality seemed completely preposterous to them!

It is likely that they paid lip service to the idea of an imminent redemption for no other reason than that such a redemption was part of their tradition. Their belief in this redemption, however, was superficial. They told their children that someday a redeemer would come and take them to the Land of Canaan. When the children grew up and asked, "Where is our redeemer?" the parents probably replied something along the lines of, "Well, that's something we tell our children, and we hope you will tell it to your children as well," like a gentile child who believes in Santa when he is young, but whose parents hope that he will eventually grow out of the fantasy.

Therefore, when Moshe informed the Jewish people, "I am he: I am the redeemer for whom you have been waiting. God has sent me," the Jews thought that he was out of his mind. They could not imagine that this old tradition had anything to do with reality. They thought, "We are here to stay. Redemption is just a legend." In their minds they were Egyptians — second-class citizens, but Egyptians nonetheless. It never occurred to them

BLESSED are You, Hashem our God, King of the world, Who separates between holy and secular, between light and darkness, between the Jewish People and the gentiles, between the seventh day and the six days of activity. You made a separation between the holiness of Yom Tov and the holiness of Shabbos, and made the seventh day more holy than the six days of activity. You separated and hallowed Your people Israel with Your holiness. Blessed are You, Hashem, who separates between one holiness and another.

When reciting *Shehecheyanu,* have in mind that it covers the Yom Tov itself and all the mitzvos of this night. Women (and men too) who recited this *berachah* when lighting the candles should not say it again during Kiddush.

---

that history would change so drastically. This is part of human nature — it is very difficult for people to believe that the reality to which they are accustomed can suddenly and inexplicably change. Twenty years ago, for example, no one would have believed that the Iron Curtain would come crashing down. The idea was utterly preposterous — everyone was convinced that Communism would last forever! The truth is that nothing lasts forever. However, the human mind naturally resists the idea of change. Thus, the Jewish people in Egypt thought, "What do you mean Pharaoh is going to let us out? It's out of the question!"

In the end Moshe finally made an impact on them. He managed to convince the Jewish people that they did not really belong in Egypt. This was the first step of the Exodus. It began to dawn on the Jews that redemption was not just a legend after all. They began to realize that their beliefs were not just remnants of some ancient tradition. Redemption was a reality: "We are going to leave — whether next year or the year after, we don't know yet — but we are going to leave!" The Torah expresses this intellectual exodus with the phrase, "I will take you out." Hence, we see that the first step of the Israelites' Exodus was coming to the realization that they were not Egyptians, that they were intrinsically different from all those who surrounded them, and that they had a unique role to play in the world.

All of these ideas are found in the words of the *Kiddush*, upon closer analysis of the text. We say in *Kiddush*, "Who chose us from all peoples." We acknowledge that we are indeed different. We

בָּרוּךְ אַתָּה יְיָ אֱלֹהֵינוּ מֶלֶךְ הָעוֹלָם שֶׁהֶחֱיָנוּ וְקִיְּמָנוּ וְהִגִּיעָנוּ לַזְּמַן הַזֶּה:

Recline on your left side and drink the whole cup, or at least most of it, without pausing in the middle. Have in mind that you are fulfilling the mitzvah of drinking the first of the Four Cups.

וּרְחַץ

Everyone washes his hands (some people's custom is that only the leader of the Seder washes): the *berachah* for hand washing is not said.

---

acknowledge as well that God's relationship with us is not the same as His relationship with the rest of the peoples of the world.

"You have elevated us above all languages" — our language, our approach to communication, is different from any other means of communication.

"You have sanctified us with Your commandments" — we are different from every other nation.

If we really mean every word we say when we recite the *Kiddush*, then the *Kiddush* portion of the Seder takes us through our own personal, inner exodus. Through it we raise ourselves from our own exiles, wherever we may be. We begin to recognize that we don't belong in exile; we belong somewhere else. The *Kiddush* therefore is actually verbalizing what is meant by "I shall take you out" — the first step in the Exodus and the redemption process. This explains how *Kiddush* on Pesach is not "just a *Kiddush*." Besides fulfilling the requirement of *Kiddush* that must be made on every Festival, it is also an expression of Israel's initial step towards redemption.

UR'CHATZ

The next step in the Seder is *Ur'chatz*, the washing of the hands. Ordinarily, at any other Shabbat or Festival meal, the bread is eaten immediately after the washing of the hands. At the Seder, however, the matzah is eaten only after the conclusion of *Maggid*. Why then do we wash our hands immediately after *Kiddush*? We do so in preparation for eating the *Karpas* (Aramaic for "vegetable"),

BLESSED are You, Hashem our God, King of the world, Who has given us life, sustained us, and brought us to this time.

Recline on your left side and drink the whole cup, or at least most of it, without pausing in the middle. Have in mind that you are fulfilling the mitzvah of drinking the first of the Four Cups.

U'RECHATZ

Everyone washes his hands (some people's custom is that only the leader of the Seder washes): the *berachah* for hand washing is not said.

---

which we dip in salt water or vinegar.

It is interesting to note that originally there was no obligation to wash the hands before eating bread; the Torah does not require this. It was only in the days of King Solomon that the Rabbis decided to institute the washing of hands. This rabbinical decree is based on the fact that a *kohen* (a priest) is obligated to eat certain foods in a state of purity. (If he would touch the carcasses of certain animals, for instance, he would be rendered impure, and he would have to undergo a process of purification before eating tithes or sacrificial offerings.) In order to cultivate within themselves a constant awareness of and sensitivity to purity, the *kohanim* always acted on the assumption that their hands were impure, whether or not this was indeed the case. The Rabbis reinforced this custom by instituting a decree *obligating* the *kohanim* to wash their hands before eating tithes or sacrificial offerings.

In time, the Rabbis realized that it would be very difficult for the *kohanim* to maintain a state of purity while living among other Jews, so for their sake they instituted a general decree obligating all Jews to wash their hands before eating bread. Every Jew who washes his hands before eating bread thus fulfills a rabbinic ordinance, and it is for this reason that a blessing is recited.

We also know that a wet fruit or vegetable becomes vulnerable to impurity. If it is dry, it will not be rendered impure even if it comes in contact with a source of impurity. However, if the food is wet, it *will* be rendered impure through contact with a source of impurity.

It is for this reason that we wash our hands prior to dipping

כַּרְפַּס

For Karpas some people use parsley, others celery, others radish, and some potato. In a pinch any vegetable will do (except the one that is going to be used for *maror*).

Everyone takes a piece of vegetable, less than a *kezayis* in size, and dips it in salt water.

Before eating it, say this *berachah*, and have in mind that it also covers the *maror* that will be eaten later.

בָּרוּךְ אַתָּה יְיָ אֱלֹהֵינוּ מֶלֶךְ הָעוֹלָם בּוֹרֵא פְּרִי הָאֲדָמָה:

The *karpas* is now eaten. Some people's custom is to eat it reclining.

---

the *Karpas* into salt water — by wetting the vegetable, we make it vulnerable to impurity, and hence, we must purify our hands to prevent contaminating it. A blessing is not recited when washing the hands before eating a wet vegetable because this was not part of the original rabbinical decree to wash one's hands before eating bread. Nevertheless, Jews throughout the ages have washed their hands prior to eating wet vegetables in order to prevent contaminating the vegetables.

KARPAS

The next step in the Seder is *Karpas.* As we have mentioned above, *Karpas* is the Aramaic name of a particular vegetable. The Rabbis included its name in the Seder because it alludes to a central aspect of the Jewish people's enslavement in Egypt.

The maximum number expressed in the Hebrew vocabulary is ten thousand, a *riboh.* There is no Hebrew word to represent a hundred thousand or a million. The only way to say 100,000 in Hebrew is "ten ten-thousands." We know that the number representing the totality of the Jewish people is 600,000 because this is the number of Jews who were counted upon Israel's departure from Egypt. (Of course, this is not an exact number, for it does not include all men above sixty or under twenty years of age, nor does it include the women and children. However, this number is said to represent the totality of the Jewish people.) According to our tradition, the number of Jews who were enslaved in Egypt was

KARPAS

For Karpas some people use parsley, others celery, others radish, and some potato. In a pinch any vegetable will do (except the one that is going to be used for *maror*).

Everyone takes a piece of vegetable, less than a *kezayis* in size, and dips it in salt water.

Before eating it, say this *berachah,* and have in mind that it also covers the *maror* that will be eaten later.

BLESSED are You, Hashem our God, King of the world, Who creates the fruit of the earth.

The *karpas* is now eaten. Some people's custom is to eat it reclining.

---

also 600,000 (again, the number is not exact).

How would one say 600,000 if ten thousand is the maximum number? One would have to say "sixty ten-thousands." The Hebrew letter which represents sixty is the *samech*. Now, we also know that our enslavement in Egypt entailed more than just hard labor. The Egyptians' main objective was to break the spirit of the Jewish people. Telling someone to do something, not because you want it done, but in order to show your domination over that person, is called in Hebrew *avodas parech.* The root of the word *parech* means "to break" — it literally breaks one's spirit.

Significantly, the letters of *Karpas* contain both the *samech* — the letter which represents sixty ten-thousands, as explained above — and *parech,* which alludes to the back-breaking and spirit-breaking labor that the Egyptians forced us to perform. It is for this reason that the name *Karpas* is included in the Seder.

The fact that these two allusions require that the word *Karpas* be read in reverse is no less significant — it symbolizes the redemption, which "turned around" our condition of hopeless enslavement to a state of eternal freedom. Therefore, when the child asks, "Why do we eat this particular vegetable?" the father can answer that the reverse of the name *Karpas* reminds us of our back-breaking enslavement, which was "turned around" by the redemption.

Why, though, do we dip the *Karpas* into salt water at this point in the Haggadah? Why not wait until after we have washed our hands to eat matzah? Furthermore, eating *Karpas* at this point in the Seder creates all sorts of problems. If, for example, a person wishes to eat an apple immediately before eating bread, he must definitely recite a blessing over the apple. However, if he would eat enough of the apple to require an after-blessing, he would encounter a difficult halachic dilemma. Since he is about to break bread, it is questionable whether he would have to recite the after-blessing over the apple. This is no simple question; there are halachic authorities who say that a blessing is required, and there are those who say that a blessing is *not* required. The same dilemma applies to eating *Karpas* on the night of Passover. Many authorities rule that one should eat less than a *kezayis* (size of an olive) of *Karpas* in order to avoid encountering this halachic problem. From this one example, it is readily evident that the dipping of vegetables on the night of Passover is problematic. Why then do we do it at all? There must be a deeper purpose behind it. What is it?

Let us begin by defining the practical purpose of eating *Karpas*. Today's equivalent of *Karpas* is the appetizer. The idea of eating an appetizer before a meal is that a light snack increases one's appetite. Somehow, the appetizer stimulates the appetite and enhances the enjoyment one derives from eating the main meal.

Why is it so important to stimulate one's appetite during the Seder? The reason given in the Talmud is that matzah should be eaten with a hearty appetite, and since people are not accustomed to eating as much matzah as one is required to eat during the Seder to fulfill the mitzvah, one must take steps to develop one's appetite. For the same reason, halachah prohibits eating a full meal on the afternoon before Passover — again, the idea is that one should develop a hearty appetite for the matzah to be eaten at the Seder. But why is so much importance ascribed to eating matzah with a hearty appetite? There must be a deeper reason.

The answer will emerge in the course of the following discussion: The Sages say, "Why do we dip the vegetable? In order that children should ask." This seems like a very strange answer. Imagine that a person dips the vegetable, and then the children — right on cue — ask the reason. What would be the correct response? Should the father answer, "Why do we dip? We dip in order that you should ask that very question," the child would be justified to respond, "Fine, Dad. I've asked. Now, why *do* we dip?"

Furthermore, why is the obligation to arouse the children's curiosity performed in this specific manner? Couldn't we just as well jump up, sit down, and turn around five times in the middle of *Kiddush*? That will certainly motivate the child to ask, "Hey, Dad! What's going on?" Is that all we are after?

The Maharal explains that one of our goals on Passover is to clarify why it was necessary for us to have undergone slavery in Egypt. The answer given is that we had to experience freedom; however, if one has never experienced the opposite of freedom — i.e., slavery — then one cannot fully experience freedom either. The idea of Passover is to drive home to the Jewish people the idea that before one is able to experience anything, one must develop a hunger for that state by experiencing the very opposite.

Slavery develops the hunger for freedom precisely because it is the exact opposite of freedom. In order to experience happiness, one must first know what it means to be sad. This is why Passover night is called "the night of opposites." Even the recitation of the Haggadah has to be preceded by questions, because unless a person has asked a question, the answers will not mean anything to him. Asking questions is parallel to the concept of developing appetite — curiosity is an intellectual form of "appetite." If a person would merely tell his children, "We were once enslaved in Egypt," this piece of dry information will not make any impression upon him. However, if he encourages them to first ask questions, his answers will become meaningful.

What then is the appropriate answer to the child's question, "Dad, why *do* we dip the vegetable?"? Something to the effect of, "Do you know why we dip? It is an appetizer. What is an appetizer and why do we need one? Just as you cannot really enjoy food unless you have first developed a hearty appetite, so too, you cannot really enjoy freedom unless you have first experienced slavery. Hence, the reason we dip the vegetable is to arouse the children's curiosity. That is the whole point — we want you to ask, children, because if you don't ask, then the answers you will hear won't mean anything to you. Just as you won't appreciate the matzah unless you've developed a hunger, so too, no experience will mean anything to you unless it is preceded by an opposite experience. That was the ultimate purpose of our enslavement in Egypt."

Anyone who attempts to teach a child something that he is

יַחַץ

Take the middle one of the three matzos and break it in two. Leave the smaller piece between the two whole matzos, and wrap the larger piece in a clean napkin and put it away to be the *afikomen*. Each piece should have in it at least a *kezayis*; if one of them doesn't, be sure to add some more to it from another *shemurah matzah*.

---

not interested in will soon realize the futility of his efforts; the material simply will not be absorbed. Even if the child does manage to remember the material for ten minutes, he will study it for the test and then forget it. Why? Because he has not developed a hunger for it. In order for any lesson to have meaning, one must develop a feeling that without this information, he is missing something of great importance. This is the deeper concept behind *Karpas* — it is the ultimate intellectual "appetizer."

Yachatz

Yachatz involves breaking one of the matzos on the Seder plate into two pieces. The smaller piece is left on the plate, while the larger piece is wrapped in a cloth and set aside to be eaten later as the *afikoman*.

There are two prevalent customs regarding the number of matzos placed on the Seder table: According to one custom, only two matzos are placed on the table, and the bottom matzah is broken in two. However, most people follow the custom of placing three matzos on the Seder plate, in which case the middle matzah is broken.

The reasoning behind these two customs is as follows: Halachah stipulates that on Shabbos and Yom Tov, the blessing over the bread served at each of the meals should be recited over two whole loaves (*lechem mishneh*). Thus, since the night of Passover is a Yom Tov, some authorities are of the opinion that two matzos are sufficient. Others, however (representing the custom followed by the majority of people), require that three matzos be placed on the Seder plate, since one matzah will be broken during *Yachatz*, and two additional whole matzos must remain on the Seder plate for *lechem mishneh*.

Having explained how *Yachatz* is performed, let us explore the deeper significance of this custom. Since one reason for breaking

YACHATZ

Take the middle one of the three matzos and break it in two. Leave the smaller piece between the two whole matzos, and wrap the larger piece in a clean napkin and put it away to be the *afikomen*. Each piece should have in it at least a *kezayis;* if one of them doesn't, be sure to add some more to it from another *shemurah matzah.*

---

the matzah is in order to set aside the larger piece for the *afikoman*, it would be appropriate to begin by defining this strange-sounding word. What is the meaning of the term *afikoman*?

Etymologically, the word *afikoman* is derived from the Greek word *epicumen*, which, loosely translated, means, "a food eaten for pleasure" — in other words, something sweet; what we today would call dessert. In the context of the Seder night, this implies that the reason we set aside the larger half of matzah for *afikoman* is so that we may eat it for dessert. This seems like a strange idea. Why eat matzah for dessert?

In order to understand this concept, we must first define the term "dessert" more precisely. Essentially, the dessert is the final portion of a meal, its crowning touch. It is an epicurean delight which brings the evening to a close and leaves us with a lingering taste that captures all that we have derived from the meal. It is for this reason that, on the night of Passover, halachah forbids the eating of any other foods after we have eaten the *afikoman* (*Shulchan Aruch, Orach Chaim* 478:1) — the only taste that should linger in our mouths following the Seder is that of matzah. This concept will be elaborated upon further at a later stage.

We now understand why the *afikoman* is eaten, but we have yet to explain why the larger half of the matzah that we set aside for *afikoman* must be wrapped in a cloth. Furthermore, why is it necessary to hide it? Some families even have the custom of hiding the *afikoman* and then encouraging their children to find and steal it. At first glance this custom seems strange — encouraging children to steal certainly does not sound like a very Jewish thing to do. There must be a deeper meaning behind this custom, for ostensibly it seems completely incongruous to a Jewish lifestyle, which regards every aspect of life as an educational tool. What kind of educational tool is it to encourage children to be devious and steal their parents' *afikoman*?

To be able to comprehend the basis for such behavior, we

must first explore the source of the custom of eating the *afikoman*. What is its origin?

In the days when the Temple stood, the entire Jewish people would convene in Jerusalem for each of the Three Festivals. On the first night of the Festival of Passover, they would begin their meal by eating matzah and bitter herbs, and then they would partake of the *korban chagigah*, the special sacrificial offering that was brought by those who made the pilgrimage to Jerusalem on each of the Three Festivals. The festive offering served as the "main course" of the meal, while the *korban Pesach* was eaten at the end of the meal — in a manner of speaking, it was the "dessert." After eating the *korban Pesach*, the Jews were forbidden to eat any other food until the following morning.

The logic behind this "menu" is that the matzah must be eaten with appetite — hence, it is eaten at the beginning of the meal. The *korban Pesach*, on the other hand, must be eaten *al hasova* (see Rashi on *Pesachim* 40a), after one's appetite has been satiated. It should not be eaten after one has gorged oneself with food to the point that one is loath to eat another bite of food, for eating the *korban Pesach* in such a state would be disrespectful of the sanctity of the sacrificial offering. Rather, it should be eaten when one feels satisfied but not overly full.

The obvious question which presents itself at this point is why the matzah must be eaten *with* appetite, while the *korban Pesach* must be eaten *without* appetite?

The commentaries explain as follows: Matzah is representative of the Jewish people's relationship with God. This is evident from the similarity in the spellings of the Hebrew words matzah (מצה) and mitzvah (מצוה). A person must cultivate within himself a hunger and a yearningto develop his relationship with God. Otherwise, he will not appreciate this relationship, and it will have no value in his eyes. We can easily relate this principle to everyday experiences in all facets of life — people generally ascribe importance only to those things that they have obtained after long periods of yearning. Only by feeling a deep longing for something can someone truly appreciate its value when it finally becomes his.

This is the idea behind the matzah/mitzvah relationship — unless a person develops that hunger, that craving for mitzvos, he will not appreciate their true value when they are within his grasp. It is for this reason that the matzah must be eaten with a hearty appetite.

Why then does the Torah require that the *korban Pesach* be eaten at the end of the meal, when one's appetite has been satiated?

The explanation is as follows: In *Pirkei Avos*, Ethics of the Fathers (1:3), we learn, "Do not be like servants who serve their master for the sake of receiving a reward; rather, be like servants who serve their master, but not for the sake of receiving any reward." In other words, mitzvos should be performed for no purpose other than to fulfill God's will. When ulterior motives are present, they detract from the merit of the mitzvah. This implies that when a person performs a mitzvah that involves some physical pleasure, such as the eating of some food for the sake of the mitzvah, the fact that he feels hungry somehow detracts from the value of that mitzvah. In order to circumvent this dilemma, the Torah stipulates that the *korban Pesach* be eaten at the end of the meal, when one is no longer hungry.

Although we have succeeded in explaining why the matzah is eaten at the beginning of the meal and why the *korban Pesach* is eaten at the end of the meal, we have also defined what appears to be a blatant contradiction: We have established above that it is preferable to develop a craving for mitzvos in order to fully appreciate their value, yet now we seem to be claiming just the opposite — that it is preferable to perform mitzvos purely for their own sake, and to preclude our personal desires to the best of our ability.

The following well-known story eloquently illustrates the point. There are two versions of the tale — according to the Chassidic version, the hero is the Baal Shem Tov, whereas according to the Misnagdic version, the hero is the Vilna Gaon. The story is relevant in either case, and all that concerns us is its moral lesson.

Less than a month remained before Sukkos, and no one had managed yet to find an *esrog* for the great *tzaddik*. The other three species necessary to fulfill the special mitzvos of Sukkos had been obtained — *hadassim* (myrtle branches), a *lulav* (a palm branch) and *aravos* (willow branches), but there was still no sign of an *esrog*.

Every year, the *tzaddik*'s followers had sent an envoy to Italy to purchase an *esrog*, and he had always returned well in advance of the festival. This year, however, the envoy had not returned. The people grew concerned.

They decided to send another envoy to purchase an *esrog* for the *tzaddik*. The man assigned to carry out this important mission arrived at the Italian city that had supplied the Northern European Jews with *esrogim* for many years. He immediately set out to make inquiries. When he told the residents what he was looking for, they burst out in raucous laughter.

"Haven't you heard?" they asked the bewildered man. "It has been a drought year, and hardly any *esrogim* grew. Only a handful of people in the entire region managed to get one. Believe us, you will not find anyone in this area who will be willing to sell you an *esrog* this year."

When the man explained who the *esrog* was for, the people sent him to the only resident of their city who possessed an *esrog*. The envoy traveled to the man's house and introduced himself. He began by asking the man whether he had ever heard of the *tzaddik*.

"Of course I've heard of him," the man answered. "Who hasn't?"

The envoy got right to the point. "Well, how would you feel if this righteous man would remain without an *esrog* this Sukkos? Do you want to have that responsibility on your shoulders?"

"Hey, listen, don't make me feel guilty!" the man protested. "I worked hard to find this *esrog*, and I have no intention of selling it to anyone."

The envoy offered him a small fortune for the *esrog*. The man adamantly refused. The envoy offered to bring him double the money immediately after Sukkos. "Sorry, I am not in the habit of selling my mitzvos," the man answered. The envoy asked him to reconsider and give him an answer by the following morning. He stressed that there were no *esrogim* at all to be found in Northern Europe, and pleaded with him to perform an act of kindness towards the *tzaddik*. "He will be completely broken-hearted if I do not return with an *esrog*," the envoy stressed.

The next morning the man approached the envoy and informed him that he had changed his mind, and that he was now willing to sell the *esrog* to the *tzaddik*.

"How much?" the envoy asked with trepidation.

"I do not want any money. But I will give you the *esrog* only on one condition — that I receive all of the *tzaddik*'s reward for fulfilling the mitzvah. He can perform the mitzvah, but I will gain all the reward."

The envoy was not sure whether he was in the position to accept such an offer. But then he remembered the *tzaddik*'s last instructions to him: "Bring back an *esrog* at any cost!" Surely he did not intend only monetary cost. And so, he accepted the *esrog* and hurried back home.

When he returned to his own town in Poland, he felt apprehensive about telling the *tzaddik* the terms of sale. What would he say? How would he react? The envoy finally mustered the courage to knock on the *tzaddik*'s door. The *tzaddik* took one look at the man's drawn face and assumed the worst.

"You were unsuccessful in your search?" he asked him.

"No, as a matter of fact, I did find an *esrog*."

"So what is the matter?" the *tzaddik* queried.

The envoy warily told the *tzaddik* the terms that accompanied the "purchase" of the *esrog*. Then, to his utter surprise, the *tzaddik*'s face lit up and he joyfully embraced him.

"Why, Rebbe?" the man asked.

"Because all my life I have wanted to perform a mitzvah purely for the sake of heaven, without being influenced by any ulterior motive whatsoever. Yet I have never succeeded, for in the back of my mind I have always been cognizant of the tremendous reward that I will receive for each mitzvah that I perform. Now, thanks to you, this Sukkos I will finally achieve my life-long dream — I will perform the mitzvah of taking the Four Species with full knowledge that I will receive absolutely nothing in return! I will not be able to have any ulterior motives whatsoever!"

The *korban Pesach* symbolizes the Jewish people's selfless devotion to fulfilling God's will, their desire to perform the mitzvos without any ulterior motives, for when the Jews in Egypt became aware of the miraculous manner in which God had "passed over" (in Hebrew, *pasach*) their houses, they realized for the first time the extent of God's love for them. It was in Egypt that God began to act towards the Jewish nation as His chosen nation. The people at that time indeed felt "chosen," and from that moment on were completely committed to Him. This absolute devotion to God was manifest in Egypt in their having risked their lives for His sake — as they slaughtered, roasted, and ate the flesh of lambs (the first performance of the mitzvah of *korban Pesach)* in full view of the Egyptians, in spite of the fact that the Egyptians considered the lamb their deity.

This is why the *korban Pesach* is referred to as a "pact" (see *Krisus* 9a). Indeed, we find a number of instances in Scripture where blood signifies the forming of a pact (e.g., Exodus 24:6–8). The Torah itself makes a connection between the mitzvah of *bris milah* (circumcision) and *korban Pesach*, for an uncircumcised male is excluded from participating in either the offering or eating of the *korban Pesach* (see Exodus 12:48). This is because both of these mitzvos, *bris milah* and *korban Pesach*, are in fact pacts between God and the Jewish people.

In view of the spirit of selfless devotion which characterized the attitude of the Jewish people whenever they formed a pact with God, it would be simply inappropriate to leave room for any ulterior motives in the performance of the mitzvos which represent such pacts. The halachah therefore stipulates that we eat the *korban Pesach* at the end of the meal, when we are no longer hungry. It is at this stage, when we neither need nor even desire additional food, that we eat the *korban Pesach* — or, in current times, the *afikoman* — for no reason other than to fulfill God's commandment.

Hence, we see that both seemingly conflicting ideas are valid, and each has its place in the Seder meal. On the one hand, developing a "hunger" for mitzvos is important — this principle is represented by the matzah, which is eaten at the beginning of the meal. On the other hand, it is equally important to be enthusiastic about performing mitzvos even when the required action will not bring us any personal gain — this principle is represented by the *korban Pesach*, and today, in the absence of the Temple, when the *korban Pesach* is not possible, by the eating of the *afikoman*.

One question which we raised earlier still remains unanswered: What is the source of the custom of hiding the *afikoman* and encouraging the children to steal it? Having broken the middle matzah in two, we wrap the larger piece in a cloth and hide it; then the children steal it and everyone searches for it. Once it is found, we sit down and eat the matzah for dessert.

The commentators explain as follows: The reason we do not eat the actual *korban Pesach* today is that we are still in a state of exile. The *korban Pesach* is therefore a symbol of redemption, of the Jewish people returning to their former glory. Matzah, on the other hand, symbolizes just the opposite, for matzah, "the bread of affliction," can be eaten even while we are in a state of exile. Hence, the *afikoman*, which we eat to commemorate the *korban Pesach*, is reminiscent of both exile and redemption, reminding us that we will indeed be redeemed from exile and will once again eat the meat of the *korban Pesach*. The act of hiding the *afikoman* is symbolic of the state of exile, in which God "hides His countenance" from us (see Deuteronomy 31:17). Searching for the *afikoman* symbolizes our yearning for the redemption. The commentators explain that the act of searching for the *afikoman* actually hastens the advent of the redemption.

There is a long-standing tradition that the redemption will come in one of two possible ways: either *be'itah*, in its appointed time, or *achishenah*, hastily, as a consequence of our worthy deeds (see *Sanhedrin* 98a). This means that if we sincerely desire the redemption, we possess the power to bring it ourselves, actually to "force" the redemption of the world! For if each individual would create a world of redemption through his own actions, the redemption would automatically manifest itself as a reality.

Measured in spiritual terms, this latter process of initiating our own redemption is the more meritorious option. It also results in the least painful method of redemption, for if we wait until the redemption comes to us of its own accord, we will not be in control of the personality changes that will be forced upon us to facilitate a world redemption. The rate at which this rectification process will be administered will be determined solely by external forces — no one will ask us whether it hurts. By contrast, if we were to create our own state of redemption, we would ourselves determine the rate of our self-rectification, and we would be able to progress at a comfortable pace.

We may now appreciate the deeper significance of the custom to search for the *afikoman*. As we have mentioned, this piece of matzah represents the *korban Pesach*, which in turn represents the state of redemption. The act of exerting ourselves in the search for the hidden *afikoman* symbolizes the manner in which we desire to usher in the Messiah and the redemption — we want to "find it" and make it a reality through our own deeds. In other words, we demonstrate through our actions that we would prefer the method of redemption that does not involve a painful process.

מַגִּיד

While reading the Haggadah we need to have in mind that telling the Pesach story on the Seder night is one of the mitzvos of the Torah.

The head of the household lifts the Seder plate, with the matzos, and says together with everyone at the table:

הָא לַחְמָא עַנְיָא דִּי אֲכַלוּ אַבְהָתַנָא בְּאַרְעָא דְמִצְרָיִם. כָּל דִּכְפִין יֵיתֵי וְיֵכֹל כָּל–דִּצְרִיךְ יֵיתֵי וְיִפְסַח. הָשַׁתָּא הָכָא. לַשָּׁנָה הַבָּאָה בְּאַרְעָא דְיִשְׂרָאֵל. הָשַׁתָּא עַבְדֵי. לַשָּׁנָה הַבָּאָה בְּנֵי חוֹרִין:

One of the Sages of the Talmud expressed this desire when he said, "Let the [days of Messiah] come, but may I not live to see them" (*Sanhedrin* 98b). This sharp remark stemmed from his ability to foresee the extreme suffering that the *be'itah* method of redemption will entail for the Jewish people. He realized that change and adjustment forced upon us from above is infinitely more painful than self-initiated rectification. The preferable scenario would be for the Jewish people to themselves rectify their deeds, thereby creating a new reality, which would automatically usher in the redemption.

This is the essence of the custom of hiding and searching for the *afikoman.*

Maggid

This is the stage of the Seder when we begin to tell the story of the Exodus from Egypt. Indeed, the name *Maggid* is derived from the Hebrew verb *lehagid*, which means "to tell." This verb also contains the root of the noun *haggadah*, which literally means "that which is told."

We begin by raising the smaller portion of the broken matzah and declaring, "*Ha lachma anya*," which means, "This is the poor bread [or, the bread of affliction]." It is so called because wealthy individuals break bread over whole, intact loaves of bread or pieces of matzah, whereas the poor eat crumbs and broken pieces of matzah. The broken piece of matzah thus symbolizes poverty. Significantly, this statement of "*Ha lachma anya*" is not proclaimed

MAGGID

While reading the Haggadah we need to have in mind that telling the Pesach story on the Seder night is one of the mitzvos of the Torah.

The head of the household lifts the Seder plate, with the matzos, and says together with everyone at the table:

THIS is the bread of poverty that our fathers ate in the land of Egypt. Anyone who is hungry, come and eat! Anyone who needs, come and make Pesach! This year, here; next year, in the land of Israel. This year, slaves; next year, free men!

---

in Hebrew, but in Aramaic. The reason for this will soon be explained.

The words that follow are "*di achalu avhasana b'ara d'Mitzrayim,*" which mean "that our fathers ate in the land of Egypt." It would appear that by way of this statement we are explaining to our guests why we eat matzah on the night of Pesach — namely, because once upon a time the Jewish people, our forefathers, used to eat matzah in the land of Egypt.

This explanation is problematic, for it seems to contradict the following passage of the Haggadah, which appears just a few pages later:

> *What is the reason behind this matzah that we eat? Because the dough of our ancestors did not have enough time to become leavened before the King of kings, the Holy One, Blessed be He, revealed Himself to them and redeemed them, as it is written, "[The Jewish people] baked the dough that they took out of Egypt into unleavened matzah-cakes, since it had not risen, for they had been driven from Egypt and could not delay; nor had they prepared any provisions for themselves" (Exodus 12:39).*

From here we see that the reason we eat matzah is not because our forefathers used to eat matzah *in* the land of Egypt, but rather because they ate matzah *on their way out* of Egypt. In no uncertain terms, the Haggadah teaches that matzah commemorates the speed of the Exodus, which occurred so quickly that our forefathers did not have sufficient time even to let their dough rise.

Why then do we begin the *Maggid* segment of the Seder by stating that the matzah symbolizes the poverty of our forefathers in Egypt? The two explanations appear to be irreconcilable. On the one hand we say that the matzah represents our forefathers' poverty in Egypt, and on the other hand, we say that it symbolizes their journey to freedom!

This apparent contradiction may be resolved by thinking of matzah as a dual-faceted symbol of poverty — in its taste as well as in its texture.

The wealthier a society becomes, the more ingredients it adds to its basic food staples. Today, everything from grain cereals to red meats is enriched with vitamins and minerals, and the plainest foods contain a long list of ingredients that supposedly enhance their taste and texture. Bread no longer consists of just flour and water — it now contains eggs, oil, sugar, and a long list of various and sundry substances that make it last longer and taste better.

Matzah represents a complete contrast to this manifestation of prosperity. Halachah stipulates that the matzah that we eat on the first night of Pesach may contain nothing at all other than flour and water (*Shulchan Aruch, Orach Chaim* 462:1). It is for this reason that we declare at the beginning of *Maggid*, "This is the poor bread that our fathers ate in the land of Egypt." Notice that we do not say "this is the bread of poverty," but rather, "this is the poor bread" — the bread itself is "poor," in that it lacks the added ingredients that are contained in, for instance, egg matzah, which in Hebrew is called *matzah ashirah* (wealthy matzah). According to many opinions this type of enriched matzah may be eaten during Pesach, but not on the night of the Seder, when we are obligated to eat only *lechem oni* (poor matzah). This "poor bread" reminds us of the miserable conditions our forefathers endured during their term of enslavement in Egypt, when they had to rely on the "poor bread" given to them by their overlords.

Later in the Haggadah, we mention the second aspect of poverty symbolized by matzah — its plain texture. In this passage, we explain that we eat this unleavened bread to commemorate the Exodus from Egypt, which occurred so suddenly that our forefathers had not even sufficient time to let their dough rise.

These two aspects of matzah are reflected in the laws of Pesach, where the requirement that it consist of unleavened dough is discussed separately from the requirement that it contain no ingredients other than flour and water. We can now readily understand why this is so: These two requirements are rooted in two separate concepts, as we have explained.

We have yet to explain why the opening passage of *Maggid* is written in Aramaic and not in Hebrew. After mentioning the poor bread eaten by our forefathers in Egypt, we go on to declare, "Let anyone who is hungry come in and eat; let anyone who is needy come in and make Pesach." An obvious question that comes to mind is why this invitation appears immediately after the passage that describes matzah as "poor bread." What essentially are we saying here? Would it make sense to say that since this is the poor bread that our forefathers ate in Egypt, let anyone who desires come and eat? The statement seems to make no sense. In any case, if this invitation is a sincere one, why do we wait to present it at the last minute, when we are already seated at the table with our door closed? If there are people wandering about looking for a place to eat, they will be outside, not in our dining rooms. It would be more logical to proclaim this offer in the street or in the synagogue. Who exactly are we inviting at this point?

The passage that follows is no less mysterious: "This year we are here; next year we will be in the Land of Israel. Now we are slaves; next year we will be free men." It is a very eloquent statement, but what does it have to do with the statement we made a moment ago about the matzah, or with the belated invitation? What is the connection between all three juxtaposed statements? Furthermore, why are they said at the beginning of the Seder?

The commentaries offer the following explanation: Since the language of the Jews in their early nationhood was only Hebrew, it is quite obvious that this passage was added to the Seder service around the time when the Jews began speaking Aramaic — during the Babylonian exile. Evidently, the Jews in exile saw fit to modify the original version of the Haggadah by inserting this clause; somehow, it made the Haggadah more relevant to the harsh realities of life in exile.

For the Jews in exile could not help but wonder why they should continue to commemorate Passover. In fact, we today could ask ourselves the same question. If Passover is merely the Jewish version of Independence Day, then does it make any sense to continue celebrating that day even after the entire nation has been conquered and the people exiled from their homeland? Do the residents of a defeated country continue to celebrate its Independence Day? When the Jewish people lived in their land and ruled themselves independently, Passover was meaningful. Perhaps now, however, when the majority of the Jewish people reside in foreign lands and strangers determine the fate of their land, Passover has lost its meaning. It is true that we were freed from Pharaoh, but in Babylon different tyrants ruled over the Jewish people with an iron hand. And has anything actually changed since then? The cast may have been altered over the years, but the script has remained the same — we are essentially still back in Egypt. Why then do we still commemorate Passover?

This is precisely the question that the leader of the Seder is addressing with the three opening statements of *Ha lachma anya*. He admits that the "poor bread" on the table symbolizes the meager condition of the Jewish people today: It is true — we are not prosperous and self-sufficient as we once were, but are rather poor and dependent upon the good will of foreign powers. Nevertheless, the leader affirms that we still have reason to celebrate Passover. To emphasize the point, he formally invites all those gathered around his table to "come in and eat."

Why do we still have reason to celebrate? Because everything that occurred to our forefathers in the past will occur to the Jewish people once again in the future, as the Sages say, "The events experienced by our forefathers foretell the fate of their descendants" (*Midrash Tanchuma* 9). In other words, Jewish history repeats itself. If our forefathers in Egypt were redeemed, it is just a matter of time until we will be redeemed as well. Therefore, even now, though we remain still mired in exile, the Exodus from Egypt is still an occasion worthy of commemoration, for it is our guarantee that we too will be redeemed. Therefore the leader states, "This year we are here; next year we will be in the Land of Israel. Now we are slaves; next year we will be free men"; and if not next year, then the year after that. The exact date of the coming redemption is irrelevant — the point is that *it is bound to take place* sooner or later (preferably sooner!).

This explains why the passage is written in Aramaic, and what one sentence has to do with the next. However, one question remains — these opening sentences seem to be somewhat repetitive. For example, "Let anyone who is hungry come in and eat; let anyone who is needy come in and make Pesach" — the first clause seems to be conveying the same message as the second clause. Similarly, "This year we are here; next year we will be in the Land of Israel. Now we are slaves; next year we will be free men." Once again, it seems as though the author of the Haggadah is using different words to say the same thing twice.

In truth, though, this is not at all the case. We learned earlier that the *korban Pesach* must be eaten *al hasova*, after one's appetite has been satiated. For this reason, the leader first proclaims, "Let anyone who is hungry come in and eat." Only then does he state, "Let anyone who is needy come in and make Pesach." These two clauses refer to two different obligations of the Seder. All who are hungry are invited to eat, and only afterwards, whoever has already satiated his appetite and now "needs" (not "desires," for he no longer feels hungry) may now come in and partake of the *korban Pesach*.

Neither is the passage beginning with the words, "This year we are here" repetitive. Rather, it alludes to the two separate stages of the redemption — that of *Mashiach ben Yosef* and that of *Mashiach ben David* (see *Midrash Tanchuma, Bereishis* 1). The redemption of *Mashiach ben Yosef* alludes to the physical redemption of the Jewish people — just as Joseph saved his father's household from perishing in the famine by providing his brothers and their children with food (see Genesis 45:11), so too *Mashiach ben Yosef* will bring about the Jewish people's physical redemption. Nevertheless, this is only the first stage — the physical redemption must necessarily lead to the spiritual redemption of the Jewish people.

We can now understand the message conveyed in the first passage of *Maggid*: "This year we are here; next year we will be in the Land of Israel" alludes to Israel's physical redemption, when all the Jewish people will be brought back safely to their home land. This alone, though, is insufficient, for it is feasible for Jews to act like gentiles even while residing in the Holy Land. In a spiritual sense, this would still constitute exile. Therefore, the second passage adds, "Now we are slaves; next year we will be free men" — it is true that we are physically free, but we are still spiritual slaves. Next year, however, we will be spiritually free as well.

Unless a person is spiritually free, he has not tasted true

The Seder plate with the matzos is taken away and the second cup poured. Then the youngest of those at the table asks:

מַה נִּשְׁתַּנָּה הַלַּיְלָה הַזֶּה מִכָּל הַלֵּילוֹת: שֶׁבְּכָל הַלֵּילוֹת אָנוּ אוֹכְלִין חָמֵץ וּמַצָּה. הַלַּיְלָה הַזֶּה כֻּלּוֹ מַצָּה: שֶׁבְּכָל הַלֵּילוֹת אָנוּ אוֹכְלִין שְׁאָר יְרָקוֹת. הַלַּיְלָה הַזֶּה מָרוֹר: שֶׁבְּכָל הַלֵּילוֹת אֵין אָנוּ מַטְבִּילִין אֲפִלּוּ פַּעַם אֶחָת. הַלַּיְלָה הַזֶּה שְׁתֵּי פְעָמִים: שֶׁבְּכָל הַלֵּילוֹת אָנוּ אוֹכְלִין בֵּין יוֹשְׁבִין וּבֵין מְסֻבִּין. הַלַּיְלָה הַזֶּה כֻּלָּנוּ מְסֻבִּין:

freedom. It is written, "The tablets were made by God, and the writing was the writing of God engraved [*charus*] upon the tablets" (Exodus 32:16), in reference to which the Sages say, "R. Acha bar Yaakov said: No nation or culture rules over them, as it is written, 'engraved [*charus*] upon the tablets.' Do not read 'engraved' [*charus*] but 'free' [*cherus*]" (*Eiruvin* 54a). A person can be either a servant to God or a slave to his own desires. One who can break out of that slavery to his desires has achieved genuine freedom. When one can overcome the resistance of one's physical tendencies and perform a mitzvah, one has performed a real act of freedom. He who rises in the morning to go to synagogue despite being tired, for example, is truly exercising his freedom.

Today we are still slaves in the spiritual sense. Real freedom of the spirit — the next step in the process of redemption — will hopefully come next year.

The Four Questions

Most Haggados preface the Four Questions with the following instructions: "The Seder plate is removed, and the second of the four cups of wine is poured. The youngest participant asks the reasons for the unusual proceedings of the evening."

The fact that the second cup of wine is poured just before the Four Questions are asked indicates that these questions are an integral component of the Haggadah. In contrast, the previous section, which begins with the words, "This is the poor bread that our fathers ate in the land of Egypt," appears to be nothing more than a preamble, for it is recited while the cup is still empty.

We see, therefore, that *Maggid* actually begins with questions, not with answers. These questions should not be regarded as mere

The Seder plate with the matzos is taken away and the second cup poured. Then the youngest of those at the table asks:

WHY is this night different from every other night? Other nights we eat *chametz* and matzah; this night, only matzah. Other nights we eat every kind of vegetable; this night, *maror.* Other nights we don't dip [vegetables] even once; this night, twice. Other nights we eat either sitting or reclining; this night we all recline.

---

pedagogical devices by which to keep the children awake and interested. If that would have been our entire purpose, it would not have been necessary for us to go into such detail, analyzing all the particulars of the Seder service. Instead, we could simply ask a general question such as, "Why is this night different from all other nights?" Furthermore, the Sages said:

> *The second cup is poured, and at this point the son asks his father [the Four Questions]. If the son lacks the knowledge to ask, the father teaches him to ask... The Rabbis taught: "If he is wise, his son asks [the Four Questions]; if he is not wise, then his wife asks him. If she cannot ask him, then he asks himself. Even two Torah scholars who are fluent in the laws of Passover must ask one another [the Four Questions]."*
>
> (*Pesachim* 115a)

If the purpose of these questions were merely to hold the children's interest, why would the Talmud stipulate that two Torah scholars having the Seder together must also ask each other the Four Questions? Would it not suffice for them to discuss the finer points of the miraculous events that led to the Exodus from Egypt? Surely we are not concerned that they will lose interest in the Seder and fall asleep! It is therefore clearly evident that the purpose of these questions is something other than simply to keep the children awake.

What then is their real function? The answer lies in under standing the ultimate purpose of the Passover Seder, the goal which we are expected to accomplish as we undergo the Seder process.

On the night of Passover, we are bidden to simultaneously experience two diametrically opposed physical and mental states — slavery and freedom. The only way to gain entry into this altered state of consciousness is through another pair of opposites

— through questions and answers. Let us now review the Four Questions and analyze them in greater detail.

In the first question, we wonder aloud that on any other night we are permitted to eat either leavened bread or matzah, and on the night of Passover we are commanded to eat only matzah.

The second question asks, "Why on any other night may we eat whichever vegetables we desire, while on the night of Passover we are commanded to eat *maror* (bitter herbs)?"

In the third question, we ask why on all other nights we may choose whether or not to dip vegetables into liquids, while on the night of Passover we are bound to do so twice — first when the *Karpas* is dipped into salt water, and again when the *maror* is dipped into the *charoses* (according to the prevalent Ashkenazic custom, a mixture of wine and apples).

The fourth question asks, "Why, on all other nights may we eat the evening meal in either a sitting or reclining position, while on the night of Passover we must recline while eating our matzah and while drinking the Four Cups?"

The Four Questions actually appear in the Mishna (*Pesachim* 10:4), although in different form. The version we find in our Haggados has been somewhat revised from the original, as has the order of the questions. According to the Mishna, the third question is, "On all other nights we may eat either roasted...or cooked meat, on this night we must eat roasted meat." Here, the term "roasted meat" refers to the *korban Pesach*, which every Jew was obligated to eat on the night of Passover in the days when the Holy Temple stood. After the Temple was destroyed, however, the author of the Haggadah substituted for this question the one concerning the fact that we eat in a reclining position. But what does the question about reclining have to do with the question regarding the eating of the *korban Pesach*? Since the one question is a substitute for the other, there must be some connection between the two mitzvos that are mentioned in these two questions.

According to many commentators, the reason that the mitzvah of leaning substitutes for that of the *korban Pesach* in the fourth question is as follows: The *korban Pesach* and the *maror* are reminders of two pivotal stages in the origins of the Jewish people. The bitter taste of *maror* symbolizes Israel's embittered state under Egyptian bondage, while the *korban Pesach* represents the pact that was formed between God and the Jewish people. We are accustomed to viewing the night of Passover as a commemoration of the Jewish people's release from their Egyptian masters and their being set "free." This, however, is not an accurate assessment of the situation, for in a sense the Jewish people merely passed from one state of "servitude" to another — before the Exodus they had been Pharaoh's servants, whereas after the Exodus they became Hashem's servants. Still "slaves," they merely exchanged masters.

This concept is represented in the two important mitzvos of the Seder: the *maror*, which symbolizes the lowly state of our nation's servitude to Pharaoh, and the *korban Pesach*, which symbolizes the glorious state of servitude to Hashem, the King of kings, which the Jews attained upon their Exodus from Egypt. Their transition from one master to the Other, which occurred on the night of Passover, is represented by the matzah we eat at the Seder. It symbolizes the speed with which we were released from Pharaoh's control when we left Egypt — we changed masters so quickly that our dough did not even have a chance to rise!

With the destruction of the Holy Temple, we unfortunately lost the ability to offer the *korban Pesach*. In order to preserve the memory of that vital pact which the Jewish people formed with God upon their Exodus from Egypt, the author of the Haggadah sought to retain an element of the *korban Pesach*, which would convey to future generations the state of spiritual freedom that became ours with the Exodus. The obvious choice was the custom of reclining during the meal — no other action symbolizes Israel's freedom more clearly than that.

At this point, the reader may be wondering, and rightfully so, "If this is the deeper symbolism behind the fourth question, why was it left until the end? Surely a concept so central to the theme of Passover should precede the question about the two dippings, which merely addresses a rabbinically ordained mitzvah!"

The answer is as follows: The question regarding reclining when we eat is left for the last in order to remind us that it is, after all, only a substitute. Ideally, we should be asking the Mishna's question, "On all other nights we may eat either roasted...or cooked meat, while on this night, we must eat roasted meat"; in other words, we would prefer to be having the Seder in the proximity of the Holy Temple in Jerusalem, with a *korban*

Pesach resting upon our table, rather than discussing the fact that we recline while in a state of exile. The very fact that this important question has been left until the end will give us cause to wonder *why* it is asked last; this in itself will serve us as a reminder that the conditions of our existence still are not ideal, for we remain in a state of exile.

Having delved into the significance of the Four Questions that appear in the Haggadah, let us consider why certain questions have deliberately been omitted. In order to better appreciate this discussion, the legal status of each of the basic components of the Seder must first be clearly understood.

When the Holy Temple stood, we were able to fulfill three Torah-ordained mitzvos during the course of the Passover Seder: matzah, *maror*, and *korban Pesach*. Today, since the destruction of the Temple, the only Torah-ordained mitzvah that we are able to fulfill during the Seder is the eating of matzah. We cannot eat the *korban Pesach* for obvious reasons, and *maror* has been demoted to the status of a rabbinically ordained mitzvah, because of its link to the *korban Pesach*, as *Rambam* writes:

> *It is a positive commandment to eat the flesh of the Passover offering on the night of the fifteenth [of Nissan], as it is written, "They shall eat the flesh on that night, roasted over the fire, and matzos; with bitter herbs shall they eat it" (Exodus 12:8). However, the fulfillment of the mitzvah of eating the Passover offering is not dependent upon the eating of matzah and maror — if matzah and maror are not to be found, one may fulfill one's obligation of the korban Pesach by eating only the flesh of the Passover offering. However, to eat maror without the Passover offering is not a [Torah-ordained] mitzvah, for it is written, "...with bitter herbs shall they eat it."*
>
> (*Hilchos Korban Pesach* 8:1)

Hence, we see that three of the Four Questions refer to actions pertaining to the fulfillment of rabbinically ordained mitzvos. If so, we may well wonder why the Haggadah *does not* have us ask questions regarding other equally central mitzvos, such as the Four Cups of wine. When else are we required to drink four cups of wine in the course of a single meal? If so, why does the youngest child not ask, "On all other nights we may choose whether or not to drink wine, while on this night we must drink four cups?"

One might be tempted to answer simply that a child cannot be expected to ask about actions that have not yet occurred, but this would not be a satisfactory explanation, for we see that the Haggadah *does* have the child ask why we dip vegetables twice, although the second dipping (*maror* into *charoses*) has yet to take place.

The real answer is as follows: People commonly refer to the mitzvah of drinking four cups of wine during the Seder. In truth this is an inaccuracy on their part, for if this is all that the fulfillment of the mitzvah entails, why do the Sages rule that a person who drinks four cups of wine consecutively, without reciting the required portions of the Haggadah between each cup, has not fulfilled his obligation? Why is he not considered to have drunk the Four Cups? Clearly, the mitzvah of drinking the Four Cups extends beyond the mere act of swallowing an unusually large volume of wine. Yet how can we define the mitzvah of the Four Cups?

The halachah does not obligate us merely to drink four cups of wine while reciting portions of the Haggadah *in between* each cup; rather, we are required to recite portions of the Haggadah *before* drinking a cup of wine. It is similar to reciting *Kiddush* on the eve of Shabbos — is the mitzvah simply to drink the wine? Obviously, one who merely drinks a cup of wine on Friday night has not fulfilled the obligation of reciting *Kiddush*. Instead, the mitzvah of *Kiddush* consists of uttering the proper words while holding a full cup of wine — the essential component of the mitzvah is the combination of the words that are to be uttered and the act of drinking the wine, which signals the completion of the mitzvah.

As we shall see through the following discussion, the Mishna lends strong support to this concept. The Mishna in *Pesachim* (10:1) rules that "[a poor person] must be provided with four cups of wine [for the Seder], even, if necessary, from the communal charity fund." One of the commentators questions this Mishna: Why does it stipulate that the poor person alone be provided with four cups of wine? What of his family? How will they fulfill the mitzvah of drinking the Four Cups? In answer to his own question, the commentator explains that as long as the leader of the Seder drinks the Four Cups, all those in attendance are also regarded as

The plate with the matzos is brought back to the table. The matzos should be partly covered while the Pesach story is being told.

Everyone says together:

עֲבָדִים הָיִינוּ לְפַרְעֹה בְּמִצְרָיִם. וַיּוֹצִיאֵנוּ יְיָ אֱלֹהֵינוּ מִשָּׁם בְּיָד חֲזָקָה וּבִזְרוֹעַ נְטוּיָה. וְאִלּוּ לֹא הוֹצִיא הַקָּדוֹשׁ בָּרוּךְ הוּא אֶת אֲבוֹתֵינוּ מִמִּצְרַיִם הֲרֵי אָנוּ וּבָנֵינוּ וּבְנֵי בָנֵינוּ מְשֻׁעְבָּדִים הָיִינוּ לְפַרְעֹה בְּמִצְרָיִם. וַאֲפִלּוּ כֻּלָּנוּ חֲכָמִים כֻּלָּנוּ נְבוֹנִים כֻּלָּנוּ זְקֵנִים כֻּלָּנוּ יוֹדְעִים אֶת הַתּוֹרָה. מִצְוָה עָלֵינוּ לְסַפֵּר בִּיצִיאַת מִצְרַיִם. וְכָל הַמַּרְבֶּה לְסַפֵּר בִּיצִיאַת מִצְרַיִם הֲרֵי זֶה מְשֻׁבָּח:

---

having fulfilled their obligation.

At first glance this opinion seems to contradict the well-established halachic principle that a mitzvah performed with one's body cannot be performed through an agent. For example, a person who has an obligation to eat matzah or to don *tefillin* cannot appoint an agent to fulfill the mitzvah in his stead, since the mitzvah requires that the individual perform the required act with his own body. One Jew may recite a blessing for another, but he cannot perform physical actions that must be done by the individual himself. How then can the mitzvah of drinking four cups of wine be fulfilled vicariously? Is it not a mitzvah performed with one's body?

The answer is that the essential requirement of the mitzvah is to utter and hear the words of the Haggadah, while the act of drinking the wine is only a peripheral requirement. It is for this reason that the other members of the poor man's household need not be provided with four cups of wine from the communal charity fund — they can fulfill the mitzvah by listening to the words of the leader of the Seder. According to this understanding, if a person has fallen asleep during the recitation of the Haggadah and is then woken up and told to drink his cup of wine, he is not considered to have fulfilled the mitzvah, for as we have explained, the mitzvah does not consist of drinking four cups of wine while mumbling some arbitrary words in between, but rather of uttering the proper words that precede the drinking of each of four full cups of wine.

The plate with the matzos is brought back to the table. The matzos should be partly covered while the Pesach story is being told.

Everyone says together:

WE were Pharaoh's slaves in Egypt, and Hashem our God took us out of there with a strong hand and an outstretched arm. But if the Holy One, Blessed be He, had not taken our fathers out of Egypt, then we and our children and grandchildren would still be enslaved to Pharaoh in Egypt. So even if we were all Sages, all wise, all elders, all learned in Torah, it would still be a mitzvah for us to tell about the Exodus; and whoever elaborates on the story of the Exodus is praiseworthy.

With this, our original question has been answered: Why does the child not ask, "On all other nights we may choose whether to drink wine; why on this night must we drink four cups?" The answer is that the Four Questions pertain only to independent mitzvos. Drinking the four cups of wine, however, is not an independent mitzvah, but only a part of the requirement to recite the Haggadah, as we have shown.

This brings us to another question; in light of the central position that the Haggadah holds relative to the Seder, why does the child not ask, "On all other nights we speak about anything that interests us, while on this night we speak only about the Exodus from Egypt?"

Truthfully, such a question has no validity, for the only reason we ask so many questions on the night of the Seder is that the Haggadah itself encourages us to do so, as it is written, "Whoever describes the Exodus at length merits praise." Hence, asking a question regarding the recitation of the Haggadah would be equivalent to someone performing a certain action while asking someone, "Why am I doing this?" For this reason, we do not ask about the mitzvah of telling the story of the Exodus as part of the Four Questions — it is the central theme of the entire Haggadah.

"WE WERE PHARAOH'S SLAVES IN EGYPT."

Having gained a deeper understanding of the questions that are asked during the Seder, it is worthwhile to ponder the answers that we offer in response. Surprisingly enough, specific answers for each question are not provided. Instead a general, all-inclusive explanation is offered: "We were slaves to Pharaoh in Egypt, and Hashem our God took us out of there with a strong hand and an outstretched arm...."

Many commentators are of the opinion that this statement includes answers to three of the four questions (the question regarding the two dippings is disregarded at this point in the Seder). "We were slaves" explains why we eat *maror*; "Hashem our God took us out of there" explains why the *korban Pesach* is eaten; and "with a strong hand and an outstretched arm" explains why we eat matzah — Hashem took us out of Egypt with "a hand" so strong that there was not even enough time for our dough to rise.

Next we declare, "Had the Holy One, Blessed be He, not taken our forefathers out of Egypt, we and our children and our grandchildren would still be enslaved to Pharaoh in Egypt." Taken at face value, this statement is difficult to understand. Even a cursory glance back through time will reveal that history is not a static entity, but a fluid continuum, in which nations periodically reach their glorious zenith of power, then decay and plummet back down to the depths of anonymity whence they came. How then can the author of the Haggadah suggest that, had Hashem not intervened, we and our offspring would still be there? It seems ludicrous to suggest that we would still be slaves to the Egyptians today, some three thousand years later. What could this passage possibly mean?

When the Torah teaches that Hashem took us out of Egypt, it is not referring only to a physical liberation, for the Exodus from Egypt transformed us as well from a tribe of lowly slaves to a free-thinking and independent nation devoted to the service of Hashem, the King of kings. We suddenly ceased to rely on our human masters for our livelihood and began to subsist through faith in God — that is what it means to be truly free.

We Jews have maintained this sense of freedom throughout the seemingly endless string of exiles, persecutions, and pogroms to which we have been subjected after having been redeemed from slavery in Egypt. It could be described as a continuous state of optimism, characterized by a feeling of imminent redemption. This mentality has enabled us to persevere through every form of adversity and to adhere proudly to our heritage throughout our tortured and blood-stained history.

How, on the other hand, would events have unfolded had Hashem not taken us out of Egypt? True, the Egyptian empire would have collapsed eventually, and their slaves — including the Jewish people — would have attained their physical freedom. But we would never have acquired this sense of mental and spiritual freedom. We today would still be functioning with the same kind of slave mentality that our forefathers had during their bondage in Egypt — assuming we would have maintained any kind of a national identity at all, which is unlikely. This is what the author of the Haggadah meant by, "Had the Holy One, Blessed be He, not taken our forefathers out of Egypt, we and our children and our grandchildren would still be enslaved to Pharaoh in Egypt" — we would have remained with the *attitude* of an enslaved people.

On a deeper level, one of the commentators points out that our notion of world events is based on a faulty premise; we assume that historical developments are "natural." In reality, however, the opposite is true — historical developments completely *defy* logic: Why do empires collapse? How do militarily inferior nations ever manage to defeat regional superpowers? Surely the ruling ethnic groups or nations possess the means to suppress their enemies and ensure that they remain weak forever. It follows that empires such as Egypt, Babylon, and Rome should never have fallen, for once they attained preeminence, they should have been able to retain their advantage forever. Why then does history develop as it does?

The answer is that Hashem has a plan for the world. In order to carry it out, He may cause a ruling class or nation to turn a blind eye to the increasing strength of its weaker enemies. Inconceivably, the strong fail to see the warning signals and neglect to take the necessary steps to prevent their own downfall. It is Hashem Who casts the mold that shapes world history. In this sense, historical developments are essentially supernatural events, for without Hashem's intervention, major changes would almost never occur.

This is the real intention behind the statement, "Had the Holy One Blessed be He, not taken our forefathers out of Egypt, we and our children and our grandchildren would still be enslaved to Pharaoh in Egypt." If Hashem would have allowed history to remain static, Egypt would still be the world's most powerful nation today, and we would have remained slaves.

The passage that follows in the Haggadah reads, "Even if all of us were wise, all of us understanding, all of us aged scholars, all of us knowledgeable in Torah, we would still be commanded to tell the story of the Exodus from Egypt."

The terms "wise," "understanding," "aged scholars," and "knowledgeable" seem to convey meanings very similar to one another. In fact, these Hebrew words are commonly used as synonyms. What lesson is the author of the Haggadah trying to impart to us through the use of these apparently redundant terms?

According to tradition, there are three levels of human understanding — *chochmah, binah* and *da'as.*

Chochmah literally means "knowledge" — for example, that two plus two equals four. A *chacham*, or "wise person," is someone who has compiled a large quantity of data about a particular field of study.

Binah is the ability to deduce previously unknown information from a given set of facts. The word *binah* is closely associated with the Hebrew word *binyan*, which means "building" or "creating." Following this analogy, *chochmah* represents the building materials, such as the bricks and the mortar, while *binah* represents the completed structure. This explains why the Hebrew word for "son" is *ben* — he represents a new generation, which his parents have "created."

Da'as indicates judgment — after compiling all the relevant facts through *chochmah* and deducing their implications with *binah*, the time comes for one to arrive at a practical decision regarding what to *do*. Except for a mathematical equation, nothing in the world is ever conclusive. Two plus two equals four, and it follows that four plus two equals six — this calculation does not require any judgment whatsoever. On the other hand, what about deciding on one's career? How should such an important decision be taken? The process involved in such a decision is called *da'as* — judgment.

Beyond these three, there is also a fourth level of knowledge — that that has been gained through experience. Sometimes, even a person who has acquired no information whatsoever about a particular topic knows instinctively what to do in a given situation. This occurs as a consequence of the aggregate lessons that he has incorporated based on his own life experiences — gradually, he has learned from his mistakes and has developed what one might term "a sixth sense." The older a person is, the more experience we assume he has acquired. This fourth level of knowledge is called *ziknah*, which literally means "advanced age."

With this understanding, the intention of the Haggadah in this passage becomes clear: "Even if all of us were wise (*chachamim*)" — that is to say, if we possessed the quality of *chochmah*; and "understanding (*nevonim*)" — if we possessed the quality of *binah*; and "aged (*zekenim*)" — if we possessed the quality of *ziknah*; and "knowledgeable in Torah" — if we possessed the quality of *da'as*; even so, "we would still be commanded to tell the story of the Exodus from Egypt."

The mitzvah to recount the Exodus entails more than simply listing the historical events that took place, for the Haggadah is much more than just a handbook on ancient Egyptian history. Rather it is a means by which to identify with the miracles that took place during the Exodus and, on a personal level, to experience it as though we had actually been there.

Imagine listening to a history professor delivering a tedious lecture on ancient Mesopotamian cultures, and then imagine someone describing in great detail how he narrowly escaped certain death in a car crash. What is the difference between the two narratives? Why is one so dull and the other so animated? The answer is self-evident — the professor is talking about an obscure subject that has very little relevance to either himself or his audience, while the car-crash survivor is relating an exciting incident that has affected him on a very personal level.

The Seder is not intended to be a history lecture, but a personal account of monumental events that have left their imprint on every Jew for all generations. Had Hashem not taken us out of Egypt, we would not be who we are today — something about us would be altogether different. The events surrounding the Exodus are personal experiences that have affected each and every one of our lives, and the Haggadah is an opportunity to relive our past and to express our gratitude to Hashem for all the miracles that He performed for *our* sake.

מַעֲשֶׂה בְּרַבִּי אֱלִיעֶזֶר וְרַבִּי יְהוֹשֻׁעַ וְרַבִּי אֶלְעָזָר בֶּן עֲזַרְיָה וְרַבִּי עֲקִיבָא וְרַבִּי טַרְפוֹן שֶׁהָיוּ מְסֻבִּין בִּבְנֵי בְרַק. וְהָיוּ מְסַפְּרִים בִּיצִיאַת מִצְרַיִם כָּל אוֹתוֹ הַלַּיְלָה. עַד שֶׁבָּאוּ תַלְמִידֵיהֶם וְאָמְרוּ לָהֶם. רַבּוֹתֵינוּ, הִגִּיעַ זְמַן קְרִיאַת שְׁמַע שֶׁל שַׁחֲרִית:

אָמַר רַבִּי אֶלְעָזָר בֶּן עֲזַרְיָה. הֲרֵי אֲנִי כְּבֶן שִׁבְעִים שָׁנָה, וְלֹא זָכִיתִי שֶׁתֵּאָמֵר יְצִיאַת מִצְרַיִם בַּלֵּילוֹת, עַד שֶׁדְּרָשָׁהּ בֶּן זוֹמָא, שֶׁנֶּאֱמַר, לְמַעַן תִּזְכֹּר אֶת יוֹם צֵאתְךָ מֵאֶרֶץ מִצְרַיִם כֹּל יְמֵי חַיֶּיךָ. יְמֵי חַיֶּיךָ הַיָּמִים, כֹּל יְמֵי חַיֶּיךָ הַלֵּילוֹת. וַחֲכָמִים אוֹמְרִים יְמֵי חַיֶּיךָ הָעוֹלָם הַזֶּה, כֹּל יְמֵי חַיֶּיךָ לְהָבִיא לִימוֹת הַמָּשִׁיחַ:

בָּרוּךְ הַמָּקוֹם, בָּרוּךְ הוּא. בָּרוּךְ שֶׁנָּתַן תּוֹרָה לְעַמּוֹ יִשְׂרָאֵל, בָּרוּךְ הוּא. כְּנֶגֶד אַרְבָּעָה בָנִים דִּבְּרָה תוֹרָה. אֶחָד חָכָם. וְאֶחָד רָשָׁע. וְאֶחָד תָּם. וְאֶחָד שֶׁאֵינוֹ יוֹדֵעַ לִשְׁאוֹל:

חָכָם מַה הוּא אוֹמֵר? מָה הָעֵדֹת וְהַחֻקִּים וְהַמִּשְׁפָּטִים אֲשֶׁר צִוָּה יְיָ אֱלֹהֵינוּ אֶתְכֶם? וְאַף אַתָּה אֱמָר-לוֹ כְּהִלְכוֹת הַפֶּסַח, אֵין מַפְטִירִין אַחַר הַפֶּסַח אֲפִיקוֹמָן:

The Wise Son

One of the Chassidic commentators points out that this is a rather incongruous query for a son whom the author of the Haggadah calls "wise," since the question implies that he lacks even a cursory knowledge of Scripture. If he is not even familiar with the basic mitzvos of Passover, in what sense is he "wise"?

In response to this observation, and based on a number of proofs from Scripture, the commentator interprets the Hebrew word *mah* to mean not "what," but rather "what is the purpose."

This sheds new light on the Wise Son's question. We see that he is actually quite familiar with the mitzvos of the Seder, and that he is aware of their importance. He has only one problem — why does God command the Jewish people to fulfill the mitzvos?

THIS is told of Rabbi Eliezer, Rabbi Yehoshua, Rabbi Elazar ben Azaryah, Rabbi Akiva, and Rabbi Tarfon: they sat once in Bnei Brak and told about the Exodus all that night, until their students came and told them, "Rabbis, the time has come to say the morning Shema!"

SAID Rabbi Elazar ben Azarya: I am like a man of seventy years, and yet I was never able to prove that the Exodus should be mentioned at night until Ben Zoma explained it: the Torah says, "so that you may remember the day you left the land of Egypt all the days of your life" [Devarim 16:3]. "Days of your life" — daytime; "*All* the days of your life" — the nights [too]. The Rabbis say: "the days of your life" — this world; "*all* the days of your life" — including the Era of Mashiach.

BLESSED be the Omnipresent; blessed be He. Blessed be He Who gave the Torah to His people Israel; blessed be He. The Torah speaks about four sons: one wise, one wicked, one simple, and one who doesn't know how to ask.

WHAT does the wise one say? "What are the principles, the laws, and the statutes that Hashem our God has commanded you?" [Devarim 6:20]. You too should answer him according to the *halachos* of Pesach: "An Afikomen may not be served as a last course after the Pesach lamb."

Since, through mitzvah observance, a person stands to earn immeasurable eternal reward in the World to Come as well as untold blessings in this world, why does God have to obligate the Jewish people to fulfill the mitzvos? Anyone who realizes the extent of the reward that can be earned through the performance of even a single mitzvah would enthusiastically perform all of them, even had God not commanded him to do so. Instead of holding the proverbial gun to our heads, God could simply have granted us the Torah and given us a glimpse of the tremendous reward to be earned by one who observes it. At that point, we would have decided voluntarily to fulfill all its commandments.

This is analogous to a ravenous individual who is served a nourishing meal — there is no need to coerce him to eat. Since mitzvah observance is so beneficial to a person, why did Hashem deem it necessary to suspend Mount Sinai above the Jewish people and threaten to crush them (see *Shabbos* 88a) unless they agreed to accept the entire Torah? Why not give us a choice? People naturally dislike being forced into doing something. It is much more satisfying to perform an action voluntarily. This is the real question of the Wise Son.

The author of the Haggadah instructs the Wise Son's father, "And you, too, should tell him the laws of Pesach: It is forbidden to eat anything after the *afikoman*." How does this response address the question as we have interpreted it above? In order to understand this, we must first digress for a moment and consider a different concept.

The great commentators often refer to the deeper reasons behind the laws of the Torah by the term *ta'amei hamitzvos.* In this context the Hebrew word *ta'am* means "reason" or "purpose," as in the verse, "Teach me the best of reason [*ta'am*] and knowledge, for I have believed in Your commandments" (Psalms 119:66). However, the word also means "taste," as in the verse, "Jonathan said, 'I have only had a taste [*ta'am*] of a bit of honey with the tip of my tongue'" (I Samuel 14:43). The term *ta'amei hamitzvos,* therefore, can also be taken to mean, "the taste of the mitzvos," obviously in the figurative sense. From the dual meaning of the word *ta'am*, it is quite evident that there is a connection — at least conceptually — between "reason" and "taste." Let us attempt to define this correlation by analyzing one of the mitzvos. Let us select as our model the well-known mitzvah of Shabbos observance.

If we were to introduce the concept of Shabbos observance to first-time listeners, and then ask them to conjecture what is the deeper reason behind this mitzvah, it is most likely that we would receive the following hypotheses: The purpose of Shabbos observance is to provide people with a day of complete rest and relaxation, for it is unhealthy for a person's physical and mental well-being to work continuously without respite; or, the purpose of Shabbos is to give people an opportunity to spend quality time with family and friends.

These are very good reasons for observing Shabbos, but are they the *essence* of Shabbos? Certainly not. These external reasons for Shabbos observance can be likened to the taste of an orange — it makes the orange very palatable, but it is not as essential a component as the nutritional value of the vitamins and minerals contained in the fruit. So too, Shabbos is composed of both "taste" and "nutritional value." Just as God injected good taste into nutritious food, in order to make it appetizing to man and easier for him to digest, He did the same with the *ta'amei hamitzvos*, the "taste" of the mitzvos; God appended external reasons to them, which man can grasp with his limited mind, in order to encourage him to perform the mitzvos and to make it easier for him to "digest" them intellectually. This explains the dual meaning of the Hebrew word *ta'am.* "Reason" and "taste" make both concepts and food more palatable to man, but they must not be confused with essence. This is an important distinction to bear in mind.

Following through with the same analogy, let us imagine for a moment that oranges suddenly and inexplicably lost their taste, yet retained their nutritional value. Would they be any less nutritious than they had been in the good old days when they tasted good? Certainly not. The essence of the orange is not affected by external qualities such as taste. Let us apply this same hypothetical situation to the mitzvah of Shabbos observance — hat would happen if Shabbos suddenly lost its peripheral bene fits? Say, for instance, that a person found himself stranded in his car on a deserted highway in the middle of nowhere on a Friday night. The prospect of spending Shabbos under these conditions holds in store neither rest nor relaxation. And how could one be expected to experience Shabbos without good food? Nevertheless, it would be prohibited for this unfortunate individual to cook food on Shabbos. Why? Because the external purposes that we attach to Shabbos observance have absolutely no effect upon the *essence* of the mitzvah.

If someone would one day decide to perform mitzvos only when they are physically and intellectually palatable to him, that day would mark the official end of Torah observance for himself and for anyone who follows his example. His children will not understand that yesterday he was in the mood to observe Shabbos and that today he is not, and his grandchildren will not even be aware that such a mitzvah exists. Torah observance cannot be maintained through the performance of mitzvos only when one feels that one understands the reasons behind such actions. Sometimes we are bidden to perform mitzvos that make abso-

רָשָׁע מַה הוּא אוֹמֵר? מָה הָעֲבוֹדָה הַזֹּאת לָכֶם? לָכֶם - וְלֹא לוֹ. וּלְפִי שֶׁהוֹצִיא אֶת עַצְמוֹ מִן הַכְּלָל כָּפַר בְּעִקָּר, וְאַף אַתָּה הַקְהֵה אֶת שִׁנָּיו וֶאֱמָר לוֹ, בַּעֲבוּר זֶה עָשָׂה יְיָ לִי בְּצֵאתִי מִמִּצְרָיִם. לִי - וְלֹא לוֹ. אִלּוּ הָיָה שָׁם לֹא הָיָה נִגְאָל:

---

lutely no sense to us, in order to ensure that future generations will also observe this mitzvah.

This is why the *korban Pesach* (and today, the *afikoman*) must be eaten at the end of the meal, when one is no longer hungry. Food tastes best when it is eaten with a hearty appetite. In contrast, the *korban Pesach* is to be eaten deliberately *without* appetite, because it represents the *essence* of mitzvos, stripped of their external purposes — their "taste." We eat the *korban Pesach* for no other reason than that God commanded us to do so in His Torah. Through this act, we give expression to our belief that there is more to mitzvos than their exterior adornments, which serve solely to make them physically and intellectually palatable to man.

With the same logic, we can understand why no other food may be eaten after the *korban Pesach* until the following morning. The taste, or to be more exact, the non-taste of this sacrificial offering that represents the essence of mitzvos must remain in one's mouth the entire night. No "artificial flavorings" must be allowed to distort the realization that the essence of God's commandments has a higher purpose than those that we are able to ascribe to them.

Now we can better appreciate the father's answer to the Wise Son. As we explained earlier, the Wise Son cannot understand why God saw fit to *obligate* the Jewish people to fulfill the laws of the Torah, for if mitzvah observance is inherently beneficial to man, he should be given the opportunity to make the obvious choice. The author of the Haggadah instructs the Wise Son's father to "tell him the laws of Pesach: It is forbidden to eat anything after the *afikoman*." We can now understand how this response addresses the son's query. Essentially the father is saying to the Wise Son, "Sometimes we have to perform mitzvos without understanding

WHAT does the wicked one say? "What is this service of yours?" [Shemos 12:26]. Yours, not his; and by disassociating himself from the community, he denies God. You, too, should set his teeth on edge by telling him, "Because of this, Hashem did [wonders] for me when I went out of Egypt" [Shemos 13:8]. For me, not for him: if he had been there he would not have been redeemed.

---

their reasons, just as we eat the *afikoman* for no other reason than that God commanded us to do so."

THE WICKED SON

One of the most popular questions asked on the Haggadah is why the Wicked Son is singled out, since at first glance it appears that he is asking exactly the same question as the Wise Son. True, by asking "What is this service *to you*," the Wicked Son does seem to be excluding himself from the obligation to perform the mitzvah, but it would seem that the same accusation could be made against the Wise Son, who asks, "What are the testimonies, the statutes, and the judgments which Hashem our God has commanded *you*?" The Wise Son does not say, "...commanded *us*," but "...commanded *you*"!

The question can be answered on many levels. First, a striking idiomatic distinction can be drawn between the two questions — while the Wise Son uses the term *es'chem* (you), the Wicked Son says *lachem*. The word *es'chem* is actually a derivative of *it'chem*, which means "with you." It conveys a sense of fidelity, which the usage of *lachem* lacks. Hence, essentially the Wise Son is saying, "Although I ask why God commanded these mitzvos to *you*, I do not exclude myself from the obligation, for I am 'with you.'" In contrast, the Wicked Son asks his question from the perspective of an outsider who feels alienated from the group.

But there is a deeper answer. Let us first ponder what the Wicked Son is really asking. Remember that although he may be wicked, he has bothered to come to the Seder table. This means that he appreciates certain aspects of the Seder, for otherwise, he would have made other plans for the evening. What is it that he likes? He likes the matzah balls, the wine, the *charoses*...all the "fun stuff."

Essentially he is asking, "Why do we have to perform all these burdensome rituals? Why do we have to read all this boring material? I'm willing to sit here with you, but why can't we make the Seder more of an appetizing banquet? Who needs to eat bitter herbs and so much matzah? Let's just enjoy ourselves and have a good time."

It is for this reason that the author of the Haggadah writes that "he denies a fundamental principle of faith" — by adhering to the exterior trappings of the mitzvos and discarding their essence, he has denied the basis of Judaism.

The author of the Haggadah advises the father to "set his teeth on edge." Some commentators interpret this to mean that he should make the Wicked Son feel uncomfortable, as though he had bitten into a sour apple. How is this to be accomplished? By talking about the Wicked Son in the third person, and by saying in reference to him, "It is because of this that God did so for me when I went out of Egypt. For *me*, but not for him. Had he been there he would not have been redeemed."

It would be futile to attempt to answer him logically, for it is impossible to enter into meaningful dialogue with a "Wicked Son." A sincere discussion can take place only in an atmosphere of mutual respect, where both parties have a positive attitude towards each other. But if one of the participants is full of hostility and resentment, the other party should not bother wasting his breath, since he will surely not be heard.

Some commentators explain that the Wicked Son is asking a rhetorical question to which he neither expects nor desires to hear a meaningful answer. There are many such people in the world, who make a pretense of asking "innocent questions" when in fact their real intention is to justify their own position. Of course, we are not referring here to people who ask such questions as "Why should I believe in God?" in all sincerity — this is obviously a valid question which deserves an adequate answer. But there are those who ask this same question with a cynical bent — first they violate all kinds of commandments, and then, when someone admonishes them, they vindicate themselves by asking the rhetorical question, "Why should I believe in God?" Someone who answers a question posed under such circumstances accomplishes nothing other than to make a complete fool of himself, for the mind of the one who has asked is already made up, and no argument will budge him from his position. The only appropriate response in such situations is to convey one's concern for the cynic's spiritual well-being.

Yet, there are situations in which one cannot afford to remain silent, for others overhearing the exchange could misinterpret one's reticence as a sign of acquiescence. What should one do?

The author of the Haggadah provides the answer: The father is advised to disengage from the dialogue with the Wicked Son, sigh with pity, and inform the other participants that, had the Wicked Son been in Egypt, he surely would have perished in the Plague of Darkness along with the other non-observant Jews of that generation. Their punishment was appropriate for their sin — they died in darkness because they intentionally kept themselves "in the dark." That is, they refused to keep an open mind and re-evaluate their outlook on life. If the Haggadah's advice were lines in a script, the actor playing the father would gesture towards the Wicked Son and say to his guests, "That poor guy! You know, if he had been in Egypt, he would not have come out alive!"

Other commentators offer a different reason to explain the fact that the Torah even bothers to address the Wicked Son altogether. In reference to the verse, "Woe to the evil, wicked man, for he shall fare ill; as his hands have dealt, so shall it be done to him" (Isaiah 3:11), the Talmud remarks, "[What is the meaning of the term 'evil, wicked man'?] Are there evil, wicked men and good, wicked men? Rather, there are two kinds of wicked men — the one who is wicked both towards Heaven and towards his fellow men is an 'evil, wicked man'; and the one who is wicked towards Heaven, but is *not* wicked towards his fellow men is a wicked man, but he is not evil" (*Kiddushin* 40a). The second type of wicked man is not completely bad, for he has a redeeming quality — he desires to live in peace with his fellow human beings.

The Hebrew word for "wicked man" is *rasha*, which closely resembles the word for evil, *ra*. The only difference between these two terms is the additional letter *shin* found in the word *rasha*. According to tradition, the letter *shin* represents the roots of the soul. This deeper meaning is also manifest in the shape of the letter, which resembles a tree or an inverted root. Hence, the *shin* of the word *rasha* signifies that although a transgressor of this sort is wicked, there is still hope that one day he will repent his sins and return to his roots.

This explains why the Wicked Son is sitting at the Seder table, and why the Torah addresses him altogether — he still has

תָּם מַה הוּא אוֹמֵר? מַה זֹּאת? וְאָמַרְתָּ אֵלָיו בְּחֹזֶק יָד הוֹצִיאָנוּ יְיָ מִמִּצְרַיִם מִבֵּית עֲבָדִים:

וְשֶׁאֵינוֹ יוֹדֵעַ לִשְׁאוֹל אַתְּ פְּתַח לוֹ. שֶׁנֶּאֱמַר וְהִגַּדְתָּ לְבִנְךָ בַּיּוֹם הַהוּא לֵאמֹר בַּעֲבוּר זֶה עָשָׂה יְיָ לִי בְּצֵאתִי מִמִּצְרָיִם:

---

potential! In contrast, the "evil, wicked man" is not present at the Seder, for he is completely beyond hope.

The Simple Son

The term *tam* is commonly taken to mean "Simple Son." His ignorance is reflected in his vapid and unimaginative question, "What is this [*mah zos*]?" Because he lacks the sophistication of the other sons who have been introduced thus far, he asks for nothing more than the basic facts, which is just about all the father gives him — a brief headline consisting of no more than seven Hebrew words, which summarizes the entire story of the Exodus.

Other commentators, however, interpret the word *tam* differently. They take it to mean "perfectly righteous," as in the verse, "Jacob was a perfectly righteous man [*ish tam*]" (Genesis 25:27). This interpretation creates a sense of symmetry in this section of the Haggadah, for now each of the Four Sons has a corresponding opposite — the Wise Son is the opposite of the Son Who Does Not Know to Ask, and the Perfectly Righteous Son is the opposite of the Wicked Son. According to this understanding, the third son represents a perfectly righteous individual who wishes to review the mitzvos that are incumbent upon him.

The Son Who Does Not Know To Ask

Various questions present themselves upon reading this passage: First, what does the phrase "open a conversation with him" mean? Second, why does the author of the Haggadah address the reader as *at*, which is the feminine form of the second person? Third, a verse is cited to prove that one must "open a conversation with" this type of son, but there is no hint to such a suggestion in the

WHAT does the simple one say — "What is this?" [Shemos 13:14]. "And you shall say to him, 'Hashem took us out of the house of bondage, Egypt, with a strong hand.' "

AS for the one who doesn't know how to ask, you open [the dialogue] for him, as the Torah says, "You shall tell your son that day thus: 'Because of this Hashem did [wonders] for me when I went out of Egypt' " [Shemos 13:8].

---

verse. Fourth, what does the term "who does not know to ask" mean? With Hashem's help, all four questions will be clarified in the course of the following discussion.

The son of the Vilna Gaon, Rabbi Avraham, points out in his commentary on the Haggadah that the verse that the author cites as proof for his directive uses the Hebrew verb *lehagid* ("*vehigadeta l'vincha*") instead of the more common *lomar*. Rabbi Avraham explains that *lehagid* implies relating a novel idea, as in the verse, "To proclaim [*lehagid*] Your steadfast love at daybreak, Your faithfulness each night" (Psalms 92:3). According to this interpretation, the father is obligated to arouse the son's interest and relate a novel idea that his son will find intellectually stimulating. To prove his point, Rabbi Avraham draws our attention to the phrase in the Haggadah, "you open a conversation with him" — in other words, the father must draw the son out of his shell and motivate him to ask questions of his own accord. Another proof is the Scriptural phrase, "On that day you will tell your son saying [*leimor*]...." Translated literally, the phrase means, "On that day you will tell your son *to say*...." What does the Torah mean by this? That a father must motivate his son to ask questions of his own, for only in this manner will he fully appreciate his answers.

Thus far, we have answered the first three questions; let us now address the matter of what is meant by the Son Who Does Not Know to Ask. To do so, we must first determine what type of person the author of the Haggadah had in mind when he wrote this passage. Undoubtedly, there are many people in the world who are of normal intelligence, who are reticent and shy, but who surely can manage to ask such a simple question as "Why?" So who is this Son Who Does Not Know to Ask? Is the Haggadah referring to someone who suffers from some mental impairment? Surely not. Perhaps it is referring to someone who is not interested in the

Seder? If so, the passage should read, "and regarding the one who does not want to ask," not "who does not know to ask."

The commentaries explain that the word *yode'a* (know) does not convey merely a general, impersonal familiarity with a concept, but rather an intimate knowledge. For example, we find that the Torah uses the word *yode'a* as a euphemism for marital relations, as in the verse, "Adam *knew* his wife Eve..." (Genesis 4:1). The term thus implies a commitment, a deep-rooted and personal relationship with a person or with a concept.

A person may, for instance, have a general knowledge of the events taking place in some remote region of the world, but he is intimately familiar with the subtlest nuances of the interpersonal dynamics unfolding between the members of his household. The term *lada'as* conveys knowledge regarding a piece of information that has great personal relevance to oneself.

This is the intent of the author of the Haggadah when he discusses the Son Who Does Not Know to Ask. He is referring to a person who does not regard the Exodus from Egypt as having personal relevance to himself. Such an individual relates to the story of the Exodus as though to the national anthem — it demands a certain measure of respect, but only on a national level. On a personal level, however, this Exodus that occurred thousands of years ago makes very little difference to him. Why should he care?

For this reason the Haggadah advises the father to tell this son, "It is because of this that God acted on my behalf when I went out of Egypt." The father is urged to portray the story of the Exodus as a personal journey to spiritual and existential freedom. To achieve this effect, he must look within himself to discover in what manner the Exodus has touched him personally, and then share his experience with those participating in his Seder. If he sincerely feels that he himself has gone out of Egypt, and if he manages to communicate this to those gathered with him around the table, then suddenly they will all start caring, and will consequently feel that God acted on their behalf when He took the Jews out of Egypt.

There is another personality alluded to in the Son Who Does Not Know to Ask. There are some people who refrain from asking too many questions, not because they do not care, but because they fear the consequences of their asking. This type of personality is concerned that the answers he will receive will complicate his comfortable lifestyle. For example, he is afraid to ask about Shabbos observance, lest the answer be so convincing that he himself will feel compelled to abandon his liberal attitudes and start observing Shabbos. At that point, who can tell what will happen next? Perhaps he will feel that he must begin to observe the laws of kashrus and all sorts of other commandments that will interfere with his pursuit of worldly pleasures. Therefore, when he feels the desire to ask a sincere question that wells up from the depths of his soul, he reins himself in and keeps his lips tightly sealed, lest his queries get him into deep trouble. This is another understanding of the term, "the one who does not know to ask" — it also means, "the one who is too scared to ask."

THE FOUR SONS AND DEVOLUTION

Thus far, the Four Sons have been portrayed as archetypal personalities, which have existed in Jewish society since time immemorial. However, they can also be understood in a more global sense as portraying the Jewish people's recurring sociological patterns as formed by the ebb and flow of world history.

As any student of Jewish history knows, the Egyptian exile marked only the beginning of Israel's three-thousand-year odyssey through a never-ending gauntlet of persecution and torture at the hands of one nation after the next. An oft-repeated question, therefore, is why does the commemoration of the Exodus occupy such a central position in the Jewish calendar? Since the Jewish people have been cast from one exile to the next, why is Passover still referred to as "the time of our freedom?" What kind of freedom is this?

The answer is that the miracles of the Exodus, which culminated on Passover, serve as the prototype of the Jewish people's ultimate redemption. In a sense, the miracles that took place in Egypt set a historical precedent, which will sooner or later repeat itself. Prior to the Exodus from Egypt, there was no practical indication that Israel would ever be redeemed; perhaps exile would become an integral component of the Jewish psyche for all eternity. With the miracles of Passover, it became clear to all the inhabitants of the earth that the Jewish people were not destined for a permanent state of exile; our identity is thus characterized by a state of redemption.

Yet more often than not, the Jewish historical cycle has consisted not of a transition from exile to freedom, but rather from exile to exile. This movement of our people from one culture to another has too often proven fatal to large segments of the Jewish nation, which bears the scars to this very day, as we see from the recurring cycle of Jewish exile.

Typically, when Jews make their entrance into a nation, they tend immediately to feel a tremendous drive to "fit in" and excel in those very same pursuits that the host society considers their own unique specialty. If the locals take pride in their superior business skills, then the first-generation Jewish immigrants strive to become superb businessmen; if the locals take pride in their scientific achievements, then the Jews strive to become superb scientists. The Jews' innate ambition to excel stems from Israel's destiny to become a "light unto the nations." This enormous spiritual potential cannot be suppressed — if it is not channeled towards spiritual endeavors, it manifests itself on the corporeal plane as a consuming ambition to excel in every field of worldly endeavor. Soon, the all-consuming yearning to excel can become so overwhelming that the Jew may be willing to sacrifice anything — including his heritage — in order to attain his goal. In a matter of a few generations, the Jew does indeed excel, but this time, to his detriment, he becomes so well adjusted to his new culture that he totally assimilates and essentially fades away as a Jew.

Who remains in exile? Only the descendants of those Jews who have resisted the temptation of assimilating and have remained faithful to the Torah. This is the only guarantee of Jewish survival. Those who embraced Torah still have Jewish descendants today; those who shunned it in the past are no longer a part of Israel.

Let us now analyze the inner workings of each cycle of exile. What type of person immigrates to a new country from the previous locale of exile? As has been explained above, it is a person who adhered to his traditions, since it stands to reason that all those who discarded their heritage assimilated completely and disappeared from the Jewish map.

These new immigrants are committed to their heritage. They know what mitzvos are and how to perform most of them; they can pray in Hebrew and can study Torah. We could safely refer to this first generation of exiles as the generation of the *chacham*, the Wise Son. It is for this reason that the author of the Haggadah mentions the Wise Son first — this son is representative of the first immigrants who enter Israel's latest exile.

What happens to the children of the *chacham*, the second generation of the new exile? They are in the greatest danger, for they find themselves walking a tightrope between two very different cultures. It is extremely difficult for them to live in both of these worlds at once. They perceive their parents' world as old and primitive in comparison to the fast and exciting world in which they have grown up. They are liable to abandon the old ways of their parents and embrace the trappings of the modern world, thinking, "These ancient laws are not for us! 'What is this service to you?' It means nothing to us!" This is the generation of the *rasha*, the Wicked Son. For this reason, the author of the Haggadah lists him as the second son — he represents the second generation of Jews in exile.

What becomes of the third generation? The children of the Wicked Son have nothing to rebel against — their parents have left no stone unturned. For the most part, they simply do what their parents tell them. From a religious perspective, the most one can expect from them is to ask, "What is this?" They may have faint memories of their grandfather opening up a Jewish book once in a while or performing some other mitzvah. Out of curiosity they will ask, "What is this? What is the Torah all about?" This third generation of immigrants is defined as the Simple Son. It is for this reason that the author of the Haggadah lists him as the third of the Four Sons.

If the Simple Son receives a Torah education, he still has a chance. If he does not, then his children will become the generation of the Son Who Does Not Know to Ask. Indeed, what have they to ask? Their father knows next to nothing, their grandfather is the rebel, and they don't remember their great-grandfather. All they know is that they are Jewish, but they have no inkling of what it means to be a Jew. The Haggadah warns that this fourth generation is the last generation — there is no Fifth Son, for the children of the Son Who Does Not Know to Ask no longer exist from a Jewish perspective. If a Jew knows nothing more than that he is Jewish, his children will not know even that.

Interestingly, people often remark that almost every Jew they

יָכוֹל מֵרֹאשׁ חֹדֶשׁ, תַּלְמוּד לוֹמַר בַּיּוֹם הַהוּא. אִי בַּיּוֹם הַהוּא יָכוֹל מִבְּעוֹד יוֹם, תַּלְמוּד לוֹמַר בַּעֲבוּר זֶה. בַּעֲבוּר זֶה - לֹא אָמַרְתִּי אֶלָּא בְּשָׁעָה שֶׁיֵּשׁ מַצָּה וּמָרוֹר מֻנָּחִים לְפָנֶיךָ:

---

know has at least a great-grandfather who was religious. They are correct — it is rare to find a Jew who has been disconnected from his heritage for five generations. This is precisely what the Haggadah teaches.

"You might think that one can [relate the Haggadah] from Rosh Chodesh..."

Upon reaching this cryptic passage an attentive reader will wonder — and justifiably so — why the author of the Haggadah considers the possibility that the mitzvah (presumably, he means the obligation to tell the story of the Exodus) is incumbent upon us from as early as the first day of Nissan, a full two weeks before the Passover Seder. He could just as well have suggested that the mitzvah is incumbent upon us from the first day of the new year!

One of the commentators points out the apparent lack of continuity between this passage and the previous passage concerning the Fourth Son. It appears as though the author of the Haggadah has suddenly sidetracked his train of thought mid-sentence — while in the midst of relating the Fourth Son's question, he suddenly begins pondering whether one should begin reading the Haggadah from the first day of Nissan. The two passages seem completely unrelated.

The commentators explain the relationship between these two passages as follows: The father of the Son Who Does Not Know to Ask — the Fourth Son — is obligated to motivate him to ask questions; should the father fail to arouse his son's interest, he would not be regarded as having fulfilled the mitzvah of telling his son about the Exodus. How can the father bring his son to ask questions during the Seder? The answer is, by arousing his curiosity and by prodding him about the unusual customs surrounding the night of Passover. This preparatory stage could be termed a *hechsher mitzvah* of the Haggadah. The term *hechsher*

YOU might think that one can [relate the Haggadah] from Rosh Chodesh Nissan onward; so the Torah says, "on *that* day." If [it can be told] "on that day," then you might think that you can [tell it] while it is still daylight; so the Torah says, "because of *this*." I cannot say "because of this" except when matzah and *maror* are lying before you.

---

mitzvah literally means, "the preparations required for the fulfillment of a mitzvah." For example, the mitzvah of sitting in a sukkah requires that a sukkah be constructed. The act of building the sukkah is not an independent mitzvah, but is rather a *hechsher mitzvah* that makes it possible to fulfill the basic mitzvah of sitting in a sukkah. Similarly, baking matzos is not a mitzvah in its own right, but a *hechsher mitzvah* that makes it possible for one to fulfill the mitzvah of eating matzah on the night of Passover. Now, when are *hechsher mitzvos* usually performed? Are they to be performed on the night of Sukkos or on the night of Passover? Obviously not — the preparations must be performed before the time when the mitzvah is to be fulfilled.

Likewise, the author of the Haggadah reasoned that since the mitzvah of telling the story of the Exodus to the Son Who Does Not Know to Ask requires that his father prepare him in advance to ask questions during the Seder, perhaps the father is obligated to begin this *hechsher mitzvah* prior to the Seder. The most logical beginning of this "training period" would be the first day of the month of Nissan, for the entire month is called "the month of redemption, the month of freedom" (see *Radak* on Ezekiel 45:18). This is the true intent of the phrase, "Perhaps [the mitzvah must be performed] from as early as the first day of the month."

However, the author of the Haggadah rejects this suggestion by citing the verse, "[You shall tell your son] *on that day*, [saying, 'It is because of this that God acted on my behalf when I left Egypt']" (Exodus 13:8).

The author of the Haggadah then raises another suggestion: "Since it is written 'on that day,' perhaps [the mitzvah must be performed] while it is still daytime." His reasoning is that we find in regard to most time-related mitzvos the concept of sanctifying the day earlier. For instance, we accept upon ourselves the sanctity of Shabbos late on Friday afternoon even though officially it only begins at dusk. This practice is called *tosefes Shabbos*, which literally means, "an addition to Shabbos." The same concept applies to Yom Kippur.

It is therefore reasonable to assume that the concept of *tosefes* might apply equally to all other time-related mitzvos, including Passover. The terminology used by Scripture in fact lends support to this idea, for it is written, "You shall tell your son *on that day....*" What does the phrase "on that day" mean? Following the analogy of Shabbos, it would be reasonable to assume that the verse is instructing us to begin reading the Haggadah on the afternoon of "that day." We could even coin a new term for this additional period of sanctification — *tosefes Pesach.*

Despite the apparent validity of this argument, the author of the Haggadah again rejects his own suggestion on the basis of a textual interpretation: "'It is because of *this* [that God acted on my behalf]' — I only said 'it is because of this' when matzah and *maror* are placed before you." Contextually, the use of the word "this" implies that the speaker is pointing to a particular object, presumably to the matzah or the *maror* placed upon the table before him, which must be eaten after dark on the night of the fifteenth of Nissan, as it is written, "At night you will eat matzos" (Exodus 12:18). This proves that the reading of the Haggadah may be performed only when it is possible to fulfill the mitzvos of matzah and *maror*, i.e., at nighttime.

One question remains unanswered: Leaving all textual interpretations aside for the moment, why should the Torah object to parents discussing the Haggadah with their children on the afternoon preceding the night of Passover or, for that matter, from the first day of Nissan? What is wrong conceptually with preparing ahead of time?

There is a crucial lesson to be gleaned here. Maimonides in his *Guide for the Perplexed* explains that the ultimate goal of all the mitzvos in the Torah is to cultivate personal growth. Each mitzvah contains a different element necessary for potential self-improvement, whether it be in the realm of character refinement or of purification of one's thoughts or values. In this sense, God's commandments rectify a person and shape his entire being. It is for this reason that the Torah required us to perform the mitzvos.

However, Maimonides warns against a potential danger that could result from misconstruing this approach: A person might reason that if he feels capable of attaining the ultimate goal of a particular mitzvah through other means, then he is no longer bound to perform that mitzvah. The mitzvos of Passover are a good example — since the ultimate purpose of Passover is to internalize the concept of freedom and to appreciate one's relationship with God, someone who thinks that he has already attained this spiritual state might feel that he does not need to go through the motions of the Seder. Shabbos is another example — since the ultimate purpose of the mitzvah is to remember that God created the universe and then rested, a person who feels he understands this concept could claim that while he accepts the ideology, he does not need to observe the prohibitions of Shabbos.

Maimonides rejects these claims by explaining that any ideology that is not attached to a specific action — such as the eating of matzah, lighting candles or abstaining from work — is bound to disappear and be forever forgotten. The ideology may endure for one or even two generations, but it will have no continuity. That is why we need the mitzvos. Without them, all our important ideological tenets will simply fade into oblivion. It is true that we sometimes overlook or forget the ultimate goal of the mitzvos, often performing them by rote, but by fulfilling them and imparting the concept of mitzvah observance to our children, we ensure that future generations will have access to our ideology — perhaps the following generation will gain the insight that we lack.

The mitzvos can be likened to a highly condensed set of codes that encapsulate a complex and multi-dimensional spiritual blueprint. Sometimes we ourselves do not know how to decipher it, but as long as we guard it and pass it on to our children, we keep alive the possibility that a future generation will one day crack the code. We may not understand the reason we don *tefillin*, but perhaps our grandchildren will. The only way to provide them with the opportunity to solve the puzzle and thereby come closer to spiritual perfection is by fulfilling the mitzvos ourselves and teaching our children to follow our example. Thus, it is the concrete action in the form of the mitzvah that guarantees the continuity of our ideology.

This insight answers the question raised above. Talking about the Exodus is very nice, but unless the discussion is linked to a tangible mitzvah, it has no substance. If a father were to tell his children about the redemption from Egypt, but would refrain from

מִתְּחִלָּה עוֹבְדֵי עֲבוֹדָה זָרָה הָיוּ אֲבוֹתֵינוּ, וְעַכְשָׁו קֵרְבָנוּ הַמָּקוֹם
לַעֲבוֹדָתוֹ. שֶׁנֶּאֱמַר, וַיֹּאמֶר יְהוֹשֻׁעַ אֶל כָּל הָעָם כֹּה אָמַר יְיָ אֱלֹהֵי
יִשְׂרָאֵל בְּעֵבֶר הַנָּהָר יָשְׁבוּ אֲבוֹתֵיכֶם מֵעוֹלָם, תֶּרַח אֲבִי אַבְרָהָם
וַאֲבִי נָחוֹר וַיַּעַבְדוּ אֱלֹהִים אֲחֵרִים. וָאֶקַּח אֶת אֲבִיכֶם אֶת אַבְרָהָם
מֵעֵבֶר הַנָּהָר וָאוֹלֵךְ אוֹתוֹ בְּכָל אֶרֶץ כְּנָעַן וָאַרְבֶּה אֶת זַרְעוֹ וָאֶתֵּן
לוֹ אֶת יִצְחָק. וָאֶתֵּן לְיִצְחָק אֶת יַעֲקֹב וְאֶת עֵשָׂו וָאֶתֵּן לְעֵשָׂו אֶת
הַר שֵׂעִיר לָרֶשֶׁת אוֹתוֹ וְיַעֲקֹב וּבָנָיו יָרְדוּ מִצְרָיִם:

attaching his narrative to a "this" that he can point to with his finger, something that the children can touch, put in their mouths and chew and taste, then his efforts will be to no avail — the lesson will be swiftly forgotten. That is why the Torah insists that the story of the Exodus begin at nighttime, "when matzah and *maror* are placed before you."

"At first our fathers were idolaters..."

The author of the Haggadah now begins to relate the story of the Exodus by describing how the Jewish people came to be enslaved in Egypt. He takes us all the way back to our ignoble past by citing the verse, "At first our ancestors were idolaters...[as] the God of Israel said, 'In the days of old your forefathers dwelt beyond the river, Terach, father of Abraham and father of Nachor, and they worshipped idols..." (Joshua 24:2). The obvious question is, Why? Of all times, why mention our dishonorable past on the night of Passover, when the Jewish people are at the pinnacle of their faith in God? Why create such an anticlimax?

The answer is that the author of the Haggadah followed the directive stipulated by the Mishna: "The father...begins with words of ignominy and concludes with words of praise" (*Pesachim* 116a). This statement is interpreted in two ways: According to Rav, it means that one must begin the account of the Exodus by citing the passage, "At first our ancestors were idolaters..."; according to Shmuel, it means that one must begin with the statement, "We were slaves unto Pharaoh..." (as in our Haggadah). The point of contention between these two Sages is which of the two

AT first our fathers were idolaters; and now the All-Encompassing has brought us to His service, as the Torah says, "Yehoshua said to the whole people, 'Thus says Hashem, the God of the Jewish People: Your fathers always lived across the Euphrates, Terach the father of Avraham and of Nachor, and they worshiped other gods. But I took your father Avraham from across the river, and sent him all over the land of Canaan. I made his descendants numerous and gave him Yitzchak; and I gave Yitzchak Ya'akov and Esav. I gave Esav Mount Seir as his inheritance, while Ya'akov and his children went down to Egypt' " [Yehoshua 24:2].

---

passages contains a stronger description of Israel's ignominy — that which describes our idolatrous roots or that which portrays our servitude to the Egyptians.

The author of the Haggadah cites both statements in order to satisfy both opinions, for after all, both are valid. The Jewish nation is characterized by both physical and spiritual aspects. If one would focus exclusively on the physical element, the Jews' lowest episode in history was when they lost their freedom and became miserable slaves to Pharaoh in Egypt. However, if one would focus on the Jewish people's spiritual element, then their most disgraceful point was in Abraham's youth, when he and his entire family worshipped idols.

These two aspects of the Jewish people are reflected in the overall structure of the Haggadah. In answer to the children's question, "Why is this night different from all other nights?" the author responds by focusing on the physical element: "We were slaves to Pharaoh in Egypt...." This is an appropriate answer to give the children, because their young minds are incapable of comprehending the more subtle spiritual elements of the Jewish people. To illustrate to the children the concluding statement, "whoever expounds much upon the tale of the Exodus merits praise," the author of the Haggadah recounts the incident in which Rabbi Akiva and five of his colleagues spent the night of Passover in Bnei Brak and stayed up until dawn recounting the Exodus. This episode marks the end of the first stage of the Seder — the children have been answered according to their level of understanding, and one of the opinions cited in the Talmud (that of Rav) has been fulfilled.

Now the "second" Haggadah begins. It will focus on the more complex theme beginning with Israel's spiritual nadir, reached in the days when Abraham the Patriarch still lived "beyond the river." This reflects the second opinion cited in the Talmud (that of Shmuel).

The question we must attempt to answer is why the Torah demands that we focus so intently on the Jewish people's moment of greatest disgrace. Isn't the night of Passover supposed to symbolize Israel's freedom? What is the purpose of delving so deeply into our ignoble past?

The Maharal of Prague refers to the night of Passover as "the night of contrasts." Dichotomy is the essence of Passover — the Seder is full of contrasts. The Maharal explains that a person who has not experienced slavery — either personally or vicariously — cannot possibly comprehend what it means to be free. The reason is that the human intellect can perceive a concept only through its opposite. With this the Maharal answers the famous theological question of the nature of evil in the world: "If God created the world, why does evil exist?" The answer is that evil must exist as a contrast to good; without evil, there would be no conception of good. Were it not for darkness, human beings would not fathom the existence of light.

This is one reason that God caused us to descend into Egypt and become enslaved to Pharaoh. Why did He make us suffer so much? Because otherwise we would never have experienced true freedom.

But there is a deeper reason why we had to be exiled into Egypt: The real goal of the Exodus was to bond Israel with God, to lead Israel to the realization that there exists only one God Who created the entire universe. It is only monotheism that obligates the believer to lead an ethical life. "Ethical polytheism" is a contradiction in terms, because pagan belief thrives on the presumption that the worshiper must bribe the gods. Why, for example, does an idol worshiper offer sacrifices to the god of rain? Is it because he loves the god of rain? Certainly not. It is because he wants it to rain. Hence, the object of worship is ultimately the worshiper himself. Sacrifice amounts to just a means of bribery by which to compel the gods to fulfill the worshiper's desires.

To idolaters, the concept of developing a personal relation ship with a god was a completely alien notion. One simply pleased the gods in order to impel them to do one's will; the god never obligated the worshiper to behave righteously or to live according to a specific set of ethical standards. Just the opposite was true — sometimes pleasing the god required that its worshipers perform abominable acts. The people willingly complied, for they reasoned that man's only goal in life is to satisfy the gods. Hence, if they thought that reprehensible acts such as slaughtering a child or tearing out the heart of a live virgin would please the gods, they would do these things without feelings of remorse. Morality was a foreign concept — there was no right or wrong. The only important consideration was what would please the gods.

Only in monotheism can an objective code of ethics exist. One God controls the entire universe, and His only desire is that man behave righteously and justly. The notion of bribing this One God fades into absurdity. The only way to serve Him is by meeting the standards of behavior that He has set out.

Monotheism is the direct opposite of idolatry. This is the true intent of this passage. The first portion of the passage contrasts the Jewish people's commitment to God with their lowly pre-Exodus spiritual condition. However, the purpose of the last sentence is less obvious. For example, what role did Esau play in the Exodus from Egypt? And if he is mentioned, why has Ishmael been omitted?

It is obvious that if Isaac originally intended to bless Esau, he could not have been completely evil. He must have had an important role to play in history. What was it?

The answer is that Isaac thought that Jacob and Esau were destined to join forces together and thereby compensate for one another's deficiencies. Esau would compensate for Jacob's lack of enthusiasm for physical endeavors, and Jacob would compensate for Esau's lack of enthusiasm for spiritual endeavors. Together, they would conquer the world and prompt all of humanity to recognize God as the sole Master of the Universe.

However, their mother Rebecca saw that this idealistic union could not work in practice. Foreseeing that Esau's physicality would gain the upper hand over Jacob's spirituality, she instructed Jacob to steal the blessings that Isaac intended to impart to Esau. In doing so, she revealed to Jacob that he would have to attain his physical requirements independently and that, despite Isaac's plans, Jacob would not be able to rely on Esau to compensate for his deficiencies. In a sense, Rebecca told Jacob that he would have to become his own "Esau."

Jacob dons Esau's hunting clothes and steals his blessings. Suddenly, the studious man who "dwells in tents" is transformed into a man of the field. Jacob now embodies both roles — he is at once Jacob and Esau. We can see, however, from Isaac's original assumption, that Esau should have had an important role to play in Jewish history and identity. It is for this reason that he is mentioned along with the Three Patriarchs.

Now let us look at another pair of opposites — Isaac and Ishmael. The commentaries explain that the relationship between them was never meant to be any closer than the relationship that existed between Sarah and Hagar, their mothers. Hagar was Sarah's maidservant. Likewise, Ishmael was never destined to be anything more than Isaac's servant. Theirs was not meant to be a partnership, but only a master-servant relationship. And just as Hagar could not bear to remain subject to Sarah, neither could Ishmael bear to remain subject to Isaac. It is for this reason that Ishmael is omitted from the genealogical lineage of the Jewish people. He was never a potential member of the quintessential Jewish nation, unlike Esau, who potentially held a significant place in Jewish history.

Esau, Laban, and Jewish Survival

We raised the question concerning the last clause of this passage — "I gave to Esau Mount Seir to inherit, and Jacob and his sons went down to Egypt" — why does the author of the Haggadah include it? How is it relevant to the story of the Jewish people's Exodus from Egypt?

In *Parashas Lech Lecha* it is written:

> *[God] said to Abram, "Know with certainty that your offspring shall be foreigners in a land that is not theirs; they will serve them, and they will oppress them for four hundred years. But I will bring judgment against the nation that enslaves them, and they will then leave with great wealth.... The fourth generation shall return here [to the Land of Canaan], for the iniquity of the Amorite people has not yet run its course."*
>
> (*Genesis* 15:13–16)

These verses teach that the land of Canaan was promised to all of Abraham's descendants — including Esau — but only on condition that they would bear the yoke of being "foreigners in a land that is not theirs" and be oppressed by its inhabitants.

Had Esau and his descendants gone down to Egypt along with Jacob and his children, they too would have earned an ancestral inheritance in the land of Canaan. For this reason, the author of the Haggadah emphasizes that God gave Mount Seir as an ancestral inheritance to Esau, while only "Jacob and his sons went down to Egypt" to bear the punishment promised to Abraham's descendants. This proves that the Jewish people — and not the descendants of Esau — are the spiritual inheritors of Abraham the Patriarch. Because they alone descended to Egypt, they alone merited to be redeemed and granted an eternal portion in the land of Canaan.

"BLESSED BE HE WHO KEEPS HIS PROMISE TO THE JEWISH PEOPLE."

Notice that the passage is written in the present tense, "Who guards," and not the past, "Who guarded." This conveys the understanding that God's promise is not just a one-time affair, but is rather a continuous, permanent commitment.

The commentators also point out that the term "Who guards His promise" is an unusual figure of speech, since in common Hebrew usage, one is said to fulfill one's promise (*lekayem havtachaso*), not to "guard" it. What is the idea behind God guarding His promise?

This concept can be illustrated through the following analogy: Imagine that you promised a child that if he will come to you at the same time on the next day, you will give him a candy. Does this promise guarantee that the child will indeed come on the following day to collect his candy? Obviously not, for you have committed yourself to give a candy to the child only if he fulfills his end of the deal — to show up on time tomorrow. What if you would promise that, in addition to giving the child a candy, you will also take steps to ensure that the child will show up the next day, even if this entails watching over the child to make sure that nothing impedes him from coming at the appointed hour. That

בָּרוּךְ שׁוֹמֵר הַבְטָחָתוֹ לְיִשְׂרָאֵל. בָּרוּךְ הוּא, שֶׁהַקָּדוֹשׁ בָּרוּךְ הוּא חִשַּׁב אֶת הַקֵּץ לַעֲשׂוֹת כְּמָה שֶׁאָמַר לְאַבְרָהָם אָבִינוּ בִּבְרִית בֵּין הַבְּתָרִים. שֶׁנֶּאֱמַר וַיֹּאמֶר לְאַבְרָם יָדֹעַ תֵּדַע כִּי גֵר יִהְיֶה זַרְעֲךָ בְּאֶרֶץ לֹא לָהֶם וַעֲבָדוּם וְעִנּוּ אוֹתָם אַרְבַּע מֵאוֹת שָׁנָה. וְגַם אֶת הַגּוֹי אֲשֶׁר יַעֲבֹדוּ דָּן אָנֹכִי וְאַחֲרֵי כֵן יֵצְאוּ בִּרְכֻשׁ גָּדוֹל:

---

would be an unusually generous promise.

This is precisely the difference between fulfilling a promise and guarding it. Fulfilling a promise means merely to be true to one's word on condition that the other party has satisfied his obligations. On the other hand, guarding a promise is a much stronger commitment; it entails taking steps to ensure that the other party's obligations are met.

God could have promised Abraham that He would redeem his descendants if they would manage somehow to survive hundreds of years of ruthless oppression and slavery. In the unlikely event that the Jewish people would still exist, God would redeem them and take them to the land of Canaan. This in itself would have been quite a generous gesture towards Abraham.

But God did much more. Not only did He vow to fulfill His promise, He also pledged to guard it — to make sure that the Jewish people survived the long years of oppression so that they would be eligible to merit the long-awaited reward promised to Abraham the Patriarch. This is what the author of the Haggadah means when he writes that God "guards His promise" — He made sure that the conditions required to fulfill the promise would be met.

"For the Holy One, Blessed Be He, Calculated the End..."

Two questions come to mind upon reading this passage: First, what does the author mean when he says that God "calculated the end"? Second, why did God tell Abraham that the oppression of the Jewish people would last for four hundred years, when in

BLESSED be He Who guards His promise to the Jewish People; blessed be He. For the Holy One, Blessed be He calculated the end when He would do as He had said to our Father Avraham at the Covenant Between the Pieces, as the Torah says: "[God] said to Avram, 'You must know that your descendants will be strangers in a land not their own. They will be slaves to [the people of the land], who will torment them for four hundred years. But I will also judge the people whose slaves they will be, and afterward they will leave with much property' " [Bereishis 15:131].

---

reality, they were in Egypt only 210 years? (See *Rashi* on Genesis 15:13.) Did God revise His promise to Abraham?

In fact, God began counting the four hundred years from the birth of Isaac, as the Sages say:

> *The decree was issued before Isaac was born. When Isaac was born, God calculated the end, as it is written, "Know with certainty that your offspring [i.e., your son Isaac] will be a foreigner..." (Genesis 15:13). Abraham, however, thought that the decree would be calculated from the time when God informed him of it.... On the fifteenth day of Nissan God spoke with Abraham at the Covenant between the Parts; on the fifteenth day of Nissan the ministering angels came to an nounce [to Abraham and Sarah] that Isaac would be born; on the fifteenth day of Nissan Isaac was born; on the fifteenth day of Nissan [the Jewish people] were redeemed from Egypt; and on the fifteenth day of Nissan Israel is destined to be redeemed [with the coming of the Messiah]....*
>
> (*Midrash Tanchuma, Parashas Bo* 9)

This is what God had to "calculate" — it was what one might call a "flexible" prophecy, for in spite of the guaranteed number of years, God alone decided which years they would be.

Likewise, during the First Temple era, God told the Jewish people that they would be exiled to Babylonia for seventy years. Theoretically, the seventy years could have been calculated from the earliest possible moment, say, when the first Israelite was banished from the territorial boundaries of Israel. However, this was not to be the case. Instead, the seventy years were calculated from the latest possible moment — the day on which the Temple was destroyed. This extended the seventy years of exile by eighteen years. Again, we see that the calculation of appointed times mentioned in the words of the Prophets are "flexible" in the sense that the prophecy itself contains a unique method of calculating the time periods that are mentioned therein.

The same can be said of the Egyptian exile — strictly speaking, God could have left the Jewish people in Egypt for a full four hundred years, without breaking His promise to Abraham. However, by that time the Jewish people would have completely assimilated and disappeared as a nation from the face of the earth. Abraham could not have held God responsible for this, since Israel's destruction would have been self-inflicted.

However, in His great mercy, God recalculated the four hundred years and pushed the beginning of the count all the way back to Isaac's birth, thereby sparing the Jewish people 190 additional years of slavery and oppression. Not coincidentally, the numerical value of the Hebrew word *keitz* (the end) is one hundred and ninety. God indeed "guarded His promise by calculating the end [*keitz*]"!

The last sentence of this passage cites God's assurance to Abraham, "But I will bring judgment against the nation that enslaves them, and they will then leave with great wealth...." Bear in mind that this sentence marks the conclusion of this passage and is intended to be directly in contrast to the opening statement, "At first our ancestors were idolaters...," for as mentioned earlier, the Seder is a night of opposites — slavery and freedom, darkness and light, questions and answers. What then is the opposite of idolatry? It is spiritual "great wealth" — in other words, the Torah. This is clearly how the author of the Haggadah understands God's assurance to Abraham.

However, this interpretation seems to contradict the Sages' understanding of the verse, for they said:

> *[It is written,] "Please [nah] speak in the ears of the people, and let each man request from his friend and each woman from her friend gold and silver vessels" (Exodus 11:2). The disciples of R. Yannai said: The Hebrew word nah indicates a plea. In essence, the Holy One, Blessed be He, said to Moses: Please say to the Israelites, "I beg you — go and request gold and silver vessels from the Egyptians in order that the righteous one [i.e., Abraham] will not say to Me, 'You have*

> *fulfilled the promise that "They will serve them and they will oppress them for four hundred years," but You have neglected to fulfill the promise, "And they will then leave with great wealth!" ' "*
>
> (*Berachos* 9a)

In truth, the Sages' interpretation itself is difficult to understand. First, if God intended to grant the Jewish people vast monetary wealth, why did He need to beg the Jews to borrow gold and silver vessels from their Egyptian neighbors? Did God have no other means at His disposal by which to fulfill His promise to Abraham? Surely He did not need their help! Secondly, the Sages' interpretation seems to imply that God did not really want to fulfill His promise to Abraham, but He had no other choice, for had He neglected to do so, Abraham would have complained. This is a truly outrageous assumption — if it were not for Abraham's complaint, would God have opted to renege on His promise? Impossible! Let us clarify the idea through an understanding of the following halachic principle.

According to Torah law, monetary value is often subjective. For example, if a person who has borrowed a hundred dollars returns only ninety-nine dollars to the lender, he has obviously not fulfilled his obligation. However, if the lender would prefer to be repaid in the form of an object owned by the borrower that is worth a hundred dollars in the lender's eyes, even though objectively the object is worth much less, the lender could give him this object and consider himself as having repaid his debt in full. The same principle applies to *pidyon haben*, the redemption of the firstborn (see Exodus 34:19; *Mishneh Torah, Hilchos Bikkurim* 11). The infant's father must give the *kohen* five units of silver, but if the *kohen* prefers to receive an object owned by the father that is worth five units of silver in his eyes, the father may fulfill the mitzvah by giving this object to the *kohen*, even if the object's market value is actually much less.

Parenthetically, this principle answers the famous philosophical question of why bad things happen to good people, and why good things happen to bad people. The commentators explain that "God does not withhold the reward of any creature" (*Sefer Ha'ikarim* 4:13). Even the wicked are rewarded for the good deeds they perform during their lives. However, they receive all of their reward in the ephemeral currency of this world, while the righteous receive all of their reward in the form of eternal bliss in the World to Come. This is the true intent of the verse, "He repays His enemies in their lifetimes to make them perish" (Deuteronomy 7:10). *Targum Onkelos* renders this verse, "He rewards the wicked for their good deeds in their lifetime in order to cause them to perish [from the World to Come]." By the time the wicked die and their souls stand in judgment before the Holy Tribunal, all of their reward has been consumed, and they have no means by which to obtain an eternal portion in the World to Come. (According to the same principle, punishment is meted out to good people in this world. Compared to the horrible punishments suffered by the wicked in the next world, the punishments of this world are, in relative terms, hardly substantial.)

In reference to the fate of the wicked, the commentaries raise the following difficulty: Since this world is nothing but an illusion in comparison with the eternal nature of the World to Come, where is the justice in giving the wicked their reward in the worthless currency of this world? The currency of this world is not just ephemeral, it is downright counterfeit! Why then do we say that "God does not withhold the reward of any creature"? The "reward" of the wicked is nothing but a sham!

Yet according to the halachic principle outlined above, the worth of an object is established by the one who desires it. It is true that the paltry currency of this world is completely worthless in objective terms, but just as the *kohen* can determine that an ordinary object is worth the equivalent of five units of silver, so too, a wicked individual can ascribe great value to this "unreal" world. In this instance, God yields to the desires of the wicked person and grants him his wish — He rewards his good deeds with money, power, and the fulfillment of physical desires.

Similarly, God promised Abraham that his descendants would leave Egypt with great "wealth." Now, what exactly did God mean by "great wealth"? Obviously, God's idea of wealth is not money but eternal spiritual reward — in other words, Torah and mitzvos. Unfortunately, however, the Jews coming out of Egypt were not at a sufficiently elevated spiritual level to appreciate the true meaning of "wealth." This is evident from the manner in which they behaved at the shores of the Red Sea before the waters parted. There they said to Moses:

> *Weren't there enough graves in Egypt? Why did you have to bring us out here to die in the desert? How could you do such a thing to us, bringing us out of Egypt? Didn't we tell you in Egypt to leave us alone and let us work for the Egyptians? It would have been better to be slaves in Egypt than to die here in the desert!*
>
> (*Exodus* 14:11–12)

In His great mercy, God took the Jews out of Egypt despite their low spiritual level, but now He encountered a problem, as it were. He had originally promised Abraham to grant his descendants great spiritual wealth (i.e., the Torah and mitzvos), but now the Jewish people, who were the rightful heirs to this promise, indicated through their behavior that they did not attach much value to this eternal gift. Their concept of "wealth" at that point was much cruder — to put it simply, they thought of wealth in terms of gold and silver. God realized that giving the Jewish people the Torah would not constitute a fulfillment of His promise to Abraham in their eyes, since they would consider the Torah more an obligation than a gift. He would also have to give them a sense of wealth in their own, coarser terms. Therefore, He begged the Jewish people to take the Egyptians' gold and silver vessels with them out of Egypt. Of course He could have granted them monetary wealth through miraculous means, but this gift would have replaced the eternal spiritual reward that He intended to give them at Mount Sinai. Therefore, in His boundless mercy, He resorted to asking the Jewish people to amass wealth through natural means.

This explains why the author of the Haggadah cites the verse, "But I will bring judgment against the nation that enslaves them, and they will then leave with great wealth..." as though it were a direct contrast to the Jewish people's idolatrous roots. In Divine terms, Israel's "great wealth" — the Torah — is indeed a sharp antithesis of their idolatrous beliefs of the past. As we read this passage, we should feel gratitude to God for removing from us the shackles of both physical slavery (that of Egypt) and spiritual slavery (that of paganism) and for granting us genuine and eternal wealth in the form of Torah and mitzvos.

Cover the matzos and pick up the cup. Then everyone says:

וְהִיא שֶׁעָמְדָה לַאֲבוֹתֵינוּ וְלָנוּ שֶׁלֹּא אֶחָד בִּלְבָד עָמַד עָלֵינוּ לְכַלּוֹתֵנוּ אֶלָּא שֶׁבְּכָל דּוֹר וָדוֹר עוֹמְדִים עָלֵינוּ לְכַלּוֹתֵנוּ וְהַקָּדוֹשׁ בָּרוּךְ הוּא מַצִּילֵנוּ מִיָּדָם:

Put down the cup and uncover the matzos. Then continue:

צֵא וּלְמַד מַה בִּקֵּשׁ לָבָן הָאֲרַמִּי לַעֲשׂוֹת לְיַעֲקֹב אָבִינוּ. שֶׁפַּרְעֹה לֹא גָזַר אֶלָּא עַל הַזְּכָרִים וְלָבָן בִּקֵּשׁ לַעֲקֹר אֶת הַכֹּל. שֶׁנֶּאֱמַר אֲרַמִּי אֹבֵד אָבִי וַיֵּרֶד מִצְרַיְמָה וַיָּגָר שָׁם בִּמְתֵי מְעָט, וַיְהִי שָׁם לְגוֹי גָּדוֹל עָצוּם וָרָב:

"THIS IS WHAT HAS STOOD BY OUR FOREFATHERS AND US."

At this point in the Seder, it is customary to cover the matzos and lift the cup of wine in one's hand. (It is important to fill the cup before starting to read the Haggadah. As we have mentioned earlier, the Haggadah should be recited before a full cup of wine.) The reason we hold the cup is because this passage is the essence of the entire Haggadah.

What does the author of the Haggadah mean by "this"? What has stood firm for our fathers and for us? The answer is, of course, God's "promise to Israel," which the author mentioned in the previous passage, the promise to Abraham that his descendants would be redeemed, not only from Egypt, but from every other form of captivity and servitude that they would endure until the end of time. This promise requires that we survive as a nation, for otherwise, God's promise would lack a most vital component — a beneficiary.

Were it not for this promise, the Jewish people would have been extinct by now. The author of the Haggadah explains the reason. Pharaoh was not the only one "who stood against us to annihilate us," for anti-Semites like Pharaoh have attempted to annihilate us "in every generation." It is possible for a nation to survive a one-time incident of "ethnic cleansing," but no nation on earth, other than Israel, has survived thousands of years of incessant hatred, persecution, and genocide. If a nation would survive

Cover the matzos and pick up the cup. Then everyone says:

THIS is what has stood by our forefathers and us. For not only one man has attempted to destroy us; in every generation they try to destroy us, but the Holy One, Blessed be He, saves us from their grasp.

Put down the cup and uncover the matzos. Then continue:

GO and learn what Lavan the Aramean sought to do to Ya'akov Avinu. For Pharaoh only decreed [death] for the male children, but Lavan sought to uproot everything, as the Torah says, "My father was a wandering Aramean, who went down to Egypt and abided there as a small group. There he became a nation, great, populous, and numerous" [Devarim 26:5].

---

one or two such incidents in the course of history, a non-believer could theoretically ascribe such a phenomenon to perseverence or just to sheer luck. But what can one say of a nation that has been banished from its homeland for some two thousand years, whose members, scattered throughout the four corners of the earth, have consistently been the targets of the most vicious and savage acts ever recorded in the dark annals of human history? How has it managed to survive this long war against such great odds? Even an ardent non-believer realizes the foolishness of ascribing Jewish survival to chance or good fortune. The only answer is Divine intervention; statistically, there can be no other explanation.

This is the essence of the Seder's purpose — to realize that God's promise to Abraham applies to the Jewish people today, every bit as much as it applied to the generation enslaved by Pharaoh. When we succeed in internalizing this thought, the Exodus suddenly becomes a pivotal event in our own lives. We suddenly realize that the Divine promise that ensured that our ancestors would be set free from the Egyptian bondage is the very same Divine promise that has kept the Jewish people in existence all these years, and that will also, we hope and pray, hasten the advent of the final redemption, speedily and in our days.

A compulsive skeptic, however, might interject at this point, "Why are you insinuating that the Jewish people have been persecuted in every generation? There are peaceful periods when, in the absence of Hitlers and Hamans, the Jews have lived peacefully and flourished in exile." The next passage addresses precisely this question.

"Go and learn..."

Let us analyze this passage carefully and see how it responds to the skeptic's question regarding the term "every generation."

The author of the Haggadah tells the skeptic to "go and learn." On the surface it is a good question — it would seem that there have been a number of generations throughout our history wherein the Jewish people have not faced imminent extinction or any perceivable danger whatsoever. Some people might say that Jewish society in America is a living example of such tranquility. However, the author of the Haggadah advises that we "go out and ascertain" — that we take a closer look — before drawing such conclusions. He is confident that if we will do so, we will find the danger threatening every generation.

To prove his point, he offers us an example of an outwardly benign but potentially fatal enemy — Laban the Aramean, the father of Jacob's two wives and the grandfather of his eleven children. (Benjamin had yet to be born when the encounter mentioned here took place.) When Jacob fled from Laban's household together with his wives and children, Laban gave chase and overtook Jacob's camp. Portraying himself as the aggrieved father, he berated Jacob for running away and not allowing him to kiss his daughters and grandchildren good-bye (see Genesis 31:25–28). Yes, the author of the Haggadah tells us, Laban seemed the very picture of a loving father, but in his sly way he almost destroyed the Jewish people; in fact he was even more dangerous than Pharaoh.

But to what specific event is the author of the Haggadah referring? It is difficult to believe that Laban actually intended to slaughter his daughters and grandchildren in cold blood following his encounter with Jacob. What then is the meaning of the verse "An Aramean tried to destroy my forefather"? There are two explanations to this confusing issue.

As we know, Abraham sent his servant Eliezer to find a suitable wife for Isaac (see Genesis 24), and he chose Rebecca, Laban's younger sister. The Oral Tradition teaches that after the wedding agreement was concluded (in absentia, for Isaac remained in the land of Canaan), Laban attempted to poison Eliezer. Miraculously, Besuel — Laban and Rebecca's father — ended up with Eliezer's portion, and so it was Besuel who drank the poison and died.

What would have happened if Eliezer had drunk the poison, as Laban had intended? A major disaster would have resulted. Halachah stipulates that a person may marry a woman by proxy. For example, an envoy may take a man's ring, travel to a different country, and marry a particular woman on behalf of the man who has sent him on this mission. This constitutes a perfectly legal marriage. But what would happen if the sender had not specified which woman to marry? What if he said simply, "Marry a woman on my behalf"? Now imagine that the envoy finds a suitable bride for the sender, marries her on his behalf, sends back a message with the words "*mazal tov*!" to the new groom, and then suddenly dies. The sender is now married, but he has no idea to whom. According to halachah, he may not marry any woman in the world, lest she be a relative of his new wife. This man would have to remain single for the rest of his life.

Likewise, had Laban succeeded in killing Eliezer, Isaac would have had to remain single for the rest of his life. He would have died childless, and that would have been the end of the Jewish people. This is the technical interpretation of the verse, "An Aramean tried to destroy my forefather."

The second interpretation is more closely associated to the actual events that are recorded in the Torah. In the Grace after Meals we say, "May the Compassionate One bless...ours and all that is ours, just as our forefathers, Abraham, Isaac, and Jacob were blessed with everything [*bakol*], from everything [*mikol*], everything [*kol*]." The Sages teach that these terms refer respectively to the blessings of Abraham, Isaac, and Jacob. "With everything [*bakol*]" refers to the verse, "Abraham was old, well advanced in years, and God blessed Abraham with everything" (Genesis 24:1). "From everything [*mikol*]" refers to the verse, "Then Isaac...said...I partook of everything [*mikol*]...and I blessed him..." (ibid. 27:33). "Everything [*kol*]" refers to Jacob's statement, "I have everything [*kol*]" (ibid. 33:11).

How could Jacob have said, "I have everything"? No human being can possibly have everything, even if he is the richest man in the world. Evidently, Jacob was speaking from a subjective perspective — he had everything he needed, and he desired nothing more, for he realized that all his possessions had been granted to him by God. Whatever he lacked was not important to him; thus, as far as he was concerned, he had everything.

Esau, on the other hand, did not say, "I have everything," but rather, "I have plenty" (ibid. 33:9), implying that he had room for more. Esau did not differentiate between his needs and his desires — to him everything was needed and desired, and the more, the better. Unlike Jacob, he did not think that whatever he lacked was not important to him; on the contrary, it was very important to him. It is for this reason that he accepted Jacob's gifts after having made a show of refusing them for the sake of outward appearances.

Only Jacob attained the spiritual level at which he could in all honesty declare, "I have everything." It stemmed from his ability to pursue nothing but truth — what the Sages refer to as *Emes LeYaakov* (the Truth of Jacob). This is indicative of the highest blessing — the blessing of truth.

Laban the Aramean was the antithesis of Jacob. The name Laban means "white," while *Arami* is closely associated with the word *rama'i*, which means "cheater." In other words, Laban was a "white cheater" — he feigned extreme righteousness while performing the most despicable acts of deceit. He was the type of liar who, when caught, does not confess, but rather attempts to convince his victims that he was actually trying to perform a mitzvah.

We see this evidenced a number of times in Scripture. For example, Laban ran out to welcome Jacob when he arrived at Aram. The Sages say that as he hugged Jacob, he searched his clothes for money. But on the surface, Laban was performing the mitzvah of *hachnasas orchim* (welcoming a guest)! Later, after Jacob had been his guest for a few days, Laban said to him, "I don't want you to work for me for free." What a nice offer, but wait — who ever mentioned working? Jacob had not been working for Laban at the time. This was Laban's diplomatic way of saying, "I'm not going to put you up forever, you slouch! It's high time you put away those books of yours and start doing some productive work around here!" Yet on the surface, Laban was altruistically refusing to accept Jacob's free service, demanding instead to pay him for his labor.

Later, when Laban cheated Jacob and gave him his eldest daughter Leah as a wife, instead of Rachel, whom Jacob had chosen, Laban justified his treachery with righteous indignation. Essentially, what he told Jacob was, "Unlike some people, in this country we show respect for older siblings." With this message, not only did he cheat Jacob, he also had the audacity to admonish him for taking Esau's blessing! This is the nature of Laban — he feigns snow-white righteousness, while at his core he remains black as ebony.

What would have resulted if Jacob and his children would have stayed in Laban's proximity? Laban certainly would have influenced them and swiftly destroyed the *Emes LeYaakov*, the trait of truth that enabled Jacob to say, in all sincerity, "I have everything."

With this insight, let us read the words of the Haggadah again and try to perceive the deeper meaning: "Go out and ascertain what Laban the Aramean intended to do to Jacob our forefather, for Pharaoh decreed destruction only of the males, while Laban intended to eradicate the whole [nation]." Pharaoh intended to slay only the Jewish males, but Laban intended to destroy Israel's essence — he would have eradicated Jacob's special characteristic, which was the source of his ability to declare, "I have everything."

Let us now return to our skeptic, who questioned the Haggadah's claim that "in every generation there are those who stand against us to annihilate us." Even in generations when the Jewish people are not threatened by visible enemies, their survival still may be at stake; the situation may, in fact, be far more dangerous in environments favorable to the Jews. When a Jew lives in a country where everyone is nice to him, he feels an overpowering desire to blend in and adopt the customs of the society. Another term for this phenomenon is "assimilation." We mourn the six million Jews who were killed by the Nazis during the Holocaust, but do we mourn the equal number of Jews who have perished spiritually since World War II as a result of assimilation and intermarriage? It is a soft, quiet Holocaust, and for this reason it is for the most part ignored. Yet, potentially, it can fell many times more Jews than the Nazis ever managed to kill.

Despite the spiritual death taking place all around us, on the night of Passover we are comforted by the knowledge that God's promise "has stood firm for our fathers and for us. For it was not one alone who stood against us to annihilate us; in every generation there are those who stand against us to annihilate us. But the Holy One, Blessed be He, saves us from their hands."

Egypt, Anti-Semitism, and Jewish Survival

There is yet another point to consider regarding the passage, "Go out and ascertain what Laban the Aramean intended to do to Jacob our forefather..." (Deuteronomy 26:5). Because the Haggadah is so familiar to us, we tend to forget the context of the verse that the author is quoting. It is actually an excerpt from the lengthy declaration that was uttered by individuals who would bring their offerings of first fruits to the Temple. The entire passage reads:

> *It will be when you enter the land that Hashem your God gives you as an inheritance, and you possess it, and dwell in it, that you shall take of the first of every fruit of the ground that you bring in from your land...and you shall put it in a basket and go to the place where Hashem your God will choose to rest His Name. You shall come to whomever will be the priest in those days, and you shall say to him, "I declare today to Hashem your God that I have come to the land that God swore to give to our forefathers." The priest shall take the basket from your hand and lay it before the altar of Hashem your God. Then you shall call out and say before Hashem your God, "An Aramean tried to destroy my forefather; and he went to Egypt with a small number of men and lived there as an immigrant, but it was there that he became a great, powerful, and populous nation. The Egyptians mistreated us, and afflicted us, and placed hard work upon us. Then we cried to Hashem, the God of our forefathers, and God heard our voice and saw our affliction, our travail, and our oppression. God took us out of Egypt with a strong hand and with an outstretched arm, with great awesomeness, and with signs and with wonders. He brought us to this place, and He gave us this land, a land flowing with milk and honey. And now, behold, I have brought the first fruit of the ground that You have given me, O God." And you shall lay it before Hashem your God, and you shall prostrate*

yourself before Hashem your God.

(Deuteronomy 26:1–10*)*

In terms of its context, it becomes clear that the excerpt cited by the author of the Haggadah is no more than a parenthetical digression from the main theme of the Biblical passage in which it appears. The passage is actually a description of the offering of the first fruit and the declaration of gratitude to be articulated by the individual bringing the offering. If so, we may rightly wonder why the author of the Haggadah chose to quote this particular verse. The Book of Exodus provides a detailed narrative of all the events that led to Israel's redemption. Would it not be more appropriate to quote one of the numerous and even more descriptive verses from there, which focuses entirely on the redemption from Egypt? Why did the author overlook those, and instead cite the verse from Deuteronomy?

The Maharal of Prague explains that the main goal of Passover night is not merely to recount the events that led to Israel's redemption from their Egyptian slavemasters, but to personally identify these events with them in such a way as to cause feelings of profound gratitude to well up from deep within ourselves. Our objective on this night is to internalize the concept that our lives would have been dramatically different had the Exodus not taken place. The focus should be not on our forefathers' experiences, but on our own emotional responses to the miracles that God performed for them.

In light of this approach, we can understand why the author of the Haggadah chose to cite the verses in the Book of Deuteron omy rather than the lengthier and more detailed descriptions of the redemption that are to be found in the Book of Exodus. The Book of Exodus offers an historical record of the redemption, whereas the verses chosen from the Book of Deuteronomy reveal how a Jew should react to these events. On the night of Passover, we are to emulate the Jewish farmer who brings a first-fruit offering. Just as he feels deeply grateful to God for having blessed his fields and having caused his trees to bloom and give forth fruit, so must we cultivate through our celebration of Passover an overwhelming sense of gratitude to God for having taken our forefathers, as well as ourselves, out of Egypt.

וַיֵּרֶד מִצְרַיְמָה: אָנוּס עַל פִּי הַדִּבּוּר.

וַיָּגָר שָׁם: מְלַמֵּד שֶׁלֹּא יָרַד יַעֲקֹב אָבִינוּ לְהִשְׁתַּקֵּעַ בְּמִצְרַיִם אֶלָּא לָגוּר שָׁם. שֶׁנֶּאֱמַר, וַיֹּאמְרוּ אֶל פַּרְעֹה לָגוּר בָּאָרֶץ בָּאנוּ כִּי אֵין מִרְעֶה לַצֹּאן אֲשֶׁר לַעֲבָדֶיךָ, כִּי כָבֵד הָרָעָב בְּאֶרֶץ כְּנָעַן, וְעַתָּה יֵשְׁבוּ נָא עֲבָדֶיךָ בְּאֶרֶץ גֹּשֶׁן:

בִּמְתֵי מְעָט: כְּמָה שֶׁנֶּאֱמַר בְּשִׁבְעִים נֶפֶשׁ יָרְדוּ אֲבוֹתֶיךָ מִצְרָיְמָה וְעַתָּה שָׂמְךָ יְיָ אֱלֹהֶיךָ כְּכוֹכְבֵי הַשָּׁמַיִם לָרוֹב.

"Who went down to Egypt..."

The next narrative in the Haggadah analyzes each clause of the verses quoted above. The author of the Haggadah explains that Jacob went to Egypt against his will. He was given no choice in the matter, for God had already decreed in the days of Abraham the Patriarch that his descendants would be cast into exile. To prove this point, the author of the Haggadah quotes the statement that Jacob's children made to Pharaoh, "We have come to sojourn in the land because there is no grazing for your servants' flocks..." (Genesis 47:4), demonstrating that they agreed to leave the land of Canaan only because of the severity of the drought. This passage teaches us that even though the Jewish people have been forced into exile, to remain there for a seemingly endless period of time, they must never forget that they have only "come to sojourn in the land," and that their true home will always be the Land of Israel.

"As a small group..."

Next the Haggadah explains that the original group of Jews who descended into Egypt consisted of only seventy souls. Only 210 years later, this "small" group of immigrants comprised 600,000 men over the age of twenty, in addition to a proportional number of women, children, and senior citizens. The Torah employs a rather demeaning term to illustrate this miraculous population

Who went down to Egypt — obliged to by the Divine command.

And abided there — [the choice of words] teaches us that Ya'akov Avinu did not go down to Egypt with the idea of settling there, only to abide there a while, as the Torah says, "They said to Pharaoh, 'We have come to abide in the land, for there is no pasturage for your servants' flocks, so severe is the famine in the land of Canaan; now let your servants dwell in the land of Goshen' " [Bereishis 47:4].

As a small group — as the Torah says, "Your fathers went down to Egypt with seventy souls, and now Hashem your God has made you as numerous as the stars in the sky" [Devarim 10:22].

---

explosion: "The Israelites were fertile and prolific [*vayishritzu*], and they increased greatly..." (Exodus 1:7). The Hebrew term *vayishritzu* is derived from the word *sheretz*, which means "small, crawling animal"; thus a colloquial rendering of the phrase would read, "The Israelites were fertile and multiplied like mice...." The obvious question that presents itself is: Why would the Torah choose such a disparaging term in reference to the Israelites?

The Torah here is describing Israel's population growth from the perspective of the Egyptians. Pharaoh had originally intended that Jacob's children live exclusively in the land of Goshen, where they would remain segregated from mainstream Egyptian society. Gradually, however, as the old generation passed away, their children thought, "Why do we have to keep living in this ugly ghetto? Let's move to a higher-class neighborhood. The better the Egyptians know us, the more they'll like us!"

However, the Israelites were in for a surprise. The better the Egyptians got to know them, the more they became utterly disgusted with them. They perceived the Jews as a plague of mice which inundated their neighborhoods, their professions, their economy, even their government. In time, every important position came to be filled by a Jew. It seemed to them that the Jews were everywhere, until Pharaoh declared, "Behold, the people, the Israelites, are more numerous and stronger than we!" (Exodus 1:9). For this reason, the Torah uses the term *vayishritzu* to describe Israel's miraculous numerical growth.

וַיְהִי שָׁם לְגוֹי: מְלַמֵּד שֶׁהָיוּ יִשְׂרָאֵל מְצֻיָּנִים שָׁם.

גָּדוֹל, עָצוּם: כְּמָה שֶׁנֶּאֱמַר: וּבְנֵי יִשְׂרָאֵל פָּרוּ וַיִּשְׁרְצוּ וַיִּרְבּוּ וַיַּעַצְמוּ בִּמְאֹד מְאֹד וַתִּמָּלֵא הָאָרֶץ אֹתָם.

וָרָב: כְּמָה שֶׁנֶּאֱמַר: רְבָבָה כְּצֶמַח הַשָּׂדֶה נְתַתִּיךְ וַתִּרְבִּי וַתִּגְדְּלִי וַתָּבֹאִי בַּעֲדִי עֲדָיִים שָׁדַיִם נָכֹנוּ וּשְׂעָרֵךְ צִמֵּחַ וְאַתְּ עֵרֹם וְעֶרְיָה. וָאֶעֱבֹר עָלַיִךְ וָאֶרְאֵךְ מִתְבּוֹסֶסֶת בְּדָמָיִךְ, וָאֹמַר לָךְ בְּדָמַיִךְ חֲיִי, וָאֹמַר לָךְ בְּדָמַיִךְ חֲיִי:

וַיָּרֵעוּ אֹתָנוּ הַמִּצְרִים וַיְעַנּוּנוּ וַיִּתְּנוּ עָלֵינוּ עֲבֹדָה קָשָׁה.

"The Egyptians did us evil."

This passage is commonly translated, "The Egyptians *did us eveil,* and afflicted us, and placed hard work upon us." If this literal translation would have been the true intention of the verse, it should have read, *vayarei'u lanu*, not *vayarei'u osanu.* Furthermore, if the verse indeed means, "The Egyptians mistreated us," then why does the author of the Haggadah cite the verse, "Come, let us devise plans against them, lest they increase..." as its proof? Surely the Egyptians' decision to "devise plans" against the Israelites was not the greatest atrocity perpetrated by them! What of the decree to cast the Israelites' male children into the sea? What of the inhumane labor to which they subjected the Jewish people?

A more accurate translation of the phrase *vayarei'u osanu* would be, "The Egyptians made evil of us," or more colloquially, "They gave us a bad name." According to this rendering, the proof offered by the author of the Haggadah is understandable — the Egyptians discredited us by accusing us of disloyalty, as it is written, "Come let us devise plans against them lest they increase, and if war will befall us, [they] too will join our enemies and wage war against us and go up out of the land" (Exodus 1:10).

The Egyptians' attempt to discredit the Jews has become a prototype for anti-Semitic propaganda. Because Jews have exhib-

There he became a nation, great... — [the fact that the Jews are called a nation] teaches us that they were distinguishable [from all others] there.

Populous... — as the Torah says, "the children of Israel multiplied, swarmed, increased, became exceedingly populous, until the land was full of them" [Shemos 1:7].

And numerous — as it says, "I made you as numerous as the shrubs of the field; you multiplied and grew until you came into choice ornaments: breasts set and your hair grown, but you were bare and naked. Then I passed by you and saw you rolling in your blood; I said to you, 'By your blood, live!' — I said to you, 'By your blood, live!' " [Yechezkel 16:7].

"The Egyptians did us evil: they tormented us and loaded us with hard work" [Devarim 26:6].

---

ited exemplary loyalty to their host nations throughout history, accusations to the contrary by the citizens of any given country where Jews abide are indicative of rising anti-Semitism. Such slander will soon escalate into explicit denunciations, which will cause Jews to be perceived as social parasites, who benefit from the labor of others without contributing anything in return. At that point, disaster is at hand. This is the true intent of this passage.

The Haggadah supports the statement, "The Egyptians... afflicted us and placed hard work upon us" with the verse, "They put over them tax officers in order to afflict them with their burdens, and they built store-cities for Pharaoh: Pisom and Ramses" (Exodus 1:11). At first glance, however, the proof seems inappropriate, for although tax officers admittedly can be quite irritating at times, surely they do not qualify as instruments of "affliction"!

Yet Pharaoh, not unlike many modern-day tyrants, wanted to annihilate Israel "legally," without violating the "bill of rights." Sensing that it would be bad for his image, as the respected leader of the most powerful nation on earth, to suddenly enslave his own subjects, he looked for a way to carry out his evil plans within the framework of the law. It was then that he thought of his tax officers.

Egyptian taxation worked according to a system different

וַיָּרֵעוּ אֹתָנוּ הַמִּצְרִים: כְּמָה שֶׁנֶּאֱמַר: הָבָה נִתְחַכְּמָה לוֹ פֶּן יִרְבֶּה וְהָיָה כִּי תִקְרֶאנָה מִלְחָמָה וְנוֹסַף גַּם הוּא עַל שֹׂנְאֵינוּ וְנִלְחַם בָּנוּ וְעָלָה מִן הָאָרֶץ.

וַיְעַנּוּנוּ: כְּמָה שֶׁנֶּאֱמַר: וַיָּשִׂימוּ עָלָיו שָׂרֵי מִסִּים לְמַעַן עַנֹּתוֹ בְּסִבְלֹתָם וַיִּבֶן עָרֵי מִסְכְּנוֹת לְפַרְעֹה אֶת פִּתֹם וְאֶת רַעַמְסֵס.

וַיִּתְּנוּ עָלֵינוּ עֲבֹדָה קָשָׁה: כְּמָה שֶׁנֶּאֱמַר: וַיַּעֲבִדוּ מִצְרַיִם אֶת בְּנֵי יִשְׂרָאֵל בְּפָרֶךְ:

וַנִּצְעַק אֶל יְיָ אֱלֹהֵי אֲבֹתֵינוּ וַיִּשְׁמַע יְיָ אֶת קֹלֵנוּ וַיַּרְא אֶת עָנְיֵנוּ וְאֶת עֲמָלֵנוּ וְאֶת לַחֲצֵנוּ.

---

from that to which we are accustomed. Egyptians were not required to pay a percentage of their earnings to Pharaoh, but rather to set aside a few days each year in which to work for him directly. The work force for all public services and federal and municipal projects was comprised entirely of such "volunteers." The system worked along the same lines as today's army draft, which, in a sense, is also a form of taxation.

However, as with the draft, there were segments of the Egyptian populace that were exempt from having to participate in public service, namely, the priests. We learn this from the passage in the Torah describing the taxation system that Joseph instituted (see Genesis 47:22). Who exactly were these priests? In ancient Egypt, whoever dedicated his entire life to the attainment of higher levels of spirituality and to providing guidance to others was considered a priest. All of the Jews living in Goshen fit this definition; therefore, due to their priestly status, all Jews were exempt from taxation during Joseph's lifetime.

This situation changed when the Jews began leaving the ghettos of Goshen and migrating to the major Egyptian cities. There, through their enormous enterprise and creativity, they worked their way up the social ladder and earned high wages, much to the displeasure of the Egyptians. It was at this point that Pharaoh said, "The Israelites are becoming too numerous and

The Egyptians did us evil — as the Torah says, "Come, let us outsmart him, lest he grow [too] numerous, and then if there is a war he might become an additional enemy, and fight us and leave the country" [Shemos 1:10].

They tormented us — as the Torah says, "They put taskmasters over [the people] so as to torment them with their burdens. [The people] built the store-cities of Pitom and Raamses for Pharaoh" [Shemos 1:11].

And loaded us with hard work — as the Torah says, "The Egyptians put the children of Israel to back-breaking labor" [Shemos 1:13].

"Then we cried to Hashem the God of our fathers. Hashem heard our voice and saw our privation, our toll, and our distress" [Devarim 26:7].

---

strong for us — we must deal wisely with them" (Exodus 1:9–10).

Pharaoh launched his "final solution" to the "Jewish problem" by revoking the priestly status of all the Jews who had abandoned their idyllic way of life in Goshen in order to enter the Egyptian marketplace. "Draft notices" were sent to such Jews; they were all ordered to report for public service on the same day. The Jews, full of ambition and enthusiasm, readily agreed to contribute their share to the society that they had come to embrace.

When they asked how long they would have to work, Pharaoh replied, "Don't worry, I'll tell you when to stop." As we all know, he never did.

The only Jews who retained their priestly status were those who had chosen to continue pursuing their spiritual aspirations in the land of Goshen. They were definitely a minority — the tribe of Levi, plus a few spiritual seekers from the other tribes. By tending their sheep and growing a modest amount of crops, they managed to learn Torah and legally avoid the draft, while their more upwardly mobile brethren were caught in Pharaoh's evil dragnet. In this manner, Pharaoh found a clean solution (or so he thought!) to the "Jewish problem." Legally speaking, the Jews were not his slaves, they were merely members of the work force who were paying their debt to Egyptian society, and it was the tax officers who ensured that they were not lax in their "payments."

וַנִּצְעַק אֶל יְיָ אֱלֹהֵי אֲבֹתֵינוּ: כְּמָה שֶׁנֶּאֱמַר: וַיְהִי בַיָּמִים הָרַבִּים הָהֵם וַיָּמָת מֶלֶךְ מִצְרַיִם וַיֵּאָנְחוּ בְנֵי יִשְׂרָאֵל מִן הָעֲבֹדָה וַיִּזְעָקוּ וַתַּעַל שַׁוְעָתָם אֶל הָאֱלֹהִים מִן הָעֲבֹדָה.

וַיִּשְׁמַע יְיָ אֶת קֹלֵנוּ: כְּמָה שֶׁנֶּאֱמַר: וַיִּשְׁמַע אֱלֹהִים אֶת נַאֲקָתָם וַיִּזְכֹּר אֱלֹהִים אֶת בְּרִיתוֹ אֶת אַבְרָהָם אֶת יִצְחָק וְאֶת יַעֲקֹב:

וַיַּרְא אֶת עָנְיֵנוּ: זוֹ פְּרִישׁוּת דֶּרֶךְ אֶרֶץ, כְּמָה שֶׁנֶּאֱמַר: וַיַּרְא אֱלֹהִים אֶת בְּנֵי יִשְׂרָאֵל וַיֵּדַע אֱלֹהִים.

וְאֶת עֲמָלֵנוּ: אֵלּוּ הַבָּנִים, כְּמָה שֶׁנֶּאֱמַר: כָּל הַבֵּן הַיִּלּוֹד הַיְאֹרָה תַּשְׁלִיכֻהוּ וְכָל הַבַּת תְּחַיּוּן.

וְאֶת לַחֲצֵנוּ: זֶה הַדְּחַק, כְּמָה שֶׁנֶּאֱמַר: וְגַם רָאִיתִי אֶת הַלַּחַץ אֲשֶׁר מִצְרַיִם לֹחֲצִים אֹתָם:

וַיּוֹצִאֵנוּ יְיָ מִמִּצְרַיִם בְּיָד חֲזָקָה וּבִזְרֹעַ נְטוּיָה וּבְמֹרָא גָּדֹל וּבְאֹתוֹת וּבְמֹפְתִים.

וַיּוֹצִאֵנוּ יְיָ מִמִּצְרַיִם: לֹא עַל יְדֵי מַלְאָךְ וְלֹא עַל יְדֵי שָׂרָף וְלֹא עַל יְדֵי שָׁלִיחַ אֶלָּא הַקָּדוֹשׁ בָּרוּךְ הוּא בִּכְבוֹדוֹ וּבְעַצְמוֹ, שֶׁנֶּאֱמַר: וְעָבַרְתִּי בְאֶרֶץ מִצְרַיִם בַּלַּיְלָה הַזֶּה וְהִכֵּיתִי כָל בְּכוֹר בְּאֶרֶץ מִצְרַיִם מֵאָדָם וְעַד בְּהֵמָה וּבְכָל אֱלֹהֵי מִצְרַיִם אֶעֱשֶׂה שְׁפָטִים אֲנִי יְיָ.

"NOT BY MEANS OF AN ANGEL..."

Understood simply, this passage teaches that God alone is responsible for having taken us out of Egypt, and that we are obligated to express our gratitude to no entity other than God. Were it not for this passage, we might have been inclined to ascribe the redemption to a *shaliach* (an envoy) — Moshe, for instance.

Then we cried to Hashem the God of our fathers — as the Torah says, "It happened during that long time that the king of Egypt died. Then the children of Israel sighed because of the work; they cried out, and their shout went up to God from the work" [Shemos 2:23].

Hashem heard our voice — as the Torah says, "God heard their cry, and God remembered His covenant with Avraham, with Yitzchak, and with Ya'akov" [Shemos 2:24].

And saw our privation — that is the cessation of family life, as the Torah says, "God saw the children of Israel, and God knew" [Shemos 2:25].

Our toil — those are the children, as the Torah says, "Every newborn son you must throw into the Nile, and every daughter you must let live" [Shemos 1:22].

And our distress — that is the pressure [of work], as the Torah says, "And also I have seen the way the Egyptians pressure them" [Shemos 3:9].

"Hashem took us out of Egypt with a strong hand and an outstretched arm, with great awe, with signs and with wonders" [Devarim 26:8].

Hashem took us out of Egypt — not by means of an angel, not by means of a *seraph,* not by means of a messenger, but the Holy One, Blessed be He, with His own Self and Presence, as the Torah says, "I will pass through the land of Egypt this night, and strike every firstborn in the land of Egypt, from man to beast, and I will execute judgment against all the gods of Egypt; I am Hashem." [Shemos 12:12].

Alternatively, we might have attributed these miracles to a *malach* or a *saraph*. What do these Hebrew terms mean? They are commonly translated as "angel" and "fiery angel," respectively, but the implications of these words remain vague. What does the author of the Haggadah want to tell us? Both terms refer to specific angels, whose names appear in the prayer that accompanies the *Shema* said at bedtime: "In the Name of the God of Israel, let Michael be at my right, Gabriel at my left, Uriel before me,

וְעָבַרְתִּי בְאֶרֶץ מִצְרַיִם בַּלַּיְלָה הַזֶּה: אֲנִי וְלֹא מַלְאָךְ.
וְהִכֵּיתִי כָל בְּכוֹר בְּאֶרֶץ מִצְרַיִם: אֲנִי וְלֹא שָׂרָף.
וּבְכָל אֱלֹהֵי מִצְרַיִם אֶעֱשֶׂה שְׁפָטִים: אֲנִי וְלֹא הַשָּׁלִיחַ.

אֲנִי יְיָ: אֲנִי הוּא וְלֹא אַחֵר:

בְּיָד חֲזָקָה: זוֹ הַדֶּבֶר, כְּמָה שֶׁנֶּאֱמַר: הִנֵּה יַד יְיָ הוֹיָה בְּמִקְנְךָ אֲשֶׁר בַּשָּׂדֶה בַּסּוּסִים בַּחֲמֹרִים בַּגְּמַלִּים בַּבָּקָר וּבַצֹּאן דֶּבֶר כָּבֵד מְאֹד.

וּבִזְרֹעַ נְטוּיָה: זוֹ הַחֶרֶב, כְּמָה שֶׁנֶּאֱמַר: וְחַרְבּוֹ שְׁלוּפָה בְּיָדוֹ נְטוּיָה עַל יְרוּשָׁלָיִם.

Rafael behind me, and upon my head, God's Divine Presence."

The name Michael literally means, "who is like God?" This angel represents the spiritual force that we refer to as "faith in God," or *emuna*. Like everything else in the universe, *emuna* is an entity that God created and one that He imparts to those who are worthy. Gabriel represents the manifestation of God's will on the physical plane of reality. Uriel means "the light of God"; as its name implies, this angel represents Divine spiritual guidance. Rafael, the last angel mentioned in this passage, represents Divine healing.

According to the Midrash, three of these four angels visited Abraham the Patriarch prior to the destruction of Sodom and Gomorrah, as it is written, "[Abraham] lifted his eyes and he saw three men standing a short distance from him" (Genesis 18:2). Michael came to inform Abraham and Sarah that they would have a son (ibid. 18:10), for as we have explained, Michael represents faith in God. In effect, God was telling Abraham and Sarah, "If you have faith in Me and believe that you will have a son by next year, then it will happen." The angel Gabriel came to overturn Sodom (ibid. 19:25), and the angel Rafael came to heal Abraham and save Lot. With the *Shema* that we say at night we ask that Rafael stand behind us, because illness always sneaks up on its victims suddenly and unexpectedly, as though "from behind." We pray that Rafael

I will pass through the land of Egypt — I, and not an angel.

And strike every firstborn — I, and not a *seraph*.

And I will execute judgment against all the gods of Egypt — I and not the messenger.

I am Hashem — I am He and no other.

With a strong hand — that is the plague, as the Torah says, "See, the hand of Hashem is on your herds in the fields, on the horses, the donkeys, the camels, the cattle, and the flocks — a very virulent plague" [Shemos 9:3].

And with an outstretched arm — that is the sword, as it says, "His sword is drawn in his hand, outstretched over Jerusalem" [Divrei Ha-yamim 21:16].

"guard the rear" and protect us from illness throughout the night.

In light of the awesome power of these angels, it might have been logical to assume that they also had a central role in performing the awesome miracles that led to Israel's Exodus from Egypt. For example, we might have thought that the merit that God granted the Israelites empowered the angel Michael to redeem them from bondage. (The Hebrew letters of the name Michael can be rearranged to spell *malach*.) For this reason, the author of the Haggadah stresses that the Israelites were redeemed "not through a *malach*" — the angel Michael had no part in bringing about their redemption. Alternatively, we might have thought that the destruction of the Egyptians was brought about by a *saraph*, "a fiery angel" — this is a reference to Gabriel, the angel of destruction who overturned Sodom in the days of Abraham. But again, the author of the Haggadah rejects this idea. "God then took us out of Egypt — not through a *malach*, nor through a *saraph*." God Himself intervened on our behalf, without the involvement of any intermediary forces.

"'AND WITH AN OUTSTRETCHED ARM' — THAT IS THE SWORD..."

This is another difficult interpretation, for where in the Torah's

וּבְמֹרָא גָדֹל: זֶה גִּלּוּי שְׁכִינָה, כְּמָה שֶׁנֶּאֱמַר: אוֹ הֲנִסָּה אֱלֹהִים לָבוֹא לָקַחַת לוֹ גוֹי מִקֶּרֶב גּוֹי בְּמַסֹּת בְּאֹתֹת וּבְמוֹפְתִים וּבְמִלְחָמָה וּבְיָד חֲזָקָה וּבִזְרוֹעַ נְטוּיָה וּבְמוֹרָאִים גְּדֹלִים כְּכֹל אֲשֶׁר עָשָׂה לָכֶם יְיָ אֱלֹהֵיכֶם בְּמִצְרַיִם לְעֵינֶיךָ.

וּבְאֹתוֹת: זֶה הַמַּטֶּה, כְּמָה שֶׁנֶּאֱמַר: וְאֶת הַמַּטֶּה הַזֶּה תִּקַּח בְּיָדֶךָ אֲשֶׁר תַּעֲשֶׂה בּוֹ אֶת הָאֹתֹת.

וּבְמֹפְתִים: זֶה הַדָּם, כְּמָה שֶׁנֶּאֱמַר: וְנָתַתִּי מוֹפְתִים בַּשָּׁמַיִם וּבָאָרֶץ:

---

narrative of the Exodus do we find a reference to a sword?

The answer is provided by the commentary of the Midrash on the verse, "Who struck Egypt by means of their firstborn, for His loving-kindness is eternal" (Psalms 136:10):

> *When the Holy One Blessed be He brought the plague of the firstborn, all the firstborn of the Egyptians came to their parents and said to them, "Do you not wish us to live? Send away these Hebrews from among us, for otherwise we will die!"*
>
> *Their fathers responded, "They will not leave here, even if it means that all of Egypt must be destroyed!"*
>
> *What did the firstborn do? Each one grasped his sword and killed his parents, as it is written, "Who strikes Egypt by means of their firstborn." Scripture does not use the words, "Who strikes the firstborn of Egypt," but "Who strikes Egypt by means of their firstborn."*
>
> *(Midrash Shochar Tov)*

It is to this sword that the author of the Haggadah is alluding — the sword with which the Egyptians destroyed one another.

"'And with wonders' — this is the blood..."

At first glance, this interpretation is also difficult to understand, for the verse in Joel has absolutely nothing to do with the Exodus.

With great awe — that is the Shechinah revealed, as the Torah says, "Or has God ever before come to take a people for Himself from the midst of another people, with miracles, signs, and wonders, with war, with a strong hand and an outstretched arm, with great and awesome happenings, such as all that Hashem your God did for you in Egypt before your eyes?" [Devarim 4:34].

With signs — that is the staff, as the Torah says, "Take this staff in your hand, with which you will do the signs" [Shemos 4:17].

And with wonders — that is the blood, as It says, "I will put My wonders in Heaven and earth:

The majority of Joel's prophecy describes the imminent approach of an earth-shattering event, which he likens to an impending plague of locusts, as it is written, "Never has there been such a vast and mighty horde, and never will there be again until the end of time. Whatever is in front of it is consumed by fire; all that is behind it, singed by a flame..." (ibid. 2:3). These fire-spitting locusts will leave in their wake "blood, fire, and pillars of smoke [*timros ashan*]." Most commentators explain that the prophet is describing the war of Gog and Magog and the heavy casualties that will ensue, incurred by the multinational force that will attack Israel. This war is to be followed by the final redemption.

According to this understanding, it seems obvious that the fire-spitting locusts represent a prophetic vision of either missiles or warplanes, and that the prophet's entire account is a portrayal of an apocalyptic battle which will be fought in modern times. Significantly, the term *timros ashan* (commonly translated as "pillars of smoke") literally means "palm trees [*t'marim*] of smoke," a clear reference to the mushroom-shaped clouds caused by the powerful explosive devices commonly used in modern warfare. For lack of a better term, the prophet refers to the missiles and fighter planes as "locusts." What else could he have called them in his day and age? The locust is an excellent analogy, for no other creature is capable of unleashing such sudden and complete large-scale devastation. This explains why the author of the Haggadah cites

While saying the next two lines spill a little wine from your cup three times:

דָּם וָאֵשׁ וְתִימְרוֹת עָשָׁן

דָּבָר אַחֵר בְּיָד חֲזָקָה שְׁתַּיִם. וּבִזְרוֹעַ נְטוּיָה שְׁתַּיִם. וּבְמוֹרָא גָּדוֹל שְׁתַּיִם. וּבְאֹתוֹת שְׁתַּיִם. וּבְמוֹפְתִים שְׁתַּיִם. אֵלּוּ עֶשֶׂר מַכּוֹת שֶׁהֵבִיא הַקָּדוֹשׁ בָּרוּךְ הוּא עַל הַמִּצְרִים בְּמִצְרַיִם. וְאֵלּוּ הֵן:

While saying the ten plagues, spill a [little] wine from your cup ten times:

דָּם

צְפַרְדֵּעַ

כִּנִּים

עָרוֹב

דֶּבֶר

שְׁחִין

בָּרָד

אַרְבֶּה

חשֶׁךְ

מַכַּת בְּכוֹרוֹת.

---

the verse from Joel to explain that "wonders" alludes to blood — blood is mentioned as a sign of redemption, as we learn from Joel's prophecy.

The Ten Plagues

At this point, one could ask a very basic question regarding the redemption from Egypt: Why did God take the time to punish the

While saying the next two lines spill a little wine from your cup three times:

"Blood, and fire, and columns of smoke" [Yoel 2:3].

AN alternative explanation: *with a strong hand* — two; *and with an outstretched arm* — two; *with great awe* — two; *with signs* — two; *and with wonders* — two — these are the ten blows that the Holy One, Blessed be He, brought upon the Egyptians in Egypt. And these are they:

While saying the ten plagues, spill a [little] wine from your cup ten times:

Blood

Frogs

Lice

Wild beasts

Pestilence

Boils

Hail

Locusts

Darkness

The Striking of the Firstborn.

Egyptians with ten plagues? Surely He could have accelerated the redemption and brought the Egyptians to their knees sooner.

The Maharal answers that the number ten carries a recurring theme all through Jewish history: God created the world through Ten Statements (*Rosh Hashanah* 32a), God redeemed the Jewish people from Egypt with the Ten Plagues, and God gave Israel the Ten Commandments at Mount Sinai. These three instances of the number ten are themselves intertwined, for God created the world

רַבִּי יְהוּדָה הָיָה נוֹתֵן בָּהֶם סִימָנִים:

While saying these next words, spill a little wine from your cup three times:

דְּצַ"ךְ עֲדַ"שׁ בְּאַחַ"ב

Top off the cups again and continue:

רַבִּי יוֹסֵי הַגְּלִילִי אוֹמֵר מִנַּיִן אַתָּה אוֹמֵר שֶׁלָּקוּ הַמִּצְרִים בְּמִצְרַיִם עֶשֶׂר מַכּוֹת וְעַל הַיָּם לָקוּ חֲמִשִּׁים מַכּוֹת. בְּמִצְרַיִם מַה הוּא אוֹמֵר, וַיֹּאמְרוּ הַחַרְטֻמִּם אֶל פַּרְעֹה אֶצְבַּע אֱלֹהִים הִוא. וְעַל הַיָּם מָה הוּא אוֹמֵר, וַיַּרְא יִשְׂרָאֵל אֶת הַיָּד הַגְּדֹלָה אֲשֶׁר עָשָׂה יְיָ בְּמִצְרַיִם וַיִּירְאוּ הָעָם אֶת יְיָ וַיַּאֲמִינוּ בַּייָ וּבְמשֶׁה עַבְדּוֹ. כַּמָּה לָקוּ בְּאֶצְבַּע עֶשֶׂר מַכּוֹת. אֱמֹר מֵעַתָּה, בְּמִצְרַיִם לָקוּ עֶשֶׂר מַכּוֹת וְעַל הַיָּם לָקוּ חֲמִשִּׁים מַכּוֹת.

רַבִּי אֱלִיעֶזֶר אוֹמֵר מִנַּיִן שֶׁכָּל מַכָּה וּמַכָּה שֶׁהֵבִיא הַקָּדוֹשׁ בָּרוּךְ הוּא עַל הַמִּצְרִים בְּמִצְרַיִם הָיְתָה שֶׁל אַרְבַּע מַכּוֹת. שֶׁנֶּאֱמַר יְשַׁלַּח בָּם חֲרוֹן אַפּוֹ עֶבְרָה וָזַעַם וְצָרָה מִשְׁלַחַת מַלְאֲכֵי רָעִים. עֶבְרָה אַחַת. וָזַעַם שְׁתַּיִם. וְצָרָה שָׁלוֹשׁ. מִשְׁלַחַת מַלְאֲכֵי רָעִים אַרְבַּע. אֱמֹר מֵעַתָּה בְּמִצְרַיִם לָקוּ אַרְבָּעִים מַכּוֹת וְעַל הַיָּם לָקוּ מָאתַיִם מַכּוֹת.

---

for only one purpose — to provide human beings with the opportunity to accept His will and strive to serve Him. The Ten Statements of Creation therefore metamorphosed into the Ten Commandments, which are essentially the ten statements of God's will. However, in order to enable human beings to grasp the significance of the Ten Commandments, God knew that they would first have to come to the realization that He alone controls the world. What event could teach humanity this lesson? God chose the Ten Plagues that He would unleash against Egypt.

The Maharal explains that the number ten represents unity. One is a unit; two through nine are not units, but merely sums of units. Nine Jews are no more than that — nine separate and distinct Jews. Ten Jews, on the other hand, constitute a united

RABBI Yehudah used to make a mnemonic for them:

While saying these next words, spill a little wine from your cup three times:

D'TZACH, adash, b'achav

Top off the cups again and continue:

RABBI Yosei the Galilean says: Where is there proof that the Egyptians suffered ten blows in Egypt, but at the Red Sea they suffered fifty blows? What does the Torah say about [the events] in Egypt? — "The sorcerers said to Pharaoh, 'It Is the finger of God.' " But at the Red Sea it says, "Israel saw the great hand that Hashem turned against Egypt, and the people feared Hashem and believed in Hashem and in Moshe His servant." Now, how much did they suffer from one finger? Ten blows. In that case there were ten blows in Egypt, and fifty at the Red Sea.

RABBI Eliezer says: Where is there proof that each blow that the Holy One, Blessed be He, brought upon the Egyptians in Egypt was composed of four elements? For it says, "He sent the blast of His anger on them, wrath, fury, and trouble, a sending-force of inimical angels" [Tehillim 78:41]. *Wrath* — one; *fury* — two; *trouble* — three; *a sending force of inimical angels* — four. In that case in Egypt there were forty blows, and at the Red Sea two hundred and forty.

---

whole, something greater by far than the sum of their parts. So too, God created a multifaceted world. On the surface it appears to be composed of a multitude of separate and distinct components, but in reality it is a single, united entity. With our limited vision, we fail to see the interconnection of the parts, the unified "one" behind the disparate "ten." It was the Ten Plagues that taught us, and continue to teach us, that the entire universe is ruled by a single all-powerful Master, and the very God Who created the universe through the Ten Statements also obligates us to fulfill the Ten Commandments. All three manifestations of "ten" are actually a single statement of His will. In them "ten" becomes "one," demonstrating the oneness of God's plan.

רַבִּי עֲקִיבָא אוֹמֵר מִנַּיִן שֶׁכָּל מַכָּה וּמַכָּה שֶׁהֵבִיא הַקָּדוֹשׁ בָּרוּךְ הוּא עַל הַמִּצְרִים בְּמִצְרַיִם הָיְתָה שֶׁל חָמֵשׁ מַכּוֹת. שֶׁנֶּאֱמַר יְשַׁלַּח בָּם חֲרוֹן אַפּוֹ עֶבְרָה וָזַעַם וְצָרָה מִשְׁלַחַת מַלְאֲכֵי רָעִים. חֲרוֹן אַפּוֹ אַחַת. עֶבְרָה שְׁתַּיִם. וָזַעַם שָׁלֹשׁ. וְצָרָה אַרְבַּע. מִשְׁלַחַת מַלְאֲכֵי רָעִים חָמֵשׁ. אֱמֹר מֵעַתָּה בְּמִצְרַיִם לָקוּ חֲמִשִּׁים מַכּוֹת וְעַל הַיָּם לָקוּ חֲמִשִּׁים וּמָאתַיִם מַכּוֹת.

כַּמָּה מַעֲלוֹת טוֹבוֹת לַמָּקוֹם עָלֵינוּ:

אִלּוּ הוֹצִיאָנוּ מִמִּצְרַיִם

וְלֹא עָשָׂה בָהֶם שְׁפָטִים דַּיֵּנוּ:

אִלּוּ עָשָׂה בָהֶם שְׁפָטִים

וְלֹא עָשָׂה בֵאלֹהֵיהֶם דַּיֵּנוּ:

Slavery, Exodus, and Gratitude

People commonly think of the Exodus from Egypt as a single event. In *Dayeinu*, the author demonstrates that the Exodus was in fact a multifaceted aggregate of fifteen miracles. We express our overwhelming sense of gratitude to God by declaring that even if He had done nothing beyond taking us out of Egypt, we would have been forever indebted to Him. We then proceed to list the fifteen "superfluous" miracles that He performed on our behalf.

The deeper message of *Dayeinu* is that the entire basis of Israel's unique commitment to God stems from the extraordinary kindness that He showed to us during the Exodus. This principle is evident in the phrasing of the first of the Ten Commandments, "I am God your Lord, Who has taken you out of the land of Egypt, from the house of bondage" (Exodus 20:2). God is essentially saying to us, "I am God your Lord because I took you out of Egypt. You are indebted to Me."

While it is true that every entity in the universe owes its existence to God and is therefore eternally indebted to Him, Israel's debt is on an entirely different level. Not only did God create us and give us life as he did to the rest of Creation, but He

RABBI Akiva says: Where is there proof that each blow that the Holy One, Blessed be He, brought on the Egyptians in Egypt was composed of five elements? It says, "He sent the blast of His anger on them, wrath, fury, and trouble, a sending force of inimical angels." *The blast of His anger* — one; *wrath* — two; *fury* — three; *trouble* — four; *a sending force of inimical angels* — five. In that case in Egypt there were fifty blows, and at the Red Sea two hundred and fifty.

HOW many goodly benefits have we had from God!

If He had taken us out of Egypt,

and not wrought judgment on them, *it would have sufficed for us*!

If He had wrought Judgment on them,

and not on their gods, *it would have sufficed for us*!

---

also transformed us from a race of lowly slaves into the most noble and distinguished nation on earth. It is for this reason that while other nations must express their gratitude to God by observing the Seven Noachide Laws and simply behaving like decent human beings, we have been charged with fulfilling an all-encompassing code of 613 laws that dictate every aspect of our lives, including our feelings, thoughts, and actions.

Hence, the ultimate goal of our reciting *Dayeinu* is for us to realize the extent of our debt to God, and thereby to heighten our sense of commitment to His laws. We accomplish this by breaking down the miracle of the Exodus into its component parts and pondering the magnitude of God's love for the Jewish people. It is not by coincidence that our list of miracles consists of fifteen levels, and not fourteen or sixteen. The number fifteen represents the fifteen steps that led to the upper level of the Holy Temple, upon which the Levites would stand and sing the fifteen Songs of Ascent that appear in the Book of Psalms (see Mishnah, *Sukkah* 5:4). King David called these psalms "Songs of Ascent" because they incorporate the fifteen levels of spiritual growth that one must surmount in order to attain a closer relationship with God.

אִלּוּ עָשָׂה בֵאלֹהֵיהֶם

וְלֹא הָרַג אֶת בְּכוֹרֵיהֶם דַּיֵּנוּ:

אִלּוּ הָרַג אֶת בְּכוֹרֵיהֶם

וְלֹא נָתַן לָנוּ אֶת מָמוֹנָם דַּיֵּנוּ:

אִלּוּ נָתַן לָנוּ אֶת מָמוֹנָם

וְלֹא קָרַע לָנוּ אֶת הַיָּם דַּיֵּנוּ:

אִלּוּ קָרַע לָנוּ אֶת הַיָּם

וְלֹא הֶעֱבִירָנוּ בְתוֹכוֹ בֶּחָרָבָה דַּיֵּנוּ:

אִלּוּ הֶעֱבִירָנוּ בְתוֹכוֹ בֶּחָרָבָה

וְלֹא שִׁקַּע צָרֵינוּ בְּתוֹכוֹ דַּיֵּנוּ:

אִלּוּ שִׁקַּע צָרֵינוּ בְּתוֹכוֹ

וְלֹא סִפֵּק צָרְכֵּנוּ בַּמִּדְבָּר אַרְבָּעִים שָׁנָה דַּיֵּנוּ:

As the worshiper ascended the fifteen steps of stone to the accompaniment of the Levites' music and song, he experienced an altered state of consciousness in which his soul would draw close and adhere to its Creator.

The fifteen levels of spiritual growth coincide with the fifteen levels of appreciation that comprise this passage of the Haggadah, as we see from the concluding paragraph of the passage:

> *How great, then, is our debt to the Almighty. For He took us out of Egypt, and inflicted judgments upon them and upon their gods, and killed their firstborn, and gave us their riches, and parted the sea for us, and let us pass through it on dry*

If He had wrought judgment on their gods,

and not slain their firstborn, *it would have sufficed for us*!

If He had slain their firstborn,

and not given us their wealth, *it would have sufficed for us*!

If He had given us their wealth,

and not split the sea for us, *it would have sufficed for us*!

If He had split the sea for us,

and not taken us through it on dry ground, *it would have sufficed for us*!

If He had taken us through the sea on dry ground,

and not sunk our oppressors in it, *it would have sufficed for us*!

If He had sunk our oppressors in it,

and not supplied our needs in the desert for forty years, *it would have sufficed for us*!

---

land, and sank our foes in it, and satisfied our needs in the desert for forty years, and fed us the manna, and gave us the Shabbos, and brought us near Him at Mount Sinai, and gave us the Torah, and brought us into the Land of Israel, and built for us the Holy Temple to atone for all of our sins.

In fact, as has been pointed out earlier, the Haggadah itself consists of fifteen steps (*Kadesh, Ur'chatz, Karpas, Yachatz, Maggid, Rachtzah, Motzi, Matzah, Maror, Korech, Shulchan Orech, Tzafun, Barech, Hallel, Nirtzah*). The reason is self-evident — the entire purpose of reciting the Haggadah is to ascend to a higher spiritual state of consciousness and cling to the Master of the Universe.

אִלּוּ סִפֵּק צָרְכֵּנוּ בַּמִּדְבָּר אַרְבָּעִים שָׁנָה

וְלֹא הֶאֱכִילָנוּ אֶת הַמָּן דַּיֵּנוּ:

אִלּוּ הֶאֱכִילָנוּ אֶת הַמָּן

וְלֹא נָתַן לָנוּ אֶת הַשַּׁבָּת דַּיֵּנוּ:

אִלּוּ נָתַן לָנוּ אֶת הַשַּׁבָּת

וְלֹא קֵרְבָנוּ לִפְנֵי הַר סִינַי דַּיֵּנוּ:

אִלּוּ קֵרְבָנוּ לִפְנֵי הַר סִינַי

וְלֹא נָתַן לָנוּ אֶת הַתּוֹרָה דַּיֵּנוּ:

אִלּוּ נָתַן לָנוּ אֶת הַתּוֹרָה

וְלֹא הִכְנִיסָנוּ לְאֶרֶץ יִשְׂרָאֵל דַּיֵּנוּ:

אִלּוּ הִכְנִיסָנוּ לְאֶרֶץ יִשְׂרָאֵל

וְלֹא בָנָה לָנוּ אֶת בֵּית הַבְּחִירָה דַּיֵּנוּ:

עַל אַחַת כַּמָּה וְכַמָּה טוֹבָה כְפוּלָה וּמְכוּפֶּלֶת לַמָּקוֹם עָלֵינוּ. שֶׁהוֹצִיאָנוּ מִמִּצְרַיִם. וְעָשָׂה בָהֶם שְׁפָטִים. וְעָשָׂה בֵאלֹהֵיהֶם. וְהָרַג אֶת בְּכוֹרֵיהֶם. וְנָתַן לָנוּ אֶת מָמוֹנָם. וְקָרַע לָנוּ אֶת הַיָּם. וְהֶעֱבִירָנוּ בְתוֹכוֹ בֶּחָרָבָה. וְשִׁקַּע צָרֵינוּ בְּתוֹכוֹ. וְסִפֵּק צָרְכֵּנוּ בַּמִּדְבָּר אַרְבָּעִים שָׁנָה. וְהֶאֱכִילָנוּ אֶת הַמָּן. וְנָתַן לָנוּ אֶת הַשַּׁבָּת. וְקֵרְבָנוּ לִפְנֵי הַר סִינַי. וְנָתַן לָנוּ אֶת הַתּוֹרָה. וְהִכְנִיסָנוּ לְאֶרֶץ יִשְׂרָאֵל. וּבָנָה לָנוּ אֶת בֵּית הַבְּחִירָה לְכַפֵּר עַל כָּל עֲוֹנוֹתֵינוּ:

If He had supplied our needs in the desert for forty years,

and not given us manna to eat, *it would have sufficed for us*!

If He had given us manna to eat,

and not given us Shabbos, *it would have sufficed for us*!

If He had given us Shabbos,

and not gathered us [to Him] at Mt. Sinai, *it would have sufficed for us*!

If He had gathered us [to Him] at Mt. Sinai,

and not given us the Torah, *it would have sufficed for us*!

If He had given us the Torah,

and not brought us into Erertz Israel, *it would have sufficed for us*!

If He had brought us into Eretz Yisrael,

and not built the Holy Temple for us, *it would have sufficed for us*!

WHAT manifold goodness, redoubled and abounding, have we had from God! For He took us out of Egypt, and executed judgment on them, and on their gods, and slew their firstborn, and gave us their wealth, and split the sea for us, and took us through it on dry land, and sank our oppressors in it, and supplied our needs in the desert for forty years, and gave us manna to eat, and gave us Shabbos, and gathered us in at Mt. Sinai, and gave us the Torah, and brought us into Eretz Yisrael, and built the Holy Temple for us to atone for all our sins.

רַבָּן גַּמְלִיאֵל הָיָה אוֹמֵר כָּל שֶׁלֹּא אָמַר שְׁלֹשָׁה דְּבָרִים אֵלּוּ בַּפֶּסַח לֹא יָצָא יְדֵי חוֹבָתוֹ. וְאֵלּוּ הֵן.

פֶּסַח מַצָּה וּמָרוֹר:

Do not pick up the communal shank from the Seder plate nor point at it while saying this:

פֶּסַח שֶׁהָיוּ אֲבוֹתֵינוּ אוֹכְלִים בִּזְמַן שֶׁבֵּית הַמִּקְדָּשׁ הָיָה קַיָּם עַל שׁוּם מָה. עַל שׁוּם שֶׁפָּסַח הַקָּדוֹשׁ בָּרוּךְ הוּא עַל בָּתֵּי אֲבוֹתֵינוּ בְּמִצְרַיִם שֶׁנֶּאֱמַר וַאֲמַרְתֶּם זֶבַח פֶּסַח הוּא לַיְיָ אֲשֶׁר פָּסַח עַל בָּתֵּי בְנֵי יִשְׂרָאֵל בְּמִצְרַיִם בְּנָגְפּוֹ אֶת מִצְרַיִם וְאֶת בָּתֵּינוּ הִצִּיל וַיִּקֹּד הָעָם וַיִּשְׁתַּחֲווּ:

"Rabban Gamliel used to say."

The Haggadah explains that we eat matzah because God was in a rush to take our forefathers out of Egypt. And why was He in a rush? Because it was an emergency situation — had our forefathers stayed a moment longer, they never again would have had the opportunity to leave Egypt. The ideological assimilation to which the Jewish people were exposed had made such deep inroads into their consciousness that they had reached the point of no return — had they stayed a moment longer, they would have refused to part with Egyptian society, for they had begun to identify with it as their national culture. The Jewish people's sense of identity with Egyptian culture became clear during Israel's forty-year odyssey in the wilderness, especially when they underwent stressful experiences. One of many examples is the following passage: "All the Israelies complained, 'Why is God bringing us to the Land to die by the sword? Our wives and young children will be taken captive! It is better for us to return to Egypt.' So they said to one another, 'Let us appoint a leader and return to Egypt!' " (Numbers 14:3–4).

It is interesting to note that Passover is the only holiday that we call by a name different from the one that appears in the Torah. The Torah calls it *chag hamatzos*, "the festival of *matzos*," whereas we refer to it as Pesach (Passover). What is the reason for

RABBAN Gamliel used to say: Whoever doesn't say these three things on Pesach has not fulfilled his obligation. These are they:

PESACH sacrifice, matzah, and *maror*.

Do not pick up the communal shank from the Seder plate nor point at it while saying this:

THE Pesach sacrifice that our fathers used to eat while the Temple still stood — what did it recall? It recalled how the Holy One, Blessed be He, skipped over our fathers' houses in Egypt, as the Torah says, "You shall say, 'It is a Pesach sacrifice to Hashem, Who skipped over the houses of the children of Israel when He struck down the Egyptians and yet saved our houses.' The people knelt and prostrated themselves" [Shemos 12:27].

---

this? Why do we accept the names that the Torah assigns to the other festivals and reject this one? No one says, "I'm going home for *chag hamatzos*." People say, "I'm going home for Passover." Why?

As we all know, a son has an obligation to honor his parents. Now, let us say that a person would ask his parents whether they would like something to drink, and they would respond, "Just water, thank you." In order to fulfill the mitzvah of honoring one's parents, all the person would have to do is fulfill his parents' request and serve them a cup of water. However, a more sensitive soul might wonder whether his parents would really prefer coffee, and the only reason they asked for water is because they do not wish to inconvenience him. What should the son do? Serve them water or coffee? Should he give them what they asked for or what he knows they really want?

The answer is that the son should serve his parents coffee. Although it is very civil of his parents to try not to inconvenience him, the son's obligation is as binding as ever — to honor his parents. Hence, he must give them what he thinks they really want.

Let us apply the same principle to a famous theosophical question: Why was man created?

The Sages explain that God created man because He desired

to bestow His goodness upon him. Paradoxically, in order to accomplish this goal, God restrained Himself from flooding the entire universe with His goodness in order to leave man a spiritual void, as it were, in which he could exercise free will and thereby earn his reward. Why? Because man inherently does not wish to live on "handouts," even if they are Divine in nature. Instead, man longs to earn his reward by fulfilling God's will. Therefore, by giving man a greater sense of satisfaction and fulfillment, God also intensifies His own pleasure in bestowing His goodness upon him.

However, we find that the Mishna counsels, "Do not be like servants who serve their master for the sake of receiving a reward; instead, be like servants who serve their master not for the sake of receiving a reward" (*Avos* 1:3). How can the Mishna say such a thing? We have just finished saying that God only created man in order to bestow His goodness upon him, and that in order to heighten man's appreciation for the Divine gift, God granted him free will. Why then does the Mishna frown upon performing mitzvos for the sake of receiving reward? Is this not the ultimate purpose of Creation?

The apparent contradiction can be reconciled with the analogy of the water and the coffee. Just as the parents asked for water out of consideration for their son, so too, from God's perspective, His purpose in creating man was to bestow His goodness on him. But just as the son perceived that his parents preferred coffee and not water, so too, we must recognize that God's ultimate purpose in creating the universe is to derive pleasure from our righteous deeds. It is for this reason that the Mishna urges us to serve our Master "not for the sake of receiving a reward" — we must reach a level of spiritual purity where the desire to please God becomes our sole motivating force.

We can now also understand why Betzalel modified the order in which he was instructed to build the Tabernacle. God commanded Moshe to finish building the Ark and the other instruments before beginning work on the main structure of the Tabernacle (see Exodus 25–26). Betzalel, however, reversed the order and built the main structure before the instruments. In reference to Betzalel's decision, the Torah states, "Betzalel son of Uri son of Hur of the tribe of Judah did everything that God commanded Moshe" (ibid. 38:22). As Rashi explains, Betzalel's great wisdom enabled him to perceive God's ultimate intention more clearly than Moshe.

What did Betzalel perceive that Moshe did not? Betzalel understood that God commanded Moshe to build the instruments first because they represent the Jewish people, and hence they are more precious in God's eyes than the main structure of the Tabernacle. Betzalel, however, decided to build the main structure of the Tabernacle first, since it represents the Divine Presence, and hence is more dear to the Jewish people than the instruments. Through his awesome wisdom, Betzalel was able to perceive the ultimate goal of building the Tabernacle from the perspective of a son trying to honor his father. In the context of our analogy, we could say that while God asked for water, Betzalel served Him coffee.

Now we can understand why God refers to Passover as *chag hamatzos* (the festival of matzah) while we refer to it as Pesach. He focuses on our mitzvah of eating matzah because from His perspective, this is the most precious aspect of the holiday. We, however, focus on the miracles that He performed on our behalf — He "passed over [*pasach*] the houses of the Israelites in Egypt when He smote the Egyptians" (ibid. 12:27) — because this is what is most precious in our eyes. While God takes pride in our mitzvos, we acclaim His goodness.

It is interesting that Rabban Gamliel lists three essential elements of the Seder and not four. In this respect, this passage is incongruous with the rest of the Seder, which is almost exclusively illustrated in fours — the Four Questions, the Four Cups, the Four Sons. At this late stage, the number three suddenly appears. Why?

The Maharal explains that the number three always represents the establishment of something. It is clearly evident, for example, that a table needs at least three legs to stand. Likewise, the Mishna teaches that "the world stands on three things — on Torah study, on the service of God, and on kind deeds" (*Avos* 1:2). This pattern continues in the halachic realm: We learn that if a person acquired a tract of land without obtaining a contract of sale from the former owner, he may establish ownership by residing on the property for three consecutive seasons. Likewise, once an ox has gored three times, the owner becomes fully liable for any damages it may commit in the future. Clearly, the number three signifies the establishment of a new legal status. It is therefore not a coincidence that the Jewish people were established by three Patriarchs.

Why then were there four Matriarchs?

The Maharal explains that foundations sometimes need to be reinforced. Using the same analogy as above, a three-legged table can theoretically stand, but only in optimum conditions. For example, if the wind were to suddenly increase in strength, the table would be in danger of toppling over. Only if a fourth leg is attached to the table will it remain standing in such unfavorable circumstances. The number three, therefore, represents the conceptual foundation of an entity, while the number four represents the practical manifestation of this foundation. In simpler terms, we can say that the number four represents the number three brought down into reality.

Let us apply this concept to the foundations of the Jewish people. We consistently find that the Patriarchs represent the true ideals of Israel. However, whenever those ideals had to be implemented in the physical world, the Patriarchs always followed the advice of the Matriarchs. Why? Because while the Patriarchs occupied themselves with the metaphysical aspects of Divine service, the Matriarchs were busy translating these lofty ideals into the corporeal language of this physical world of ours.

For instance, when Abraham realized that Ishmael would have a negative influence upon Isaac, he decided to keep Ishmael at home and try to rectify his character. This was undoubtedly the ideal solution to the problem. But Sarah saw things differently — she demanded that Ishmael be banished from Abraham's household altogether. In a sense, she was more in touch with the physical manifestation of Abraham's ideals than Abraham himself. Recognizing this, Abraham complied and followed his wife's advice.

The same concept is apparent in the account of Isaac and Rebecca. Isaac wished to give Esau the blessing of the firstborn because, ideally, Esau's role in the Divine plan was to help Jacob attain spiritual perfection by providing him with a livelihood and taking care of all his physical needs. It is for this reason that Isaac intended to bestow upon Esau the blessing, "May God grant you the dew of heaven and the fat of the earth, much grain and wine" (Genesis 27:28).

Rebecca, however, realized that Isaac's ideal plan was destined to fail. In the real world, Esau and Jacob can never live in unison — they must dwell far apart from each other and lead completely separate lives. Who, then, would provide Jacob with a livelihood? Rebecca concluded that Jacob would have to fend for himself. Hence, she advised him to steal the blessing that Isaac had intended to give to Esau. It is true that realism lacks the aesthetic beauty of the realm of lofty ideals, but it has proven itself as an equally vital component of Israel's survival throughout history.

Again, we see evidence of the same pattern in the relationship between Jacob and Rachel. Ideally, Jacob was meant to have only one wife — Rachel. However, by the time Jacob met Rachel, he was no longer purely in the realm of the ideal. He had followed his mother's advice and plunged into the coarse environment of reality. He became a dual-faceted personality, a spiritual alloy composed of Jacob's idealism and Esau's pragmatism. Jacob's newly acquired nature required a different soulmate — Leah. She had originally been destined to marry Esau, but once Jacob took Esau's blessing, she became Jacob's soulmate. Indeed, there is a clearly recognizable correspondence between Esau's blessing and Jacob's marriage to Leah — just as Jacob obtained the blessing through deception (see Genesis 27:18), so too, Leah married him through deception (Genesis 29:25). And who helped to arrange Jacob's marriage to Leah? It was Rachel (see *Bava Basra* 123a). She perceived that the attainment of Jacob's spiritual goals required that he first marry Leah. Once again, we see how the Matriarchs ensured that the ideals of the Patriarchs became safely and permanently entrenched in reality. This explains why the Jewish people have three Patriarchs and four Matriarchs.

We also find the theme of the three and four "legs" in the text of the Haggadah. As we have mentioned earlier, the original version of the Four Questions as it appears in the Mishna (*Pesachim* 10:4) was slightly different from our present one. The third question was, "On all other nights we may eat either roasted...or cooked meat, why on this night must we eat roasted meat?" Here, the term "roasted meat" refers to the *korban Pesach*, which every Jew was obligated to eat on the night of Passover in the days when the Holy Temple stood. After the Temple was destroyed, however, the author of the Haggadah substituted this question with the one concerning our eating the meal while reclining. Therefore,

Pick up the middle matzah so that everyone can see it, and continue:

מַצָּה זוּ שֶׁאָנוּ אוֹכְלִים עַל שׁוּם מָה. עַל שׁוּם שֶׁלֹּא הִסְפִּיק בְּצֵקָם שֶׁל אֲבוֹתֵינוּ לְהַחֲמִיץ עַד שֶׁנִּגְלָה עֲלֵיהֶם מֶלֶךְ מַלְכֵי הַמְּלָכִים הַקָּדוֹשׁ בָּרוּךְ הוּא וּגְאָלָם. שֶׁנֶּאֱמַר וַיֹּאפוּ אֶת הַבָּצֵק אֲשֶׁר הוֹצִיאוּ מִמִּצְרַיִם עֻגֹת מַצּוֹת כִּי לֹא חָמֵץ כִּי גֹרְשׁוּ מִמִּצְרַיִם וְלֹא יָכְלוּ לְהִתְמַהְמֵהַּ וְגַם צֵדָה לֹא עָשׂוּ לָהֶם:

Now pick up the *maror* so that everyone can see it, and continue:

מָרוֹר זֶה שֶׁאָנוּ אוֹכְלִים עַל שׁוּם מָה. עַל שׁוּם שֶׁמֵּרְרוּ הַמִּצְרִים אֶת חַיֵּי אֲבוֹתֵינוּ בְּמִצְרַיִם. שֶׁנֶּאֱמַר וַיְמָרְרוּ אֶת חַיֵּיהֶם בַּעֲבֹדָה קָשָׁה בְּחֹמֶר וּבִלְבֵנִים וּבְכָל עֲבֹדָה בַּשָּׂדֶה אֵת כָּל עֲבֹדָתָם אֲשֶׁר עָבְדוּ בָהֶם בְּפָרֶךְ:

---

we see that in the past, the three things that Rabban Gamliel considered to be of central importance in the Seder — its "three legs," as it were — were mentioned in the youngest son's questions. However, a fourth element existed even in the days of Rabban Gamliel — the question concerning the dipping. In light of the concept we have outlined above, how is this question "the fourth leg" of the Seder? In what manner does it bring down to reality the concepts established through the other three questions?

As we have mentioned earlier, the question concerning the two dippings of vegetables (*karpas* into salt water and maror into *charoses*) is the only one of the Four Questions that discusses a mitzvah that is purely rabbinical in nature. Why indeed did the Sages enact this decree to dip vegetables on the night of the Seder? The dipped vegetables serve as an appetizer. Because it is a mitzvah to eat matzah with a healthy appetite, we eat *karpas* as an appetizer to increase our hunger prior to eating the matzah. The Sages prohibited eating a large meal on the afternoon preceding the Seder (see *Shulchan Aruch*, *Orach Chaim* 471:1) for the same reason — in order to ensure that we eat the matzah with a healthy appetite.

Pick up the middle matzah so that everyone can see it, and continue:

THIS matzah that we eat — what does it recall? It recalls how our ancestors' dough had not even time to rise, before the Holy One, Blessed be He, appeared to them and redeemed them, as the Torah says, "They baked the dough that they had brought out of Egypt into matzah cakes, for it had not risen. For they had been driven out of Egypt with no chance to linger; they had not even packed themselves provisions for the way' [Shemos 12:39].

Now pick up the *maror* so that everyone can see it, and continue:

THIS *maror* that we eat — what does it recall? It recalls how the Egyptians made our ancestors' lives bitter in Egypt, as the Torah says, "[The Egyptians] made their lives bitter with hard work at bricks and mortar and every kind of field work: all their work that [the Jews] broke their backs doing for them" [Shemos 1:14].

Just as the *karpas* serves as a physical appetizer, the question regarding the dipping of vegetables serves as an intellectual appetizer. It can be likened to the advice the Haggadah gives regarding the Son Who Does Not Know to Ask — "you open a conversation with him." In other words, the father must prompt him to ask, to develop an interest in the mitzvos that we fulfill during the night of the Seder. Likewise, the dipping of vegetables prompts the participants to wonder why this night is different from all other nights. The ultimate goal of eating *karpas* and asking why we dip vegetables is to strengthen the other three questions by stimulating everyone's curiosity. It is in this sense that the fourth question is the "fourth leg" of the Seder.

With this understanding, we may answer our original question: On this night of "fours," why does Rabban Gamliel say that the Seder is composed of only three essential elements?

By carefully analyzing Rabban Gamliel's words, we will discover that even he agrees that there is a fourth element. "Rabban Gamliel used to say, 'Whoever has not explained these three things on Pesach has not fulfilled his obligation: Pesach, matzah, and *maror*.'" The explaining is the heretofore concealed fourth element. It is the "fourth leg" that brings the concepts of Pesach,

Cover the matzos and pick up the cup. Then everyone says.

בְּכָל דּוֹר וָדוֹר חַיָּב אָדָם לִרְאוֹת אֶת עַצְמוֹ כְּאִלּוּ הוּא יָצָא מִמִּצְרַיִם. שֶׁנֶּאֱמַר וְהִגַּדְתָּ לְבִנְךָ בַּיּוֹם הַהוּא לֵאמֹר בַּעֲבוּר זֶה עָשָׂה יְיָ לִי בְּצֵאתִי מִמִּצְרָיִם. לֹא אֶת אֲבוֹתֵינוּ בִּלְבָד גָּאַל הַקָּדוֹשׁ בָּרוּךְ הוּא אֶלָּא אַף אוֹתָנוּ גָּאַל עִמָּהֶם. שֶׁנֶּאֱמַר וְאוֹתָנוּ הוֹצִיא מִשָּׁם לְמַעַן הָבִיא אוֹתָנוּ לָתֶת לָנוּ אֶת הָאָרֶץ אֲשֶׁר נִשְׁבַּע לַאֲבֹתֵינוּ:

לְפִיכָךְ אֲנַחְנוּ חַיָּבִים לְהוֹדוֹת לְהַלֵּל לְשַׁבֵּחַ לְפָאֵר לְרוֹמֵם לְהַדֵּר לְבָרֵךְ לְעַלֵּה וּלְקַלֵּס. לְמִי שֶׁעָשָׂה לַאֲבוֹתֵינוּ וְלָנוּ אֶת כָּל הַנִּסִּים הָאֵלֶּה. הוֹצִיאָנוּ מֵעַבְדוּת לְחֵרוּת. מִיָּגוֹן לְשִׂמְחָה. וּמֵאֵבֶל לְיוֹם טוֹב. וּמֵאֲפֵלָה לְאוֹר גָּדוֹל. וּמִשִּׁעְבּוּד לִגְאֻלָּה. וְנֹאמַר לְפָנָיו שִׁירָה חֲדָשָׁה הַלְלוּיָהּ:

---

matzah, and *maror* down into reality, making them manifest and enabling us to internalize the deeper message contained in these mitzvos.

Exaltation and Unconditional Love

On the night of Passover, *Hallel* is recited in a unique way — the first two paragraphs are read before the meal, and the remaining passages are read after the meal. The reasoning behind this unusual practice is that the first two paragraphs of *Hallel* contain a series of verses that significantly embellish our account of the Exodus from Egypt. Since the part of the Seder that is dedicated to recounting the story of the Exodus (*Maggid*) is still in full swing, we "borrow" the first two paragraphs of *Hallel* to heighten our awareness of the miracles that God performed on our behalf.

The relevance of the second paragraph of *Hallel* to the night of Passover is self-evident. It begins with the words, "When Israel went out of Egypt, the House of Jacob from a foreign nation..." and goes on to mention a number of other miracles that God performed on the Jewish people's behalf.

However, the relevance of the first paragraph of *Hallel* to the night of Passover is less obvious. Neither the word "Egypt" nor

Cover the matzos and pick up the cup. Then everyone says.

IN every generation a person is obligated to imagine that he himself had come out of Egypt, as the Torah says, "you shall tell your son on that day thus: 'Because of this, Hashem did [wonders] for me when I went out of Egypt' " [Shemos 13:8]. Not only did the Holy One, Blessed be He, redeem our fathers; He redeemed us, too, along with them, as the Torah says, "He took us out of there so as to bring us [here] and give us the land that He swore to our fathers" [Devarim 23:6].

THEREFORE we have a duty to thank, laud, praise, glorify, exalt, extol, bless, adulate, and celebrate the One Who did all these miracles for us and our ancestors. He took us out of slavery to freedom, from misery to joy, from mourning to festival, from gloom to a great light, from servitude to redemption. Let us say a new song before Him: Halleluyah!

"Israel" appears even once in the entire section. Why then did the author of the Haggadah decide to include the first paragraph in *Maggid*? Could it be that he included the first paragraph only because he desired to insert the second one? Surely there must be more reason than that. Indeed, as we will now see, the first paragraph is as vital a component to our account of the Exodus as the second.

The Hebrew word *Halleluy-a* is actually a compound of two words: *hallel* and *Y-a*. *Hallel* means "praise," while *Y-a* is one of the Divine Names composed of the first two letters (*yud* and *heh*) of the Tetragrammaton. What we are in effect saying, then, is "May God's Name be praised." Implicit in our words is that God's Name is currently not being praised. Our prayer reflects our fundamental belief that the day will come when God's Name will be recognized and praised by all the inhabitants of the earth. When will this occur? We all know the answer — in the days of the Messiah.

In reference to the Messianic era it is written, "God will be King over all the world; on that day, God will be One and His Name will be One" (Zechariah 14:9). We recite this verse three times a day, in the *Aleinu* prayer. But do we ever stop to consider the meaning of our words? What exactly do we mean when we say that "God will be King," and that "on that day" He will be One?

Is He not King now? Furthermore, are we implying that He is not One now? This sounds downright heretical!

What we mean is that in the Messianic era the entire world will recognize that God is King of the universe. The term "king" in this context means dominion or control. In mankind's present low level of spirituality, it is difficult to perceive that God indeed controls the world. Even though we know this to be true, at present, it is not an obvious fact. Certain things in the world are incontestable — if today would be Tuesday, one would not need to prove this to anyone, for it is a self-evident and unquestionable fact. This is what we mean when we say that "God will be King" — it will be a self-evident fact to all of mankind that a greater Power controls all events and runs the world exclusively according to His design. This unquestionable recognition of God's existence is actually what we are praying for when we say *Halleluy-a* (May God's Name be praised), for in order to praise God, one must first acknowledge His existence.

We then make an additional request: "May the Name of God be blessed from now to eternity." What do we mean by this?

The problem is that we Jews have gone through many ups and downs in the course of our long and tortured history. We were redeemed from Egypt on clouds of glory only to be deposited in the trash heap of Babylonian exile a few hundred years later. We were redeemed from that exile and returned to our Land, where we merited to rebuild the Holy Temple; however, four centuries later, we found ourselves mired in a darker and deeper exile than the first. This has been the pattern of Jewish history since time immemorial — an eternal roller coaster oscillating between exhilarating redemption and torturous exile.

In light of all this, we pray that God's Name "be blessed from now to eternity." We ask that the next redemption be complete, final, and eternal. May it not be followed by another descent into exile.

To illustrate the point, we say, "From the rising of the sun in the east to its setting place, praised is the Name of God." In effect we are saying, "May God's Name be praised from sunrise to sunset." But again, we must ask ourselves what we mean by this — does this imply that God's Name does not need to be praised after sunset, only before?

Obviously, the reference to sunrise and sunset symbolizes a

deeper concept: that the nature of God's praise in a state of spiritual "daylight" differs greatly from the nature of His praise amid the shadows of spiritual "darkness."

This concept is evident in the words of the prayer service that follow the recital of the *Shema*. In the morning we conclude the recital of *Shema* with the words, "I am God your Lord — it is true and certain, established and enduring...." At night, however, we say, "I am God your Lord — it is true and faithful...." The morning version conveys certainty and confidence; we have absolutely no doubts that the Almighty is our God. In contrast, the nighttime version suggests uncertainty; we are plagued by doubts and incertitude, yet nevertheless we express our faith that the Almighty is our God. A person who understands something clearly does not need to rely on faith; faith only comes into play when one has doubts about something.

By reading the next verse in *Hallel*, "May God be exalted above all the nations," we emphasize that we yearn to see the day when this "daylight consciousness" will be perceived not only by the Jewish people, but by all the inhabitants of the earth. For we must remember that the advent of the Messiah will not be an exclusively Jewish experience. People mistakenly believe that the Messiah will only come to us, but not to the rest of mankind. This is a mistaken notion.

Messiah is in fact a universal concept that will profoundly transform all of reality, including the gentile nations of the world. For while it is true that the redemption will be focused primarily on the Jewish people, the entire world will also be brought to a new level of spiritual awareness. When we say, "May God be exalted above all the nations," we are expressing our fervent hope that all of humanity will come to the realization that "coincidence" and "chance" are nothing but foolish notions, and that Someone above is moving all the pieces of the puzzle and controlling every event.

We then express our gratitude to God for all the goodness He bestows on us by declaring, "Who is like Hashem our God, Who dwells on high, Who lowers Himself to scrutinize the heavens and the earth?" God is so very exalted, yet He descends to this lowly world to care for us lowly beings, as He descended to Egypt for the sake of our forefathers.

"He raises the impoverished from the dust. From the trash

heaps He lifts the indigent, to seat them with nobles, with the noblemen of His people." God raised us from a state of abject poverty and misery to become the most distinguished nation on earth.

"He transforms a barren woman into a happy mother of children, *Halleluy-a*!" A barren woman is constantly enveloped by an all-encompassing and overwhelming state of despair. She feels that she has failed to fulfill her most fundamental purpose as a woman — to bear children and raise a new generation of Jewish souls. She feels unproductive and worthless. But God can change her entire reality at the blink of an eye — one minute she could be a barren woman wallowing in self-pity, and the next, she could be carrying a child in her womb. We pray that just as God can transform the reality of a barren woman at a moment's notice, so will He redeem the Jewish people speedily and in our day.

As we have explained above at length, the Passover Seder is a night of contrasts. The underlying theme of the first paragraph of *Hallel* is that God can change any situation. He can take us out of the deepest recesses of exile to the heights of heaven in the blink of an eye. Why? Because He is in absolute control of all contrasts and opposite forces. He is the ultimate Master of the universe, before whom nothing is irreconcilable.

The second paragraph of *Hallel* begins with the words, "When Israel went out of Egypt, the House of Jacob from a foreign nation..." It focuses on the last stage of the Exodus — the seventh day of Passover, when God parted the Red Sea and enabled the Israelites to cross safely to the opposite shore while the mighty Egyptian army was drowned. This event is considered the concluding act of the Exodus because until then, the Jewish people had not achieved true freedom from their Egyptian slave masters. For as long as Pharaoh remained alive, the Jews feared (and they indeed were proven correct!) that the Egyptians would regret having set them free and would pursue them into the desert. The Jews therefore subconsciously felt and behaved as though Pharaoh were still "the boss" even after they left Egypt and entered the wilderness.

The Torah, in its account of the Exodus, writes, "When Pharaoh let the people [*am*] leave..." (Exodus 13:17). This is indeed a strange statement, for surely Pharaoh was not the one who decided to "let the people leave" — it was all God's doing!

Why then does the Torah ascribe the Exodus to Pharaoh? Furthermore, according to tradition, whenever the Torah uses the word *am*, it is referring to the Great Multitude, a large group of Egyptians and other gentiles who followed the Jews out of Egypt. (When the Torah refers to the Jews, it uses the term *b'nei Yisrael.*) If so, the verse cited above implies that Pharaoh only let "the people" go — i.e., the Great Multitude — but not the Jewish people. What is the meaning of this verse?

The question itself provides part of the answer. The verse reflects the attitude of the people who comprised the Great Multitude. From their limited spiritual perspective, they were convinced that Pharaoh, and not God, had let them out of Egypt. Hence, the verse ascribes the Exodus of "the people" (i.e., the Great Multitude) to Pharaoh. However, we must keep in mind that the Great Multitude were not the only ones under this delusion — the Jewish people also felt that Pharaoh was still "the boss," albeit to a lesser degree than did the Great Multitude.

When was this misconception finally shattered? At the parting of the Red Sea, as we will now explain.

Ezekiel the prophet saw a vision of God's throne and the manner in which He controls the world (see Ezekiel 1:26). The Sages refer to this prophecy as "the Vision of the Chariot." Why? What is the symbolism of a chariot?

Now notice how many times the word "chariot" appears in the Torah passages describing the events preceding the parting of the Red Sea — "Pharaoh harnessed his *chariot* and summoned his people to go with him" (Exodus 14:6); "He took six hundred *chariots* with chosen crews" (ibid. 14:7); and so on.

The Jews thought that Pharaoh was sitting in the driver's seat of the universal "Chariot," and that they were therefore under his control. For this reason, when the waters of the Red Sea crashed down upon the Egyptian army and drowned every last man, the Jewish people raised their voices in prophetic song and exclaimed, "Pharaoh's chariots and army He cast in the sea" (ibid. 15:4). At first glance, this particular expression of gratitude seems somewhat bizarre, for it would have been sufficient to say, "Pharaoh's army He cast in the sea." Why make special mention of Pharaoh's chariots?

The answer is that when the Israelites said "Pharaoh's chariots," they were not just referring to a horse-drawn buggy.

They had seen Pharaoh, whom they thought was in the driver's seat of the Chariot of the universe, drown in the sea and God taking his place. The experience constituted the shattering of a national collective consciousness — Pharaoh was no longer in control!

This is the true intent of the Sages' statement, "A maidservant at the Red Sea saw more than the prophet Ezekiel" (*Mechilta*; cited in *Rashi* on Exodus 15:2). Why did the Sages specifically mention Ezekiel's name? They could just as well have used the name of any number of prophets to make their point. The answer is that Ezekiel's name hints at the true nature of the Israelites' vision at the shores of the Red Sea — it was comparable to Ezekiel's vision of the Chariot.

As we read further in the second paragraph of *Hallel*, the psalmist figuratively asks the Red Sea, "O sea, why do you flee?" and the sea answers, "From the presence of the Master Who created the earth; from the presence of the God of Jacob...."

Notice that the psalmist refers to the Israelites by two different names: "When Israel went out of Egypt, the House of Jacob from a foreign nation...." What is the significance of these two names? And why does the psalmist seemingly shift at random from one to the other?

In order to understand, we must first investigate the root of the name "Israel." Jacob was assigned this name after his all-night struggle with Esau's guardian angel, from which he emerged victorious at dawn (see Genesis 32:24; *Rashi*; *Bereishis Rabbah* 77). The name "Israel" is actually an acronym of the phrase "*Sarisa im elokim v'im anashim vatuchal* — You have become great before God and man, and you have won" (Genesis 32:29). "Israel" therefore represents that aspect of the Jewish people which is capable of overcoming the evil spiritual powers of the world — characterized by the dawn of a new day. The name "House of Jacob," on the other hand, represents the Jewish people in the midst of their struggle with the evil powers. It represents the aspect of grasping evil and not letting go in the same determined way as Jacob grasped Esau's heel while emerging from the womb. This facet of our national persona is characterized by the darkness of night.

Let us now read the passage with this insight in mind and see it take on new meaning. "When Israel went out of Egypt, the House of Jacob from a foreign nation...." The first half of the verse is understandable — after overcoming the forces of evil, the Jewish people attained the level of "Israel" and "went out of Egypt." However, the second half of the verse is less comprehensible. How could "the House of Jacob" — i.e., the Jewish people in their fallen state — have succeeded in going out from the midst of "a foreign nation"? How could anyone have convinced the assimilating masses to abandon Egyptian society, in which they had lived for over two centuries? Just as surprising is the sea's response to the psalmist's question, "What makes you flee?" We would expect the sea to answer, "the God of Israel," but instead, the sea answers, "the God of Jacob."

What the sea is really saying is, "I am parting not only on the merit of the 'Israel' Jews who adhere to the Torah and overcome the forces of evil, but also on the merit of the 'Jacob' Jews who are still struggling with evil and have yet to overcome it. Even they have sufficient merit to warrant my splitting on their behalf." This same merit also enabled the assimilated masses to abandon Egyptian society.

What exactly is the merit of the "Jacob" Jews? It is God's unconditional love for the Jewish people. When He commanded the sea to part, the angels at first refused to comply, saying, "These [Egyptians] are idol worshipers, and these [Israelites] are also idol worshipers! Why do You wish to save them?" Did God listen to them? No, He did not. And why? Because His love for Israel is not conditional on the Jewish people's righteous deeds. We follow God's will and fulfill His commandments because we have a commitment towards Him, not because our relationship depends upon it.

Another proof of God's unconditional love for Israel is found in the Torah's account of Moshe's sin of striking the rock (see Numbers 20:10). We see that water emerged from the rock even though Moshe did not follow God's instructions. Why? Since Moshe violated God's word, He should have punished him by withholding water from the people. The fact that He did not punish the Jewish people by withholding water from them serves as additional proof that His love for Israel is unconditional.

Now we can understand the intent of the last verse in this paragraph: "From the presence of the God of Jacob, Who turns the rock into a pond of water, the flintrock into a fountain of water." The Red Sea answers the psalmist's question by saying, "If God

Put down the cup, uncover the matzos and continue:

הַלְלוּיָהּ הַלְלוּ עַבְדֵי יְיָ הַלְלוּ אֶת שֵׁם יְיָ. יְהִי שֵׁם יְיָ מְבֹרָךְ מֵעַתָּה וְעַד עוֹלָם. מִמִּזְרַח שֶׁמֶשׁ עַד מְבוֹאוֹ מְהֻלָּל שֵׁם יְיָ. רָם עַל כָּל גּוֹיִם יְיָ עַל הַשָּׁמַיִם כְּבוֹדוֹ. מִי כַּיְיָ אֱלֹהֵינוּ הַמַּגְבִּיהִי לָשָׁבֶת. הַמַּשְׁפִּילִי לִרְאוֹת בַּשָּׁמַיִם וּבָאָרֶץ. מְקִימִי מֵעָפָר דָּל מֵאַשְׁפֹּת יָרִים אֶבְיוֹן. לְהוֹשִׁיבִי עִם נְדִיבִים עִם נְדִיבֵי עַמּוֹ. מוֹשִׁיבִי עֲקֶרֶת הַבַּיִת אֵם הַבָּנִים שְׂמֵחָה הַלְלוּיָהּ:

בְּצֵאת יִשְׂרָאֵל מִמִּצְרָיִם בֵּית יַעֲקֹב מֵעַם לֹעֵז. הָיְתָה יְהוּדָה לְקָדְשׁוֹ יִשְׂרָאֵל מַמְשְׁלוֹתָיו. הַיָּם רָאָה וַיָּנֹס הַיַּרְדֵּן יִסֹּב לְאָחוֹר. הֶהָרִים רָקְדוּ כְאֵילִים גְּבָעוֹת כִּבְנֵי צֹאן. מַה לְּךָ הַיָּם כִּי תָנוּס הַיַּרְדֵּן תִּסֹּב לְאָחוֹר. הֶהָרִים תִּרְקְדוּ כְאֵילִים גְּבָעוֹת כִּבְנֵי צֹאן. מִלִּפְנֵי אָדוֹן חוּלִי אָרֶץ מִלִּפְנֵי אֱלוֹהַּ יַעֲקֹב. הַהֹפְכִי הַצּוּר אֲגַם מָיִם חַלָּמִישׁ לְמַעְיְנוֹ מָיִם:

Cover the matzos and pick up the cup. Then everyone says:

בָּרוּךְ אַתָּה יְיָ אֱלֹהֵינוּ מֶלֶךְ הָעוֹלָם אֲשֶׁר גְּאָלָנוּ וְגָאַל אֶת אֲבוֹתֵינוּ מִמִּצְרָיִם. וְהִגִּיעָנוּ הַלַּיְלָה הַזֶּה לֶאֱכוֹל בּוֹ מַצָּה וּמָרוֹר. כֵּן יְיָ אֱלֹהֵינוּ וֵאלֹהֵי אֲבוֹתֵינוּ יַגִּיעֵנוּ לְמוֹעֲדִים וְלִרְגָלִים אֲחֵרִים הַבָּאִים לִקְרָאתֵנוּ לְשָׁלוֹם שְׂמֵחִים בְּבִנְיַן עִירֶךָ וְשָׂשִׂים בַּעֲבוֹדָתֶךָ. וְנֹאכַל שָׁם מִן הַזְּבָחִים וּמִן הַפְּסָחִים (במוצשק אומרים מִן הַפְּסָחִים וּמִן הַזְּבָחִים) אֲשֶׁר יַגִּיעַ דָּמָם עַל קִיר מִזְבַּחֲךָ לְרָצוֹן וְנוֹדֶה לְּךָ שִׁיר חָדָשׁ עַל גְּאֻלָּתֵנוּ וְעַל פְּדוּת נַפְשֵׁנוּ: בָּרוּךְ אַתָּה יְיָ גָּאַל יִשְׂרָאֵל:

---

caused water to emerge from the rock even though the Jewish people were not deserving of such a miracle, then certainly I must part on their behalf!"

The Sages say, "Any love that is conditional, in the absence of that condition, the love is gone; but if it is unconditional, it will never cease" (*Avos* 5:17). God's love for Israel is unconditional —

Put down the cup, uncover the matzos and continue:

PRAISE Hashem! Praise, servants of Hashem, praise Hashem's name. May Hashem's name be blessed from now until eternity. From the sun's shining until its setting Hashem's name is praised. Hashem is exalted over all nations; His glory is above heaven. Who is like Hashem our God, Who sits on high, yet sees down low in heaven and on earth? Who lifts a poor man from the dust, raising the needy from the trash heap to seat him with great men, with the great men of his people? Who makes the childless woman dwell in her household as a joyful mother of children? Praise Hashem!

WHEN Israel went out of Egypt, the family of Ya'akov from a foreign people, Yehudah became His holy one and Israel His subjects. The sea saw and fled, the Jordan turned backward. The mountains pranced like rams, the hills like young sheep. "What is the matter, sea, that you flee? Jordan, that you turn backward? Mountains, that you prance like rams, and hills like young sheep?" "Shudder, earth, before the Master, before the God of Ya'akov, Who turns a rock into a pool of water, flint into a water spring."

Cover the matzos and pick up the cup. Then everyone says:

BLESSED are You, Hashem our God, King of the world, Who redeemed us and redeemed our fathers from Egypt, and brought us to this night to eat matzah and *maror*. So, Hashem our God and God of our fathers, bring us to other festivals and pilgrimage times that will arrive in peace, [while we are] happy with Your rebuilt city and rejoicing to serve You. There we will eat sacrifices and Pesach lambs whose blood You will accept as it touches the altar, and we will thank You with a new song of our redemption and our soul's deliverance. Blessed are You, Hashem, Who redeemed Israel.

---

hence, it will never cease.

THE CONCLUDING BLESSING OF MAGGID

We conclude *Maggid* by reciting the blessing, "Blessed are You, God, Who redeemed Israel." Interestingly, this is the same

Everyone drinks the second cup. The whole cup, or at least most of it, should be drunk without pause while leaning on the left side. Have in mind that this is the mitzvah of drinking the second of the Four Cups.

בָּרוּךְ אַתָּה יְיָ אֱלֹהֵינוּ מֶלֶךְ הָעוֹלָם בּוֹרֵא פְּרִי הַגָּפֶן:

רַחְצָה

Everyone washes his hands and recites the *berachah*:

בָּרוּךְ אַתָּה יְיָ אֱלֹהֵינוּ מֶלֶךְ הָעוֹלָם אֲשֶׁר קִדְּשָׁנוּ בְּמִצְוֹתָיו וְצִוָּנוּ עַל נְטִילַת יָדָיִם:

מוֹצִיא-מַצָּה

בָּרוּךְ אַתָּה יְיָ אֱלֹהֵינוּ מֶלֶךְ הָעוֹלָם הַמּוֹצִיא לֶחֶם מִן הָאָרֶץ:

Pick up the two whole matzos with the broken one between them, and say *Hamotzi*. Let the bottom matzah fall to the table, and recite the *berachah* for matzah only on the top one (the whole one) and the broken one. Then immediately break off a *kezayis* from the whole matzah and a *kezayis* from the broken one. Everyone must take two *kezeysim* for himself (or at least one *kezayis*) plus a small piece from the leader's matzos. Have in mind that this *berachah* on matzah will cover the matzah eaten for Korech and for the *afikomen*.

---

blessing that we say after the recital of the *Shema* in both morning and evening prayer services. Apparently, there is a connection between this stage of the Seder and the *Shema*. What is it?

By the end of *Maggid*, we have come to the realization that Pharaoh — and everything he represents — is not in control of the world. We have seen his "chariot" broken by the hand of God, and he along with it has sunk to the depths of the sea. We have become truly free of the spiritual fetters that keep us enslaved to our physical and spiritual slave masters, for it has become clear to

Everyone drinks the second cup. The whole cup, or at least most of it, should be drunk without pause while leaning on the left side. Have in mind that this is the mitzvah of drinking the second of the Four Cups.

BLESSED are You, Hashem our God, King of the world, Who creates the fruit of the vine.

RACHTZAH

Everyone washes his hands and recites the *berachah*:

BLESSED are You, Hashem our God, King of the world, Who has made us holy with His mitzvos and commanded us about washing hands.

MOTZI-MATZAH

BLESSED are you, Hashem our God, King of the world, Who brings bread out of the earth.

Pick up the two whole matzos with the broken one between them, and say *Hamotzi*. Let the bottom matzah fall to the table, and recite the *berachah* for matzah only on the top one (the whole one) and the broken one. Then immediately break off a *kezayis* from the whole matzah and a *kezayis* from the broken one. Everyone must take two *kezeysim* for himself (or at least one *kezayis*) plus a small piece from the leader's matzos. Have in mind that this *berachah* on matzah will cover the matzah eaten for Korech and for the *afikomen*.

---

us that God is in the driver's seat of the greater "Chariot," and that the entire world is controlled solely by Him. In this mental state of redemption, we recite the blessing, "Who redeemed Israel."

So too, by declaring the oneness of God in the *Shema*, we realize that everything is controlled by God. Having attained a mental state of redemption equivalent to that which we strive to reach on the night of Passover, we also recite the blessing, "Who redeemed Israel."

בָּרוּךְ אַתָּה יְיָ אֱלֹהֵינוּ מֶלֶךְ הָעוֹלָם אֲשֶׁר קִדְּשָׁנוּ בְּמִצְוֹתָיו וְצִוָּנוּ עַל אֲכִילַת מַצָּה:

Recline on your left side to eat the two *kezeysim*, and do not interrupt the mitzvah until you are finished eating both. Have in mind that this is the Torah's mitzvah of eating matzah on Pesach night.

מָרוֹר

Everyone takes a *kezayis* of *maror*; dips it into the *charoses*, and then shakes off the excess *charoses*. Have in mind that this *berachah* also covers the *maror* eaten at Korech.

בָּרוּךְ אַתָּה יְיָ אֱלֹהֵינוּ מֶלֶךְ הָעוֹלָם. אֲשֶׁר קִדְּשָׁנוּ בְּמִצְוֹתָיו וְצִוָּנוּ עַל אֲכִילַת מָרוֹר

The whole *kezayis* of *maror* must be eaten without any interruptions. The best way is to chew up the whole amount and then swallow it all at once. Do no recline while eating the *maror*.

כּוֹרֵךְ

Everyone takes a *kezayis* of *shemurah matzah* for himself (the leader of the Seder takes a *kezayis* from his third matzah). Then everyone takes a *kezayis* of *maror* and bundles it together with the matzah. This is then dipped into *charoses*, and the excess *charoses* is shaken off. Then it is eaten while reclining on the left side. Before eating it, say this:

זֵכֶר לְמִקְדָּשׁ כְּהִלֵּל. כֵּן עָשָׂה הִלֵּל בִּזְמַן שֶׁבֵּית הַמִּקְדָּשׁ הָיָה קַיָּם הָיָה כּוֹרֵךְ מַצָּה וּמָרוֹר וְאוֹכֵל בְּיַחַד לְקַיֵּם מַה שֶּׁנֶּאֱמַר עַל מַצּוֹת וּמְרוֹרִים יֹאכְלֻהוּ:

"IN MEMORY OF THE TEMPLE, ACCORDING TO HILLEL'S OPINION."

As this passage implies, only Hillel would fulfill the mitzvos of the Seder in this fashion. His contemporaries objected to eating the

BLESSED are You, Hashem our God, King of the world, Who has made us holy with His mitzvos and commanded us about eating matzah.

Recline on your left side to eat the two *kezeysim,* and do not interrupt the mitzvah until you are finished eating both. Have in mind that this is the Torah's mitzvah of eating matzah on Pesach night.

MAROR

Everyone takes a *kezayis* of *maror;* dips it into the *charoses,* and then shakes off the excess *charoses.* Have in mind that this *berachah* also covers the *maror* eaten at Korech.

BLESSED are You, Hashem our God, King of the world, Who has made us holy with His mitzvos and commanded us about eating *maror.*

The whole *kezayis* of *maror* must be eaten without any interruptions. The best way is to chew up the whole amount and then swallow it all at once. Do no recline while eating the *maror.*

KORECH

Everyone takes a *kezayis* of *shemurah matzah* for himself (the leader of the Seder takes a *kezayis* from his third matzah). Then everyone takes a *kezayis* of *maror* and bundles it together with the matzah. This is then dipped into *charoses,* and the excess *charoses* is shaken off. Then it is eaten while reclining on the left side. Before eating it, say this:

IN memory of the Temple, according to Hillel's opinion. This is what Hillel used to do while the Holy Temple still stood: he would roll the Pesach sacrifice, matzah, and *maror* together and eat them all at once, so as to fulfilll what the Torah says: "You shall eat [the Pesach sacrifice] on matzos and *maror"* [Bemidbar 9:11].

---

korban Pesach together with the matzah and the bitter herbs because they were of the opinion that the taste of each mitzvah must remain distinct — just as eating matzah with mayonnaise would not be regarded as a fulfillment of the mitzvah to eat matzah, so too, eating matzah with *korban Pesach* or bitter herbs would not be considered a fulfillment of the mitzvah.

Hillel did not disagree with the other Sages in principle. He acknowledged that the taste of one food does indeed interfere with that of another, and he would readily have admitted that eating matzah with mayonnaise would not be considered a fulfillment of the mitzvah. His only point of contention was that the concept of one food interfering with the taste of another applies only in a case where the act of eating the interfering food is not a mitzvah, and does not apply when there is a mitzvah to eat each of the different foods, such as on Passover, when the eating of the *korban Pesach*, matzah, and bitter herbs are mandatory.

This means that nowadays even Hillel would not eat matzah and bitter herbs together. (Obviously, eating the *korban Pesach* today is out of the question because we have no Holy Temple in which to offer the sacrifice.) The reason is that following the destruction of the Holy Temple, *maror* was demoted from a Torah-ordained mitzvah to a rabbinically ordained one. Therefore, from the Torah's perspective *maror* is equivalent to mayonnaise in the sense that it, too, is a foreign substance interfering with the taste of eating matzah, which remains a Torah-ordained mitzvah.

It is for this reason that we first eat matzah and bitter herbs independently. Afterwards we make a "sandwich" purely as a commemorative gesture of the times when the Holy Temple stood, but not as a means of fulfilling the mitzvah of eating matzah or *maror*.

Now that we understand the basic reasoning behind this part of the Seder, we must ask ourselves a deeper question: Why has *maror* lost its Torah-ordained status? Why has God taken away this mitzvah from us? We can understand the logic of why we cannot eat the *korban Pesach* — as long as the Holy Temple remains unbuilt, we cannot offer the sacrifice in the prescribed manner. But why should the destruction of the Holy Temple have affected the status of *maror*? It should not differ from the mitzvah of matzah, which has retained its Torah-ordained status despite the destruction of the Holy Temple. Just as we are obligated to eat matzah in order to remember the Exodus from Egypt, we should have the same obligation to eat *maror* in order to remember the bitterness of our enslavement. Why then does the Torah no longer obligate us to eat *maror*?

In reference to the verse, "Jacob lived in the land of Egypt seventeen years..." (Genesis 47:28), Rashi writes, "Why is this *parashah* sealed? [In the Torah scroll, most paragraphs begin on a new line; this one does not.] To indicate that following the death of Jacob the Patriarch, the hearts and eyes of the Jewish people became sealed to the hardship of the subjugation." Understood simply, Rashi's statement teaches that the eyes and the hearts of the Jewish people became sealed as a consequence of the hardships they endured at the hands of the Egyptians.

If we would think about it for a moment, however, we would realize that this cannot be Rashi's intent. This interpretation of Rashi's words would imply that the Jewish people's enslavement began immediately after Jacob's death, yet the Torah explicitly teaches that the enslavement began many years later, after all of Jacob's children died (Exodus 1:6–7). What is Rashi really saying?

By reading Rashi carefully, we will discover that he is not saying that the hearts and eyes of the Jewish people became sealed *due* to the hardships of the subjugation, but rather, that they became sealed *to* the hardships of the subjugation. In other words, as soon as Jacob ceased influencing his children, they began enjoying life in exile. Suddenly, it wasn't so bad to be living in Egypt anymore; they actually began to like it.

Thus Rashi means to teach us that as long as Jacob was alive, he kept reminding his children that Egypt was not their home, that they really belonged in Canaan, the land of their forefathers. Upon Jacob's death, however, the Jewish people began to forget that they were living in exile. Gradually, they began to feel at home. Thoughts of returning to their homeland became increasingly indistinct.

This is analogous to the youth who, upon being informed that the Messiah was coming, said, "Wait! I have to get my driver's license first!" The concept applies to every generation — the main reason the Jews do not make an effort to get out of exile is because they do not perceive exile as being necessarily all that bad. This attitude is self-perpetuating, for the more we remain in exile, the less sensitive we become to "the hardships of the subjugation."

This is why there is no longer a Torah-ordained obligation to eat bitter herbs on the night of Passover. By annulling the mitzvah of *maror*, the Torah is essentially telling us that we have become desensitized to the bitterness of exile, and therefore, going through the motions of eating *maror* would not serve any purpose. Before we can hope to taste the bitterness of exile, we must first recognize our inability to feel the bitterness of exile.

Now that we have gained deeper insight into the nature of *maror*, let us reconsider Hillel's opinion. As we have explained, Hillel held that in the days of the Holy Temple, matzah should be eaten together with *maror* (and the *korban Pesach*). The question is, "Why?" Matzah is clearly a symbol of Exodus, of leaving Egypt, while we have just established that *maror* is a symbol of wishing to remain in exile and trying to forget oneself there. Since these two foods represent such diametrically opposed attitudes, why did Hillel deem it fit to eat them in the same mouthful? The answer will emerge in the following discussion.

The Sages say:

> *A person must accept the bad in the same manner as he accepts the good, as it is written, "You shall love Hashem your God with all your heart, with all your soul, and with all your resources" (Deuteronomy 6:5). "With all your heart" means [that you must love God] with both your inclinations — the good inclination as well as the evil one. "With all your soul" means [that you must love God] even if He takes your life. "With all your resources" means [that you must love God] regardless of how He may treat you.*
>
> (*Mishna, Berachos* 9:5)

Life is indeed far from perfect. Job's wife, after losing all her children and possessions, said to her husband, "You still keep your integrity? Blaspheme God and die!" (Job 2:9). Job's response was, "Should we accept only good from God and not accept evil?" (ibid. 2:10). Job's wife expressed the attitude felt by the large majority of mankind — when everything is going well, enjoy and praise God, but when things start to get tough, start bickering and question God. Job was one of the few individuals on earth who recognized that we must be willing to accept both sides of life, the good as well as the bad. He ultimately rose to a level of spiritual purity where he was able to accept hardship with love. This is a level that very few people reach. It requires that one realize that since God controls the entire world, even unfortunate events that occur to us must be for our ultimate benefit. Many people pay lip service to God by flippantly saying, "Well, I guess we have to accept the good with the bad," but deep down, they are resentful and are consumed with sorrow and self-pity.

The following story illustrates this idea: A man once came to a certain Chassidic Rebbe and said to him, "The Sages say that one must accept the bad in the same manner that one accepts the good. This would seem to imply that a person must feel the same degree of happiness upon hearing bad tidings as when he hears good tidings. Who can ever reach this level? How can the Torah demand such a reaction from us? It is humanly impossible!"

The Rebbe said to the man, "I don't have an answer for you. However, I know who can help you. Go to Reb Zusha of Anapoli. He'll provide an answer to your question."

So the man went to find Reb Zusha of Anapoli. He found him living in indescribably wretched conditions and writhing in pain from the symptoms of a severe illness. The man approached Reb Zusha's sickbed and whispered to him, "I have been told that you can answer my question."

Reb Zusha opened his eyes and said, "What is your question, my son?"

The man repeated the question he had asked the first Rebbe: "How can God expect us to feel the same degree of happiness upon hearing bad tidings as we feel when hearing good tidings? It seems like a totally unreasonable demand."

Reb Zusha thought for a long time and then answered, "I'm sorry, my son, but I am not qualified to answer your question, for I've never had a bad day in my life. Nothing but good things have happened to me throughout my life. I have been extremely fortunate. I think you should ask someone who has endured a measure of suffering during his life."

This story gives us a better idea of what it means to "accept the bad in the same manner as the good." A person who has attained this high spiritual level does not perceive "bad" things as being bad. His attitude is that since God determines every event in the world, nothing can be termed "bad"; even painful experiences are ultimately for one's own good.

The Talmud teaches that Hillel was such a person. As the Sages said, "A person should always be humble like Hillel, and he should not be stern like Shammai" (*Shabbos* 30b). Hillel was able to accept everything. His attitude was, "Who am I to judge if something is good or bad? Since God has decreed that it should

שֻׁלְחָן עוֹרֵךְ

Set the table for a Yom Tov meal with joy and a feeling of freedom. But do not eat too much so as to leave room for the *afikomen*. Some people eat the whole meal while reclining on the left side.

צָפוּן

Take a *kezayis* from the piece of matzah that was put away after Yachatz, and distribute the rest of it among the company. Each one should then add some more *shemurah matzah* to his piece so as to make a *kezayis*. (Some say that each person should take two *kezeysim*.) This matzah is called collectively the *afikomen*. Eat the piece of matzah while reclining on the left side, and be careful not to interrupt the mitzvah until the whole *kazayis* is eaten. Have in mind that eating this too is a mitzvah and is done in memory of the Pesach sacrifice.

---

happen to me, it must ultimately be for my own good!"

It is for this reason that Hillel ate the matzah together with the *maror* despite the fact that these two foods symbolize diametrically opposed concepts. From Hillel's perspective, there was absolutely no difference between the positive associations connected with matzah and the negative associations connected with *maror* — since both the Exodus and the Jewish people's reluctance to leave Egypt were decreed by God, both must ultimately be good. Indeed, Hillel believed that the greatest manifestation of this principle takes place on the night of Passover, when the Torah commands us to make a synthesis of good and bad by eating both matzah and bitter herbs. He believed that in order to attain a truly unified perception of good and bad, it would not only be necessary to eat these two foods in the same meal, but also to eat them simultaneously. Only by savoring the tastes of these two opposite concepts blending in one's mouth can one hope to truly internalize the idea that "bad" is just a different form of "good," and thereby fulfill the Sages' instruction, "A person must accept the bad in the same manner as he accepts the good." This is the deeper significance of *Korech*, "Hillel's sandwich."

Shulchan Orech

We are presented with the opportunity to practice the attitude exemplified by Hillel in the very next stage of the Seder, *Shulchan Orech*. The term literally means, "setting the table," and it involves

SHULCHAN ORECH

Set the table for a Yom Tov meal with joy and a feeling of freedom. But do not eat too much so as to leave room for the *afikomen.* Some people eat the whole meal while reclining on the left side.

TZAFUN

Take a *kezayis* from the piece of matzah that was put away after Yachatz, and distribute the rest of it among the company. Each one should then add some more *shemurah matzah* to his piece so as to make a *kezayis.* (Some say that each person should take two *kezeysim.*) This matzah is called collectively the *afikomen.* Eat the piece of matzah while reclining on the left side, and be careful not to interrupt the mitzvah until the whole *kazayis* is eaten. Have in mind that eating this too is a mitzvah and is done in memory of the Pesach sacrifice.

---

a most mundane activity — eating the festive meal. In fact, this activity is so mundane that several commentators wonder why *Shulchan Orech* is even considered part of the Seder. What does eating food have to do with the Exodus from Egypt?

The answer lies in the concept that we outlined above. Just as we recognize that everything that happens to us is ultimately for our own good, and that the concept of "bad" is nothing but an illusion, so too, we come to the realization that it makes no difference to us whether we serve God by eating or by praying or by studying. Our only goal is to do His will — how this is to be accomplished is irrelevant to us. If we eat for the right purpose, then the meal becomes a spiritual experience, for the very fact that we have fulfilled His will has brought us closer to Him. In this sense, the mundane act of eating the meal on the night of Passover is as great an expression of praise as the recitation of *Hallel.*

This is one of the most fundamental beliefs of Torah — that the physical can be utilized to enhance one's spiritual development. In this manner, the physical becomes sanctified and elevated.

TZAFUN

Tzafun means "the hidden thing." As we know, it is a reference to the *afikoman*, the half-matzah that we hide at the very beginning of the meal. Why do we leave half of the matzah on the table and hide the other half? Besides symbolizing poverty, the

בָּרֵךְ

The cups are filled.

שִׁיר הַמַּעֲלוֹת בְּשׁוּב יְיָ אֶת שִׁיבַת צִיּוֹן הָיִינוּ כְּחֹלְמִים: אָז יִמָּלֵא שְׂחוֹק פִּינוּ וּלְשׁוֹנֵנוּ רִנָּה אָז יֹאמְרוּ בַגּוֹיִם הִגְדִּיל יְיָ לַעֲשׂוֹת עִם אֵלֶּה: הִגְדִּיל יְיָ לַעֲשׂוֹת עִמָּנוּ הָיִינוּ שְׂמֵחִים: שׁוּבָה יְיָ אֶת שְׁבִיתֵנוּ כַּאֲפִיקִים בַּנֶּגֶב: הַזֹּרְעִים בְּדִמְעָה בְּרִנָּה יִקְצֹרוּ: הָלוֹךְ יֵלֵךְ וּבָכֹה נֹשֵׂא מֶשֶׁךְ הַזָּרַע בֹּא יָבֹא בְרִנָּה נֹשֵׂא אֲלֻמֹּתָיו:

When three men have eaten together start here (when there are ten men all together say the parts in parantheses):

המזמן אומר: רַבּוֹתַי נְבָרֵךְ (מִיר וֶועלְן בֶּענְטְשִׁין)

המסובין: יְהִי שֵׁם יְיָ מְבוֹרָךְ מֵעַתָּה וְעַד עוֹלָם

המזמן: בִּרְשׁוּת מָרָנָן וְרַבָּנָן וְרַבּוֹתַי נְבָרֵךְ (בעשרה אֱלֹהֵינוּ) שֶׁאָכַלְנוּ מִשֶּׁלּוֹ.

המסובין: בָּרוּךְ (בעשרה אֱלֹהֵינוּ) שֶׁאָכַלְנוּ מִשֶּׁלּוֹ וּבְטוּבוֹ חָיִינוּ.

המזמן: בָּרוּךְ (בעשרה אֱלֹהֵינוּ) שֶׁאָכַלְנוּ מִשֶּׁלּוֹ וּבְטוּבוֹ חָיִינוּ.

---

half-matzah — over which we say, "This is the bread of affliction that our forefathers ate in Egypt..." — also suggests that we have only heard "half" the story; the other "half" will be revealed later, when we will eat the *afikoman*.

What is the other half of the story? The redemption. We hide the *afikoman* in order to convey that the exact date when the redemption will transpire remains hidden from us. Will it come tomorrow or the next day? Next year or in one hundred years from now? We have no way of knowing — the advent of the redemption

BARECH

The cups are filled.

A song of ascent. When Hashem will return the captivity of Zion, we will seem to have been dreaming. Then our mouths will be filled with laughter and our tongues with song: then people will say among the nations: "Hashem has done great things for them." "Hashem has indeed done great things for us, and we are happy. Hashem, bring us back from our captivity like streams in the Negev. Those who sowed with tears will reap with song; though he wept as he walked carrying the pack of seed, yet he will come back singing, carrying his sheaves.

When three men have eaten together start here (when there are ten men all together say the parts in parantheses):

The leader says: My friends, let us say the blessing.

Everyone answers: May Hashem's name be blessed from now until eternity.

The leader repeats the above verse and says: With your permission, let us bless (our God) of Whose bounty we have eaten.

Everyone answers: Blessed be (our God) of Whose bounty we have eaten and by Whose goodness we live.

The leader repeats the above verse and says: Blessed is He and blessed Is His name.

---

remains concealed from us.

However, because we know it is there, somewhere, we send the children to search for it, and at the very end of the meal they find it. Hence, by eating the second half of the matzah, we bring the events of the Exodus full circle — "the bread of poverty" with which we began has now become transformed into "the bread of redemption." By finding it and eating it, we can hasten the advent of the Messiah.

בָּרוּךְ אַתָּה יְיָ אֱלֹהֵינוּ מֶלֶךְ הָעוֹלָם הַזָּן אֶת הָעוֹלָם כֻּלּוֹ בְּטוּבוֹ בְּחֵן בְּחֶסֶד וּבְרַחֲמִים הוּא נוֹתֵן לֶחֶם לְכָל בָּשָׂר כִּי לְעוֹלָם חַסְדּוֹ. וּבְטוּבוֹ הַגָּדוֹל תָּמִיד לֹא חָסַר לָנוּ וְאַל יֶחְסַר לָנוּ מָזוֹן לְעוֹלָם וָעֶד. בַּעֲבוּר שְׁמוֹ הַגָּדוֹל כִּי הוּא אֵל זָן וּמְפַרְנֵס לַכֹּל וּמֵטִיב לַכֹּל וּמֵכִין מָזוֹן לְכָל בְּרִיּוֹתָיו אֲשֶׁר בָּרָא. בָּרוּךְ אַתָּה יְיָ הַזָּן אֶת הַכֹּל:

נוֹדֶה לְּךָ יְיָ אֱלֹהֵינוּ עַל שֶׁהִנְחַלְתָּ לַאֲבוֹתֵינוּ אֶרֶץ חֶמְדָּה טוֹבָה וּרְחָבָה וְעַל שֶׁהוֹצֵאתָנוּ יְיָ אֱלֹהֵינוּ מֵאֶרֶץ מִצְרַיִם וּפְדִיתָנוּ מִבֵּית עֲבָדִים וְעַל בְּרִיתְךָ שֶׁחָתַמְתָּ בִּבְשָׂרֵנוּ וְעַל תּוֹרָתְךָ שֶׁלִּמַּדְתָּנוּ וְעַל חֻקֶּיךָ שֶׁהוֹדַעְתָּנוּ וְעַל חַיִּים חֵן וָחֶסֶד שֶׁחוֹנַנְתָּנוּ וְעַל אֲכִילַת מָזוֹן שָׁאַתָּה זָן וּמְפַרְנֵס אוֹתָנוּ תָּמִיד בְּכָל יוֹם וּבְכָל עֵת וּבְכָל שָׁעָה:

וְעַל הַכֹּל יְיָ אֱלֹהֵינוּ אֲנַחְנוּ מוֹדִים לָךְ וּמְבָרְכִים אוֹתָךְ יִתְבָּרַךְ שִׁמְךָ בְּפִי כָּל חַי תָּמִיד לְעוֹלָם וָעֶד כַּכָּתוּב וְאָכַלְתָּ וְשָׂבָעְתָּ וּבֵרַכְתָּ אֶת יְיָ אֱלֹהֶיךָ עַל הָאָרֶץ הַטּוֹבָה אֲשֶׁר נָתַן לָךְ. בָּרוּךְ אַתָּה יְיָ עַל הָאָרֶץ וְעַל הַמָּזוֹן:

רַחֵם נָא יְיָ אֱלֹהֵינוּ עַל יִשְׂרָאֵל עַמֶּךָ וְעַל יְרוּשָׁלַיִם עִירֶךָ וְעַל צִיּוֹן מִשְׁכַּן כְּבוֹדֶךָ וְעַל מַלְכוּת בֵּית דָּוִד מְשִׁיחֶךָ וְעַל הַבַּיִת הַגָּדוֹל וְהַקָּדוֹשׁ שֶׁנִּקְרָא שִׁמְךָ עָלָיו אֱלֹהֵינוּ אָבִינוּ רְעֵנוּ זוּנֵנוּ פַּרְנְסֵנוּ וְכַלְכְּלֵנוּ וְהַרְוִיחֵנוּ וְהַרְוַח לָנוּ יְיָ אֱלֹהֵינוּ מְהֵרָה מִכָּל צָרוֹתֵינוּ וְנָא אַל תַּצְרִיכֵנוּ יְיָ אֱלֹהֵינוּ לֹא לִידֵי מַתְּנַת בָּשָׂר וָדָם וְלֹא לִידֵי הַלְוָאָתָם כִּי אִם לְיָדְךָ הַמְּלֵאָה הַפְּתוּחָה הַקְּדוֹשָׁה וְהָרְחָבָה שֶׁלֹּא נֵבוֹשׁ וְלֹא נִכָּלֵם לְעוֹלָם וָעֶד:

On Shabbos add this:

BLESSED are You, Hashem our God, King of the world, who in His goodness nourishes the whole world with boundless love, with kindness and mercy. He gives bread to all that lives, for His kindness is eternal. Because of His great goodness we have never lacked, and may we never lack of nourishment for all eternity for the sake of His great name. For He nourishes and supports everything, and benefits everything, and provides nourishment for all the creatures He has created. Blessed are You, Hashem, who nourishes everything.

WE thank You, Hashem our God, for having given our fathers a coveted land, good and spacious; for having brought us, Hashem our God, out of the land of Egypt and redeemed us from the house of bondage; for Your *bris* that You have sealed in our flesh; for Your Torah that You have taught us and Your laws that You have informed us; for a life of utter kindness that You grant us out of love; and for the food we eat as You nourish and support us constantly, every day, at all times, in every hour.

FOR everything, Hashem our God, we thank You and bless You: may Your name be blessed by every living mouth, constantly for all eternity, as the Torah says, "You shall eat and be satisfied, and bless Hashem your God for the good land that He gave you. Blessed are You, Hashem, for the Land and for nourishment.

HAVE mercy, Hashem our God, on Your people Israel, on Your city Jerusalem, on Zion where Your glory dwells, on the dominion of the House of David Your anointed, and on the great and Holy House that is called by Your name. Our God, our Father, care for us, nourish us, support and sustain us, give us relief; bring us relief soon, Hashem our God, from all our troubles. And please, Hashem our God, do not let us come to need charity or assistance from flesh and blood; only Your abounding, open, holy, and generous hand, so we need never be ashamed or humiliated.

On Shabbos add this:

On Shabbos add this:

רְצֵה וְהַחֲלִיצֵנוּ יְיָ אֱלֹהֵינוּ בְּמִצְוֹתֶיךָ וּבְמִצְוַת יוֹם הַשְּׁבִיעִי הַשַּׁבָּת הַגָּדוֹל וְהַקָּדוֹשׁ הַזֶּה כִּי יוֹם זֶה גָּדוֹל וְקָדוֹשׁ הוּא לְפָנֶיךָ לִשְׁבָּת בּוֹ וְלָנוּחַ בּוֹ בְּאַהֲבָה כְּמִצְוַת רְצוֹנֶךָ וּבִרְצוֹנְךָ הָנִיחַ לָנוּ יְיָ אֱלֹהֵינוּ שֶׁלֹּא תְהֵא צָרָה וְיָגוֹן וַאֲנָחָה בְּיוֹם מְנוּחָתֵנוּ וְהַרְאֵנוּ יְיָ אֱלֹהֵינוּ בְּנֶחָמַת צִיּוֹן עִירֶךָ וּבְבִנְיַן יְרוּשָׁלַיִם עִיר קָדְשֶׁךָ כִּי אַתָּה הוּא בַּעַל הַיְשׁוּעוֹת וּבַעַל הַנֶּחָמוֹת:

אֱלֹהֵינוּ וֵאלֹהֵי אֲבוֹתֵינוּ יַעֲלֶה וְיָבֹא וְיַגִּיעַ וְיֵרָאֶה וְיֵרָצֶה וְיִשָּׁמַע וְיִפָּקֵד וְיִזָּכֵר זִכְרוֹנֵנוּ וּפִקְדוֹנֵנוּ וְזִכְרוֹן אֲבוֹתֵינוּ וְזִכְרוֹן מָשִׁיחַ בֶּן דָּוִד עַבְדֶּךָ וְזִכְרוֹן יְרוּשָׁלַיִם עִיר קָדְשֶׁךָ וְזִכְרוֹן כָּל עַמְּךָ בֵּית יִשְׂרָאֵל לְפָנֶיךָ, לִפְלֵיטָה לְטוֹבָה לְחֵן וּלְחֶסֶד וּלְרַחֲמִים לְחַיִּים וּלְשָׁלוֹם בְּיוֹם חַג הַמַּצּוֹת הַזֶּה. זָכְרֵנוּ יְיָ אֱלֹהֵינוּ בּוֹ לְטוֹבָה, וּפָקְדֵנוּ בוֹ לִבְרָכָה, וְהוֹשִׁיעֵנוּ בוֹ לְחַיִּים טוֹבִים. וּבִדְבַר יְשׁוּעָה וְרַחֲמִים חוּס וְחָנֵּנוּ וְרַחֵם עָלֵינוּ וְהוֹשִׁיעֵנוּ כִּי אֵלֶיךָ עֵינֵינוּ כִּי אֵל מֶלֶךְ חַנּוּן וְרַחוּם אָתָּה:

וּבְנֵה יְרוּשָׁלַיִם עִיר הַקֹּדֶשׁ בִּמְהֵרָה בְיָמֵינוּ בָּרוּךְ אַתָּה יְיָ בּוֹנֵה בְרַחֲמָיו יְרוּשָׁלָיִם. אָמֵן:

בָּרוּךְ אַתָּה יְיָ אֱלֹהֵינוּ מֶלֶךְ הָעוֹלָם הָאֵל אָבִינוּ מַלְכֵּנוּ אַדִּירֵנוּ בּוֹרְאֵנוּ גּוֹאֲלֵנוּ יוֹצְרֵנוּ קְדוֹשֵׁנוּ קְדוֹשׁ יַעֲקֹב רוֹעֵנוּ רוֹעֵה יִשְׂרָאֵל הַמֶּלֶךְ הַטּוֹב וְהַמֵּטִיב לַכֹּל שֶׁבְּכָל יוֹם וָיוֹם הוּא הֵטִיב הוּא מֵטִיב הוּא יֵטִיב לָנוּ הוּא גְמָלָנוּ הוּא גוֹמְלֵנוּ הוּא יִגְמְלֵנוּ לָעַד לְחֵן וּלְחֶסֶד וּלְרַחֲמִים וּלְרֶוַח הַצָּלָה וְהַצְלָחָה בְּרָכָה וִישׁוּעָה נֶחָמָה פַּרְנָסָה וְכַלְכָּלָה וְרַחֲמִים וְחַיִּים וְשָׁלוֹם וְכָל טוֹב וּמִכָּל טוּב לְעוֹלָם אַל יְחַסְּרֵנוּ:

On Shabbos add this:

MAY it be Your pleasure to deliver us with the merit of Your mitzvos, and with the mitzvah of this seventh day, the great and holy Shabbos. For this day is great and holy in Your estimation, for us to desist and rest on lovingly, according to the mitzvos You have willed. May Your desire be to give us rest, Hashem our God, with neither trouble nor sorrow nor pain on our day of rest. And let us see, Hashem our God, the consolation of Your city Zion and the rebuilding of Your holy city Jerusalem; for salvation and consolation come from You.

OUR God and God of our fathers, may the thought and consideration of us, and our fathers, and of Mashiach the child of Your servant David, and of Your city Jerusalem, and of Your whole people, the Family of Israel, rise and come and arrive and be seen with favor and heard and remembered and considered before You. May salvation, goodness, loving and merciful kindness, life and peace come of it on this day of the Festival of Matzos. Remember us this day, Hashem our God, and do us good and send us blessing; save us this day and give us life. With a word of salvation and mercy, spare us and have loving mercy on us: save us, for we look to You, since You are a loving and merciful God.

AND build Your holy city of Jerusalem soon, in our days. Blessed are You, Hashem, Who mercifully builds Jerusalem. Amen.

BLESSED are You, Hashem our God, King of the world, the God who is our Father, our King, our mighty Creator, our Savior, our holy Maker, the Holy One of Ya'akov; our Shepherd, the Shepherd of Israel, the good King Who does good to everything. For every day He has done good, He does good, He will do us good; He has granted us, He grants us, He will forever grant us loving and merciful kindness, relief, rescue, and success, blessing, and salvation, consolation, support, and sustenance, mercy, life, peace, and every good; and may He never deprive us of any good.

הָרַחֲמָן הוּא יִמְלֹךְ עָלֵינוּ לְעוֹלָם וָעֶד. הָרַחֲמָן הוּא יִתְבָּרַךְ בַּשָּׁמַיִם וּבָאָרֶץ. הָרַחֲמָן הוּא יִשְׁתַּבַּח לְדוֹר דּוֹרִים וְיִתְפָּאַר בָּנוּ לָעַד וּלְנֵצַח נְצָחִים וְיִתְהַדַּר בָּנוּ לָעַד וּלְעוֹלְמֵי עוֹלָמִים. הָרַחֲמָן הוּא יְפַרְנְסֵנוּ בְּכָבוֹד. הָרַחֲמָן הוּא יִשְׁבּוֹר עֻלֵּנוּ מֵעַל צַוָּארֵנוּ וְהוּא יוֹלִיכֵנוּ קוֹמְמִיּוּת לְאַרְצֵנוּ. הָרַחֲמָן הוּא יִשְׁלַח לָנוּ בְּרָכָה מְרֻבָּה בַּבַּיִת הַזֶּה וְעַל שֻׁלְחָן זֶה שֶׁאָכַלְנוּ עָלָיו. הָרַחֲמָן הוּא יִשְׁלַח לָנוּ אֶת אֵלִיָּהוּ הַנָּבִיא זָכוּר לַטּוֹב וִיבַשֶּׂר לָנוּ בְּשׂוֹרוֹת טוֹבוֹת יְשׁוּעוֹת וְנֶחָמוֹת.

הָרַחֲמָן הוּא יְבָרֵךְ אֶת (אָבִי מוֹרִי) בַּעַל הַבַּיִת הַזֶּה וְאֶת (אִמִּי מוֹרָתִי) בַּעֲלַת הַבַּיִת הַזֶּה. אוֹתָם וְאֶת בֵּיתָם וְאֶת זַרְעָם וְאֶת כָּל אֲשֶׁר לָהֶם. (אם הוא סמוך על שלחן עצמו אומר(הָרַחֲמָן הוּא יְבָרֵךְ אוֹתִי וְאֶת אִשְׁתִּי (וְאֶת אָבִי מוֹרִי וְאֶת אִמִּי מוֹרָתִי) וְאֶת אִשְׁתִּי וְזַרְעִי וְכָל אֲשֶׁר לִי) אוֹתָנוּ וְאֶת כָּל אֲשֶׁר לָנוּ כְּמוֹ שֶׁנִּתְבָּרְכוּ אֲבוֹתֵינוּ אַבְרָהָם יִצְחָק וְיַעֲקֹב בַּכֹּל מִכֹּל כֹּל, כֵּן יְבָרֵךְ אוֹתָנוּ כֻּלָּנוּ יַחַד בִּבְרָכָה שְׁלֵמָה וְנֹאמַר אָמֵן:

בַּמָּרוֹם יְלַמְּדוּ (עֲלֵיהֶם וְ)עָלֵינוּ זְכוּת שֶׁתְּהֵא לְמִשְׁמֶרֶת שָׁלוֹם. וְנִשָּׂא בְרָכָה מֵאֵת יְיָ וּצְדָקָה מֵאֱלֹהֵי יִשְׁעֵנוּ וְנִמְצָא חֵן וְשֵׂכֶל טוֹב בְּעֵינֵי אֱלֹהִים וְאָדָם:

On Shabbos:

הָרַחֲמָן הוּא יַנְחִילֵנוּ יוֹם שֶׁכֻּלּוֹ שַׁבָּת וּמְנוּחָה לְחַיֵּי הָעוֹלָמִים:

הָרַחֲמָן הוּא יַנְחִילֵנוּ יוֹם שֶׁכֻּלּוֹ טוֹב יוֹם שֶׁכֻּלּוֹ אָרוּךְ יוֹם שֶׁצַּדִּיקִים יוֹשְׁבִים וְעַטְרוֹתֵיהֶם בְּרָאשֵׁיהֶם וְנֶהֱנִים מִזִּיו הַשְּׁכִינָה וִיהִי חֶלְקֵנוּ עִמָּהֶם:

הָרַחֲמָן הוּא יְזַכֵּנוּ לִימוֹת הַמָּשִׁיחַ וּלְחַיֵּי הָעוֹלָם הַבָּא. מִגְדּוֹל יְשׁוּעוֹת מַלְכּוֹ וְעֹשֶׂה חֶסֶד לִמְשִׁיחוֹ לְדָוִד וּלְזַרְעוֹ עַד עוֹלָם: עֹשֶׂה שָׁלוֹם בִּמְרוֹמָיו הוּא יַעֲשֶׂה שָׁלוֹם עָלֵינוּ וְעַל כָּל יִשְׂרָאֵל וְאִמְרוּ אָמֵן:

MAY the Merciful One reign over us forever and ever. May the Merciful One be blessed in heaven and in earth. May the Merciful One be praised through all generations; may He be glorified through us for all eternity and revered through us for ever and ever. May the Merciful One support us with honor. May the Merciful One break the yoke off our necks and bring us unbowed to our Land. May the Merciful One send abundant blessing on this house and on this table where we have eaten. May the Merciful One send us Eliyahu the Prophet, of goodly memory, who will bring us good tidings of salvation and comfort.

MAY the Merciful One bless (my father and teacher the master of this house, [my mother and teacher the mistress of this house]), me, (my wife/husband and children) and all that is mine, and all that sit here, both them, their house, their children, and all that is theirs, and us and all that is ours, as our fathers, Avraham, Yitzchak, and Ya'akov were blessed: "with everything, of every thing, to have everything." So may He bless all of us together, an all-encompassing blessing, and let us say, Amen.

ON high the angels will speak well of them and of us, so that we will have enduring peace and receive blessing from Hashem and generosity from God Who saves us. So we will have favor and good opinion from Hashem and man.

On Shabbos:

MAY the Merciful One give us as our heritage a day made all of Shabbos and rest as we live eternally.

MAY the Merciful One give us as our heritage a day made all of good, a day made all unending, a day when the *tzaddikim* sit with their crowns on their heads and bask in the splendor of the *Shechinah* — and may our portion be among them.

MAY the Merciful One make us worthy of the era of Mashiach and life in the World to Come. [He is] a tower of salvation for His king and does kindness for His anointed, David and his children until eternity. He Who makes peace in His heights will make peace for us and for all Israel, and say, Amen.

יְראוּ אֶת יְיָ קְדֹשָׁיו כִּי אֵין מַחְסוֹר לִירֵאָיו: כְּפִירִים רָשׁוּ וְרָעֵבוּ וְדֹרְשֵׁי יְיָ לֹא יַחְסְרוּ כָל טוֹב: הוֹדוּ לַייָ כִּי טוֹב כִּי לְעוֹלָם חַסְדּוֹ: בָּרוּךְ הַגֶּבֶר אֲשֶׁר יִבְטַח בַּייָ וְהָיָה יְיָ מִבְטַחוֹ: פּוֹתֵחַ אֶת יָדֶךָ וּמַשְׂבִּיעַ לְכָל חַי רָצוֹן: נַעַר הָיִיתִי גַּם זָקַנְתִּי וְלֹא רָאִיתִי צַדִּיק נֶעֱזָב וְזַרְעוֹ מְבַקֶּשׁ לָחֶם יְיָ עֹז לְעַמּוֹ יִתֵּן יְיָ יְבָרֵךְ אֶת עַמּוֹ בַשָּׁלוֹם:

בָּרוּךְ אַתָּה יְיָ אֱלֹהֵינוּ מֶלֶךְ הָעוֹלָם בּוֹרֵא פְּרִי הַגָּפֶן:

Everyone drinks the cup. The whole cup, or at least most of it, should be drunk without interruption while we are reclining on the left side. Have in mind that this is the mtzvah of the third of the Four Cups.

The Third Cup: A Responsible Freedom

Earlier, we mentioned that the four cups of wine that we drink on the night of Passover contain powerful symbolic meaning, and that there is an underlying logic behind the order in which they are to be drunk. Let us briefly review their deeper significance.

The Four Cups are to be drunk at the conclusion of four of the fifteen steps of the Seder — *Kadesh* (*Kiddush*), *Maggid* (recounting the story of the Exodus), *Barech* (the recitation of Grace after Meals), and *Hallel* (the recitation of the Song of Praise). The commentators explain that the Four Cups were instituted to commemorate the four expressions of redemption contained in the verse, "I [God] shall *take you out* from under the burdens of Egypt; I shall *rescue you* from their service; I shall *redeem you* with an outstretched arm and with great judgments. I shall *take you to Me* for a people..." (Exodus 6:6–7). This would indicate that there is a conceptual correlation between the four steps of the Seder and the four expressions of redemption to which each one corresponds.

The recitation of *Kiddush* corresponds to the first expression of redemption, "I [God] shall *take you out* from under the burdens of Egypt." As we have explained earlier, the *Kiddush* recited on the night of Passover is an integral part of the Haggadah. One sign of the unique characteristic of the *Kiddush* that is recited on the night of Passover is the dual role of the first cup of wine — it is at once the

REVERE Hashem, His holy ones, for those who revere Him lack nothing. Lions have been impoverished and hungry, but those who seek Hashem lack nothing good. Thank Hashem, for He is good, for His kindness is eternal. You open Your hand and satisfy every living thing's desire. Blessed is the man who trusts Hashem, so that Hashem is his refuge. I have been a child and have grown old, and I have not seen a tzaddik abandoned and his children begging bread. Hashem will give His people courage; Hashem will bless His People with peace.

BLESSED are You, Hashem our God, King of the world, Who creates the fruit of the vine.

Everyone drinks the cup. The whole cup, or at least most of it, should be drunk without interruption while we are reclining on the left side. Have in mind that this is the mtzvah of the third of the Four Cups.

Kiddush cup and the first of the Four Cups of wine that are to be drunk during the Seder. If the *Kiddush* were unrelated to the Seder, one would have to drink the cup of *Kiddush* and, afterwards, an additional Four Cups. The fact that the cup of wine that is drunk during *Kiddush* is counted as one of the Four Cups proves that the *Kiddush* of Passover is an essential component of the Seder.

Further proof of the special quality of the Passover *Kiddush* is that on all other occasions, custom dictates that one person recite *Kiddush* for all the participants, and then each person be given a sip of wine from the *Kiddush* cup. On the Seder night, however, custom dictates that each of the participants should drink his own cup of wine. The reason is that the *Kiddush* recited on Passover is not just a technical requirement of the Festival, but an integral component of the Four Cups of wine that each participant is obligated to drink.

In order to grasp the correlation between *Kiddush* and its corresponding expression of redemption — "I will take you out from Egypt" — we must first understand the true intent of this verse. Upon reading it, a question immediately arises: Why does the expression "I will take you out from Egypt" appear before the expression "I will rescue you from their service"? These two statements seem to be chronologically out of order, for we know that the Jews were released from their labor a full six months before they actually left Egypt.

The Maharal of Prague explains that the expression "I will take you out" does not refer to the physical Exodus, but rather to the spiritual and intellectual redemption of the Jewish people. This spiritual Exodus was far more crucial to the continuing existence of the Jewish people than their physical Exodus. The Torah underscores this idea by writing "I will take you out" before "I will rescue you." This teaches that the Jewish people had first to be redeemed from their intellectual exile before they could be freed from the burden of their physical slavery.

The Maharal defines the term "intellectual exile" to mean that the Jewish people were convinced that they were in Egypt to stay. Pharaoh had never given anyone permission to leave the country, and the Jews could not fathom trying to leave of their own accord. Furthermore, after living in Egypt for over two centuries, the Jews felt quite at home there and identified with the local culture. Despite all their hardships, they had no real desire to leave Egypt. All they wanted were civil rights and equality.

God "took them out" of this exile mentality by sending Moshe to redeem them. At first they thought Moshe was out of his mind, but eventually he managed to convince the Jewish people that they really did not belong in Egypt. This was the crucial first step of the Exodus. It began to dawn on the Jews that redemption was not just a legend to be passed on to one's children, but a very real Divine process that would soon begin to manifest itself. The Torah expresses this intellectual Exodus with the phrase, "I will take you out." Hence, we see that the first step of the Exodus was to make the Israelites realize that they were not Egyptians, that they were intrinsically different from all other nations, and that they had a unique role to play in the world.

Upon closer analysis, we find that all of these ideas are encapsulated in the words of *Kiddush*. When we say, "Who chose us from all peoples," we are in essence acknowledging that we differ from all other peoples, and that our relationship with God is qualitatively different from that of any other nation. The phrase "You have sanctified us with Your commandments" conveys the same message.

We then say, "You have elevated us above all languages." Even our language and our entire way of communicating with one another is different from that of any other nation.

We see, therefore, that *Kiddush* commemorates the same concept contained in the verse "I shall take you out" — i.e., the intellectual redemption of the Jewish people. This is the central theme of the first cup.

The correlation between the second expression of redemption ("I shall *rescue you* from their service") and *Maggid* is self-evident — just as the verse refers to Israel's redemption from their physical slavery, so too, all of *Maggid* is dedicated to recounting the miraculous manner in which God freed us from our Egyptian slavemasters.

Now we come to the third cup, which is to be drunk at the conclusion of *Birkas Hamazon*. Here, it is more difficult to perceive the correlation. What does the third expression of redemption, "I shall *redeem you* with an outstretched arm" have in common with *Birkas Hamazon*? In fact, we could ask a more basic question: Why does *Birkas Hamazon* qualify as a distinct step of the Seder altogether? We recite this prayer on almost every day of the year! What in the world does it have to do with Passover?

The answer will emerge in the following discussion. The blessing immediately preceding the *Shemoneh Esreh* (the Silent Prayer) in the morning and evening prayer services is "Blessed are You...Who redeemed Israel." An unprecedented degree of importance is ascribed to this blessing throughout the writings of the Sages. One example is the statement, "R. Yossi ben Elyakim said in the name of the holy congregation of Jerusalem, 'Whoever recites the redemption blessing contiguously with the Silent Prayer will not suffer harm that entire day' " (*Berachos* 9b). The most telling proof of this blessing's importance is the fact that R. Yossi ben Elyakim's advice has earned the status of an outright obligation, as the *Shulchan Aruch* states, "It is an obligation to recite the redemption blessing contiguously with the Silent Prayer. One may not commit an interruption [by speaking] after having said 'Who redeemed Israel' [unless special circumstances arise]" (*Orach Chaim* 66:7). Even answering "*amen*" to someone else's redemption blessing is considered an interruption between these two portions of the prayer service. As a consequence, a custom has developed in many synagogues that the person leading the prayer service whispers the last word of the redemption blessing in order to avoid evoking an involuntary response of "*amen*" from the congregants.

The scope of this halachic stringency is truly unprecedented.

What is the reasoning behind it? Why did the Sages attribute such importance to reciting the redemption blessing contiguously to the first words of *Shemoneh Esreh*?

The lesson is that redemption and prayer are interdependent — one without the other is devoid of meaning. Redemption essentially means the attainment of freedom. Not freedom as a goal unto itself, but as a means to an end. For while freedom enables one to carry out very important and worthwhile responsibilities, it can also be misused for destructive purposes, such as harming other individuals and society as a whole. When freedom is viewed as an end in itself and dispensed indiscriminately, it can bring about the demise of civilized society.

Nevertheless, the positive potential of freedom outweighs the negative by a large margin, for freedom can breed the highest of human virtues — a true sense of responsibility. A slave cannot become responsible for his own actions because he has grown accustomed to leading his life according to the orders he receives from his master. Only the initiative that naturally emerges from a sense of personal freedom can lead one to become a truly responsible human being.

Pesach represents freedom, while Shavuos represents the acceptance of responsibility. Had God taken the Jewish people out of Egypt and not brought them to Mount Sinai to receive the Torah, Pesach would lose its central importance — in fact, it might not even have become a religious holiday. Its only significance is that it is a prelude to Shavuos, when the Jewish people accepted upon themselves the responsibility of fulfilling God's commandments. To unlock the hidden spiritual potential of Pesach, one must relate to it as an opportunity to foster a greater sense of responsibility towards God.

In this light, the forty-nine days that elapse between Pesach and Shavuos are not to be regarded as a separation but as a link. Indeed, Ramban writes that these seven weeks correspond to the seven days of *Chol Hamo'ed*, the seven days that connect the first Yom Tov of Pesach with the last.

With this understanding, we must qualify what we said earlier, that Pesach has significance only as a prelude to Shavuos. For while it is true that Pesach would not have been an important event without Shavuos, let us remember that Shavuos could never have occurred without Pesach. For how could a nation of slaves have reached the degree of personal freedom that is required in order to declare, "Everything that God has said, we will do and we will hear!" (Exodus 24:7)? How could the Jewish people have accepted the tremendous responsibility of leading their lives according to God's will while still bearing the yoke of servitude to Pharaoh?

It is because of this conceptual interdependency of the two festivals that Pesach and Shavuos are regarded as aspects of a single unit. We count each of the forty-nine days that elapse between the two holidays as if to say, "Wait, Passover is not over yet." It is in this sense that the forty-nine days of the *omer* are the links that bond the two festivals together.

The same concept applies to the redemption blessing and the beginning of the *Shemoneh Esreh*. Prayer implies dependency on God. We stand up before God and we say to Him, "God, I need health, food, a livelihood." A person who believes deeply that his livelihood comes from his employer or from his business associates cannot pray sincerely to God. It would be a contradiction in terms. There is a very fine distinction between feeling appreciation towards the people who provide one's livelihood and believing oneself to be completely dependent upon them. The former attitude is praiseworthy, but the latter constitutes a serious lack of faith in God. One should be thankful to a physician who alleviates one's suffering, but not feel that one would not be able to continue living without him. The only entity that we are completely dependent upon is God — employers, business associates, and doctors are merely the agents He uses to bestow His goodness upon us.

Therefore, in order to pray with heartfelt sincerity, a person must cast off the yoke of human beings from upon himself and come to the realization that he is dependent upon no entity in the universe other than God. Only after "redeeming" oneself from conceptual "bondage" to others can one utter words of prayer with sincerity. It is for this reason that the redemption blessing must be contiguous to *Shemoneh Esreh*. This halachic requirement emphasizes that personal "redemption" is a prerequisite to meaningful prayer.

What is the greatest instrument that people use to make others their "slaves"? At first one may think, "the sword." But there is something even more powerful than the sword — physical

Everyone pours the fourth cup. In addition to his own cup, the leader pours an extra cup to be the cup of Eliyahu. Open the door of the house and say this:

שְׁפוֹךְ חֲמָתְךָ אֶל הַגּוֹיִם אֲשֶׁר לֹא יְדָעוּךָ וְעַל מַמְלָכוֹת אֲשֶׁר בְּשִׁמְךָ לֹא קָרָאוּ. כִּי אָכַל אֶת יַעֲקֹב וְאֶת נָוֵהוּ הֵשַׁמּוּ. שְׁפָךְ עֲלֵיהֶם זַעְמֶךָ וַחֲרוֹן אַפְּךָ יַשִּׂיגֵם. תִּרְדוֹף בְּאַף וְתַשְׁמִידֵם מִתַּחַת שְׁמֵי יְיָ:

---

needs. A person who can make others dependent upon him for their physical needs has made them his slaves. The sword is not nearly as powerful as a piece of bread, the symbol of physical needs. It sounds almost like Marxist dogma — "bread is the greatest instrument of servitude." The similarity between the words *lechem* (bread) and *milchama* (war) is a fascinating allusion to this concept — bread can be used as a weapon to wage war against one's enemies.

It is for this reason that God commands us, "When you eat [bread] and are satisfied, bless Hashem your God for the good land that He has given you" (Deuteronomy 8:10). By praising God after we eat bread, we acknowledge that He is the One Who provides our livelihood, and not our employers or business associates, or for that matter, any other human being. As we have explained in reference to prayer, this expression of gratitude to God requires that we truly feel free and independent from all potential corporeal "slavemasters."

Each portion of *Birkas Hamazon* conveys a different declaration of personal independence. The first blessing ends with the words, "for He nourishes and sustains all" — God is the only true source of sustenance; human beings under various guises are merely His envoys. We should definitely express gratitude to our employers for being such benevolent agents, but we must never forget that ultimately everything comes from God. As we can see, this blessing deals with our personal independence.

The second blessing deals with our national independence. We express our gratitude to God for having given us our own land, for one cannot feel truly free living on someone else's land. Our national independence demands that we have a homeland. We therefore thank God for the good land that He gave to our

Everyone pours the fourth cup. In addition to his own cup, the leader pours an extra cup to be the cup of Eliyahu. Open the door of the house and say this:

POUR out Your wrath on the nations who do not know You, and on kingdoms that do not call on Your name; for they have devoured Ya'akov and laid his home waste [Tehillim 79:6–7]. Pour out Your fury on them, and may the blast of Your anger overtake them [Ibid. 69:25]. Pursue them in anger and wipe them out from under Hashem's sky [Eichah 3:66].

---

forefathers, and we conclude with the words, "Blessed are You...for the land and the nourishment."

But this degree of independence is still not sufficient. A person can have personal freedom and own his own land, but still lack freedom. An example of this condition was Jewish society in the Second Temple era. The Jews were free to go where they chose, and no one contested their ownership of the land, but the Persians were in control of the government. Then came the Greeks, and after them, the Romans. In the third passage of *Birkas Hamazon*, we pray for a third level of independence — control over national governmental affairs. The Jewish people will only attain this degree of independence when the royal lineage of King David will be re-established in Jerusalem. For this reason, we conclude this passage of *Birkas Hamazon* with the blessing, "Blessed are You...Who rebuilds Jerusalem in His mercy, *amen*."

This passage also parallels the fourteenth blessing of the *Shemoneh Esreh*, which expresses our yearning to see Jerusalem rebuilt. It is interesting to note that although separate blessings are dedicated to the re-establishment of the Davidic royal lineage and for the reconstruction of Jerusalem, we nevertheless add the clause, "May You speedily establish the throne of Your servant David within [Jerusalem]" in the blessing for the reconstruction of Jerusalem. This insertion conveys that Jerusalem will only become the fulcrum of Jewish life when the throne of David is re-established within it.

Therefore, we see that the third expression of redemption — "I shall *redeem you* with an outstretched arm and with great judgments" — shares a common theme with *Birkas Hamazon*, the yearning to lead our lives independently at all levels, whether it be on the personal, national, governmental, intellectual, or spiritual

Close the door and continue (while sitting, not reclining):

הַלֵּל

לֹא לָנוּ יְיָ לֹא לָנוּ כִּי לְשִׁמְךָ תֵּן כָּבוֹד עַל חַסְדְּךָ עַל אֲמִתֶּךָ. לָמָּה יֹאמְרוּ הַגּוֹיִם אַיֵּה נָא אֱלֹהֵיהֶם. וֵאלֹהֵינוּ בַשָּׁמָיִם כֹּל אֲשֶׁר חָפֵץ עָשָׂה. עֲצַבֵּיהֶם כֶּסֶף וְזָהָב מַעֲשֵׂה יְדֵי אָדָם. פֶּה לָהֶם וְלֹא יְדַבֵּרוּ עֵינַיִם לָהֶם וְלֹא יִרְאוּ. אָזְנַיִם לָהֶם וְלֹא יִשְׁמָעוּ אַף לָהֶם וְלֹא יְרִיחוּן. יְדֵיהֶם וְלֹא יְמִישׁוּן רַגְלֵיהֶם וְלֹא יְהַלֵּכוּ לֹא יֶהְגּוּ בִּגְרוֹנָם. כְּמוֹהֶם יִהְיוּ עֹשֵׂיהֶם כֹּל אֲשֶׁר בֹּטֵחַ בָּהֶם. יִשְׂרָאֵל בְּטַח בַּייָ עֶזְרָם וּמָגִנָּם הוּא. בֵּית אַהֲרֹן בִּטְחוּ בַייָ עֶזְרָם וּמָגִנָּם הוּא. יִרְאֵי יְיָ בִּטְחוּ בַייָ עֶזְרָם וּמָגִנָּם הוּא:

---

plane. For this reason, the Sages mandated that the third cup of the Seder come at the conclusion of *Birkas Hamazon*.

"Pour out Your wrath..."

This passage does not appear in the original version of the Haggadah, but was added at some later point in time. What does it mean? And what does Elijah have to do with the Seder? And why do we choose this particular moment to rouse God's wrath against the nations?

According to one theory, this passage was added in response to the blood libels that have always plagued the Jews at Passover time. The nations concocted a theory that Jews require the blood of a Christian child to bake matzah for Passover. For many centuries, anti-Semitic demagogues in Europe utilized this incredible lie to stir up the masses and incite acts of violence against Jews. Our prayer is an anguished plea to God to relieve our suffering and put an end to the pogroms and persecutions which have continuously ravaged us at this time of the year.

However, there is a deeper explanation. It is written, "Behold, I will send the prophet Elijah to you before the arrival of God's great and awesome day" (Malachi 3:23). The verse teaches

Close the door and continue (while sitting, not reclining):

HALLEL

NOT for our sake, Hashem, not for our sake; give honor only to Your name for Your kindness and faithfulness. why should the nations say, "Where, then, is their God?" when our God is in heaven and does all that He pleases? Their odious idols are of silver and gold, the work of men's hands: they have a mouth but do not speak, eyes but do not see, ears but do not hear, a nose but do not smell. Hands are theirs — they do not feel; feet are theirs — they do not walk; they cannot speak from their throats. Just so shall be those who make them and all who have faith in them. Israel, trust Hashem. He is their help and shield. Family of Aharon, trust Hashem! He is their help and shield. God-fearing people, trust Hashem! He is their help and shield.

---

that Elijah will announce the advent of the final redemption. Hence, by filling "Elijah's Cup," we express our faith that Elijah will soon reveal himself. In the meantime, however, we say to God, "Why do You not punish the nations that persecute us? We have faith that Elijah will come, but these nations should be punished for their transgressions now!"

We utter this prayer on the night of Passover because a precedent was established on this night. It is an opportune time to punish wicked nations (such as Egypt) and redeem Israel. In essence we say, "Why can't the experience of redemption be repeated again now?" We recite this passage before pouring the fourth cup because the verse that corresponds to it is, "I shall *take you to Me* for a people." The fourth cup, therefore, represents God's loving relationship with Israel. In essence, we are saying to God, "Do You want us to be close with You? Then how about helping us now that we are in trouble?"

HALLEL

At this point, we begin reciting the second half of *Hallel* (the first two paragraphs were recited prior to the meal), which alludes to the final redemption. We declare, "Not for us, O God, not for us,

יְיָ זְכָרָנוּ יְבָרֵךְ יְבָרֵךְ אֶת בֵּית יִשְׂרָאֵל יְבָרֵךְ אֶת בֵּית אַהֲרֹן. יְבָרֵךְ יִרְאֵי יְיָ הַקְּטַנִּים עִם הַגְּדֹלִים. יֹסֵף יְיָ עֲלֵיכֶם וְעַל בְּנֵיכֶם. בְּרוּכִים אַתֶּם לַייָ עֹשֵׂה שָׁמַיִם וָאָרֶץ. הַשָּׁמַיִם שָׁמַיִם לַייָ וְהָאָרֶץ נָתַן לִבְנֵי אָדָם. לֹא הַמֵּתִים יְהַלְלוּיָהּ וְלֹא כָּל יֹרְדֵי דוּמָה. וַאֲנַחְנוּ נְבָרֵךְ יָהּ מֵעַתָּה וְעַד עוֹלָם הַלְלוּיָהּ:

אָהַבְתִּי כִּי יִשְׁמַע יְיָ אֶת קוֹלִי תַּחֲנוּנָי. כִּי הִטָּה אָזְנוֹ לִי וּבְיָמַי אֶקְרָא. אֲפָפוּנִי חֶבְלֵי מָוֶת וּמְצָרֵי שְׁאוֹל מְצָאוּנִי צָרָה וְיָגוֹן אֶמְצָא. וּבְשֵׁם יְיָ אֶקְרָא אָנָּה יְיָ מַלְּטָה נַפְשִׁי. חַנּוּן יְיָ וְצַדִּיק וֵאלֹהֵינוּ מְרַחֵם. שֹׁמֵר פְּתָאִים יְיָ דַּלּוֹתִי וְלִי יְהוֹשִׁיעַ. שׁוּבִי נַפְשִׁי לִמְנוּחָיְכִי כִּי יְיָ גָּמַל עָלָיְכִי. כִּי חִלַּצְתָּ נַפְשִׁי מִמָּוֶת אֶת עֵינִי מִן דִּמְעָה אֶת רַגְלִי מִדֶּחִי. אֶתְהַלֵּךְ לִפְנֵי יְיָ בְּאַרְצוֹת הַחַיִּים. הֶאֱמַנְתִּי כִּי אֲדַבֵּר אֲנִי עָנִיתִי מְאֹד. אֲנִי אָמַרְתִּי בְחָפְזִי כָּל הָאָדָם כֹּזֵב:

מָה אָשִׁיב לַייָ כָּל תַּגְמוּלוֹהִי עָלָי. כּוֹס יְשׁוּעוֹת אֶשָּׂא וּבְשֵׁם יְיָ אֶקְרָא. נְדָרַי לַייָ אֲשַׁלֵּם נֶגְדָה נָּא לְכָל עַמּוֹ. יָקָר בְּעֵינֵי יְיָ הַמָּוְתָה לַחֲסִידָיו. אָנָּה יְיָ כִּי אֲנִי עַבְדֶּךָ אֲנִי עַבְדְּךָ בֶּן אֲמָתֶךָ פִּתַּחְתָּ לְמוֹסֵרָי. לְךָ אֶזְבַּח זֶבַח תּוֹדָה וּבְשֵׁם יְיָ אֶקְרָא. נְדָרַי לַייָ אֲשַׁלֵּם נֶגְדָה נָּא לְכָל עַמּוֹ. בְּחַצְרוֹת בֵּית יְיָ בְּתוֹכֵכִי יְרוּשָׁלָיִם הַלְלוּיָהּ:

---

but for Your Name....Why should the nations say, 'Where is their God?'" Even though we ourselves may not deserve to be redeemed, we implore God to bring about the redemption for the sake of His Name, for when the Jewish people are visited by strife, God's esteem is significantly diminished among the nations.

Abraham used the same argument when he begged God to spare the city of Sodom:

HASHEM is mindful of us, He will bless; He will bless the Family of Israel, He will bless the Family of Aharon. He will bless God-fearing people both great and small. May Hashem increase you, you and your children. You are blessed by Hashem Who makes heaven and earth. Heaven belongs to Hashem, but He has given earth to men. The dead do not praise God, nor any that sink into silence; but we will bless God from now until eternity. Praise God!

WOULD that Hashem would hear my pleading voice! For He has bent His ear to me, and all my days I cry. Deadly wounds have wrapped me around, mortal pains visit me; pain and grief are upon me. But I call on Hashem's name: "Please, Hashem, rescue my soul." Hashem is kind and just; our God has mercy. Hashem guards fools; though I have fallen low, He will save me. Come back, my soul, to your rest, for Hashem has bestowed good upon you. For You rescued my soul from death, my eye from tears, my foot from slipping. Now I walk before Hashem in the lands of the living. I believed what I said when I was greatly impoverished; I said in my hurry, "Every man is deceitful."

WHAT can I give back to Hashem for all that He has bestowed upon me? I lift up the cup of salvation and call on Hashem's name; now I pay my vows to Hashem before all His people. Hashem is distressed by the death of His pious men. Thank You, Hashem, that I am Your servant, the son of Your handmaiden; You have loosed my bonds. I make a sacrifice of thanks to You and call on Hashem's name. Now I pay my vows to Hashem before all His people, in the courts of Hashem's house in the midst of Jerusalem. Praise God!

Will You actually wipe out the innocent with the guilty? Suppose there are fifty innocent people in the city. Would You still destroy it?... It would be a sacrilege even to ascribe such an act to You — to kill the innocent with the guilty... It would be a sacrilege to ascribe this to You! Shall the whole world's Judge not act justly?

(*Genesis* 18:23–25)

הַלְלוּ אֶת יְיָ כָּל גּוֹיִם שַׁבְּחוּהוּ כָּל הָאֻמִּים. כִּי גָבַר עָלֵינוּ חַסְדּוֹ וֶאֱמֶת יְיָ לְעוֹלָם הַלְלוּיָהּ:

The leader of the Seder says each of the next four lines out loud, and everyone answers him after each time with "Thank Hashem, for He is good for His kindness endures forever."

הוֹדוּ לַייָ כִּי טוֹב כִּי לְעוֹלָם חַסְדּוֹ.

יֹאמַר נָא יִשְׂרָאֵל כִּי לְעוֹלָם חַסְדּוֹ.

יֹאמְרוּ נָא בֵית אַהֲרֹן כִּי לְעוֹלָם חַסְדּוֹ.

יֹאמְרוּ נָא יִרְאֵי יְיָ כִּי לְעוֹלָם חַסְדּוֹ.

מִן הַמֵּצַר קָרָאתִי יָּהּ עָנָנִי בַמֶּרְחָב יָהּ. יְיָ לִי לֹא אִירָא מַה יַּעֲשֶׂה לִי אָדָם. יְיָ לִי בְּעֹזְרָי וַאֲנִי אֶרְאֶה בְשֹׂנְאָי. טוֹב לַחֲסוֹת בַּייָ מִבְּטֹחַ בָּאָדָם. טוֹב לַחֲסוֹת בַּייָ מִבְּטֹחַ בִּנְדִיבִים. כָּל גּוֹיִם סְבָבוּנִי בְּשֵׁם יְיָ כִּי אֲמִילַם. סַבּוּנִי גַם סְבָבוּנִי בְּשֵׁם יְיָ כִּי אֲמִילַם. סַבּוּנִי כִדְבֹרִים דֹּעֲכוּ כְּאֵשׁ קוֹצִים בְּשֵׁם יְיָ כִּי אֲמִילַם. דַּחֹה דְחִיתַנִי לִנְפֹּל וַייָ עֲזָרָנִי. עָזִּי וְזִמְרָת יָהּ וַיְהִי לִי לִישׁוּעָה. קוֹל רִנָּה וִישׁוּעָה בְּאָהֳלֵי צַדִּיקִים יְמִין יְיָ עֹשָׂה חָיִל. יְמִין יְיָ רוֹמֵמָה יְמִין יְיָ עֹשָׂה חָיִל. לֹא אָמוּת כִּי אֶחְיֶה וַאֲסַפֵּר מַעֲשֵׂי יָהּ. יַסֹּר יִסְּרַנִּי יָּהּ וְלַמָּוֶת לֹא נְתָנָנִי. פִּתְחוּ לִי שַׁעֲרֵי צֶדֶק אָבֹא בָם אוֹדֶה יָהּ. זֶה הַשַּׁעַר לַייָ צַדִּיקִים יָבֹאוּ בוֹ.

Moshe, too, used this argument to convince God not to annihilate Israel following the Sin of the Golden Calf. Moshe said:

God, why unleash Your wrath against Your people...? Why

PRAISE Hashem, all nations; laud Him, all peoples! For His kindness to us has been so great, and Hashem's truth is forever. Praise Hashem!

The leader of the Seder says each of the next four lines out loud, and everyone answers him after each time with "Thank Hashem, for He is good for His kindness endures forever."

THANK Hashem, for He is good for His kindness endures forever.

LET Israel now say that His kindness endures forever.

LET the Family of Aharon now say that His kindness endures forever.

LET God-fearing people now say that His kindness endures forever.

FROM the midst of distress I called Hashem; Hashem answered me with liberation. Hashem is mine, I do not fear: what can man do to me? Hashem is here to help me, and I shall see my hateful enemies punishment. Better to take shelter with Hashem than to trust in man; better to take shelter with Hashem than to trust in the great. All nations mill around me — in Hashem's name I will wipe them out. They surround me, milling about — in Hashem's name I will wipe them out. They surround me like bees, guttering like burning thorns — in Hashem's name I will extirpate them. You push me down to fall, but Hashem helps me. Hashem, my strength and praise, became my salvation. The sound of song and salvation is in the tents of the *tzaddikim*: "Hashem's right hand does valiantly! Hashem's right hand is supernal, Hashem's right hand does valiantly!" I will not die, for I live to tell of Hashem's deeds. Hashem sent me much suffering, but did not give me over to death. Open the gates of justice for me. I will enter through them and thank Hashem. This is Hashem's gate, where *tzaddikim* enter.

---

should Egypt be able to say that You took [Israel] out with evil intentions...Withdraw Your display of anger, and refrain from doing evil to Your people.

(*Exodus* 32:11–12)

The next verses are said twice.

אוֹדְךָ כִּי עֲנִיתָנִי וַתְּהִי לִי לִישׁוּעָה. אודך: אֶבֶן מָאֲסוּ הַבּוֹנִים הָיְתָה לְרֹאשׁ פִּנָּה. אבן: מֵאֵת יְיָ הָיְתָה זֹּאת הִיא נִפְלָאת בְּעֵינֵינוּ. מאת: זֶה הַיּוֹם עָשָׂה יְיָ נָגִילָה וְנִשְׂמְחָה בוֹ. זה:

The leader says each of the following two verses out loud and everyone says them over again.

אָנָּא יְיָ הוֹשִׁיעָה נָּא. אָנָּא יְיָ הוֹשִׁיעָה נָּא.

אָנָּא יְיָ הַצְלִיחָה נָא. אָנָּא יְיָ הַצְלִיחָה נָא.

From here on the verses are said twice.

בָּרוּךְ הַבָּא בְּשֵׁם יְיָ בֵּרַכְנוּכֶם מִבֵּית יְיָ. ברוך: אֵל יְיָ וַיָּאֶר לָנוּ אִסְרוּ חַג בַּעֲבֹתִים עַד קַרְנוֹת הַמִּזְבֵּחַ. אל: אֵלִי אַתָּה וְאוֹדֶךָּ אֱלֹהַי אֲרוֹמְמֶךָּ. אלי: הוֹדוּ לַיְיָ כִּי טוֹב כִּי לְעוֹלָם חַסְדּוֹ. הודו:

יְהַלְלוּךָ יְיָ אֱלֹהֵינוּ כָּל מַעֲשֶׂיךָ וַחֲסִידֶיךָ צַדִּיקִים עוֹשֵׂי רְצוֹנֶךָ וְכָל עַמְּךָ בֵּית יִשְׂרָאֵל בְּרִנָּה יוֹדוּ וִיבָרְכוּ וִישַׁבְּחוּ וִיפָאֲרוּ וִירוֹמְמוּ וְיַעֲרִיצוּ וְיַקְדִּישׁוּ וְיַמְלִיכוּ אֶת שִׁמְךָ מַלְכֵּנוּ תָּמִיד. כִּי לְךָ טוֹב לְהוֹדוֹת וּלְשִׁמְךָ נָאֶה לְזַמֵּר כִּי מֵעוֹלָם וְעַד עוֹלָם אַתָּה אֵל:

Notice, however, the incongruous word in the Hebrew rendition of the nations' mockery — the word *na* (please). Because it is so problematic, it is usually left untranslated. However, a literal translation of the verse would read, "*Please* tell us where is Your God." What is going on? Since when do those who mock us speak so politely to us?

Chasam Sofer points out that the word *na* is omitted in a parallel verse in Psalms 79:10. From this omission we see that

The next verses are said twice.

I thank You for having answered me and having been my salvation. I.... The stone despised by the builders is now the corner foundation-block. The.... This came from Hashem; we marvel at it. This.... This is the day that Hashem made, on which we rejoice and attain happiness. This....

The leader says each of the following two verses out loud and everyone says them over again.

PLEASE, Hashem, please save! Please, Hashem, please save!

PLEASE, Hashem, please bring success! Please, Hashem, please bring success!

From here on the verses are said twice.

BLESSED be the one who comes in Hashem's name; we bless you from Hashem's house. Blessed.... God is all-powerful, He enlightens us; bind the sacrifice with ropes until it comes to the horns of the altar. God.... You are my God and I thank you, my God, and I exalt you. You.... Thank Hashem, for He is good, for His kindness endures forever. Thank...

ALL Your works shall proclaim Your praise, Hashem our God, and Your devoted ones, the righteous who do Your will, and all Your people, the House of Israel, render homage with jubilation and bless and laud and extol and exalt, praise and sanctify and glorify Your Name, our King. For it is good to render You homage and it is pleasant to sing to Your Name, for from eternity to eternity You are God.

---

there are two kinds of gentiles — the impolite gentile who does not say "please," and the polite gentile who does say "please." The impolite gentile of verse 79:10 does not expect or desire to hear an answer to his question. He is asking a rhetorical question to mock us and our God. In effect he is saying, "Look how we torture you! If your God exists, why doesn't He come and help you? Where is He? Is He asleep?"

In contrast, the polite gentile of *Hallel* sincerely wants to

הוֹדוּ לַיְיָ כִּי טוֹב כִּי לְעוֹלָם חַסְדּוֹ

הוֹדוּ לֵאלֹהֵי הָאֱלֹהִים כִּי לְעוֹלָם חַסְדּוֹ

הוֹדוּ לַאֲדֹנֵי הָאֲדֹנִים כִּי לְעוֹלָם חַסְדּוֹ

לְעֹשֵׂה נִפְלָאוֹת גְּדֹלוֹת לְבַדּוֹ כִּי לְעוֹלָם חַסְדּוֹ

לְעֹשֵׂה הַשָּׁמַיִם בִּתְבוּנָה כִּי לְעוֹלָם חַסְדּוֹ

לְרוֹקַע הָאָרֶץ עַל הַמָּיִם כִּי לְעוֹלָם חַסְדּוֹ

לְעֹשֵׂה אוֹרִים גְּדֹלִים כִּי לְעוֹלָם חַסְדּוֹ

אֶת הַשֶּׁמֶשׁ לְמֶמְשֶׁלֶת בַּיּוֹם כִּי לְעוֹלָם חַסְדּוֹ

אֶת הַיָּרֵחַ וְכוֹכָבִים לְמֶמְשְׁלוֹת בַּלָּיְלָה כִּי לְעוֹלָם חַסְדּוֹ

לְמַכֵּה מִצְרַיִם בִּבְכוֹרֵיהֶם כִּי לְעוֹלָם חַסְדּוֹ

וַיּוֹצֵא יִשְׂרָאֵל מִתּוֹכָם כִּי לְעוֹלָם חַסְדּוֹ

בְּיָד חֲזָקָה וּבִזְרוֹעַ נְטוּיָה כִּי לְעוֹלָם חַסְדּוֹ

לְגֹזֵר יַם סוּף לִגְזָרִים כִּי לְעוֹלָם חַסְדּוֹ

וְהֶעֱבִיר יִשְׂרָאֵל בְּתוֹכוֹ כִּי לְעוֹלָם חַסְדּוֹ

---

know the truth. However, we will be unable to provide it for him. This verse represents the pre-Messianic period. The gentiles will seek truth and spirituality from us, but we will not be able to supply them with it. Why? Because we ourselves will have ab-

THANK Hashem, for He is good, for His kindness endures forever.

THANK the God of gods, for His kindness endures forever.

THANK the Master of masters, for His kindness endures forever.

WHO alone does great wonders, for His kindness endures forever.

WHO makes the heavens with insight, for His kindness endures forever.

WHO spreads the earth over the water, for His kindness endures forever.

WHO makes the great lights, for His kindness endures forever.

THE sun to reign in the day, for His kindness endures forever.

THE moon and stars to reign at night, for His kindness endures forever.

WHO struck the Egyptians through their firstborn, for His kindness endures forever.

AND took Israel out from among them, for His kindness endures forever.

WITH a strong hand and with an outstretched arm, for His kindness endures forever.

WHO split the Red Sea in pieces, for His kindness endures forever.

AND led Israel through it, for His kindness endures forever.

---

sorbed their culture so thoroughly that our mentality will not differ greatly from theirs. It is in this era that the Messiah will come — speedily and in our day!

וְנִעֵר פַּרְעֹה וְחֵילוֹ בְיַם סוּף כִּי לְעוֹלָם חַסְדּוֹ

לְמוֹלִיךְ עַמּוֹ בַּמִּדְבָּר כִּי לְעוֹלָם חַסְדּוֹ

לְמַכֵּה מְלָכִים גְּדֹלִים כִּי לְעוֹלָם חַסְדּוֹ

וַיַּהֲרֹג מְלָכִים אַדִּירִים כִּי לְעוֹלָם חַסְדּוֹ

לְסִיחוֹן מֶלֶךְ הָאֱמֹרִי כִּי לְעוֹלָם חַסְדּוֹ

וּלְעוֹג מֶלֶךְ הַבָּשָׁן כִּי לְעוֹלָם חַסְדּוֹ

וְנָתַן אַרְצָם לְנַחֲלָה כִּי לְעוֹלָם חַסְדּוֹ

נַחֲלָה לְיִשְׂרָאֵל עַבְדּוֹ כִּי לְעוֹלָם חַסְדּוֹ

שֶׁבְּשִׁפְלֵנוּ זָכַר לָנוּ כִּי לְעוֹלָם חַסְדּוֹ

וַיִּפְרְקֵנוּ מִצָּרֵינוּ כִּי לְעוֹלָם חַסְדּוֹ

נֹתֵן לֶחֶם לְכָל בָּשָׂר כִּי לְעוֹלָם חַסְדּוֹ

הוֹדוּ לְאֵל הַשָּׁמָיִם כִּי לְעוֹלָם חַסְדּוֹ

נִשְׁמַת כָּל חַי תְּבָרֵךְ אֶת שִׁמְךָ יְיָ אֱלֹהֵינוּ וְרוּחַ כָּל בָּשָׂר תְּפָאֵר וּתְרוֹמֵם זִכְרְךָ מַלְכֵּנוּ תָּמִיד מִן הָעוֹלָם וְעַד הָעוֹלָם אַתָּה אֵל וּמִבַּלְעָדֶיךָ אֵין לָנוּ מֶלֶךְ גּוֹאֵל וּמוֹשִׁיעַ פּוֹדֶה וּמַצִּיל וּמְפַרְנֵס וּמְרַחֵם בְּכָל עֵת צָרָה וְצוּקָה אֵין לָנוּ מֶלֶךְ אֶלָּא אָתָּה. אֱלֹהֵי הָרִאשׁוֹנִים וְהָאַחֲרוֹנִים. אֱלוֹהַּ כָּל בְּרִיּוֹת אֲדוֹן כָּל תּוֹלָדוֹת הַמְהֻלָּל בְּרוֹב הַתִּשְׁבָּחוֹת הַמְנַהֵג עוֹלָמוֹ בְּחֶסֶד וּבְרִיּוֹתָיו בְּרַחֲמִים.

AND shook Pharaoh and his army in the Red Sea, for His kindness endures forever.

WHO led His people in the desert, for His kindness endures forever.

WHO struck down great kings, for His kindness endures forever.

AND slew mighty kings, for His kindness endures forever.

SICHON king of the Emorites, for His kindness endures forever.

AND Og king of Bashan, for His kindness endures forever.

AND gave their land as a heritage, for His kindness endures forever.

A heritage for Israel, His servant, for His kindness endures forever.

WHO remembered us when we were abased, for His kindness endures forever.

AND freed us from our oppressors, for His kindness endures forever.

WHO gives bread to all that lives, for His kindness endures forever.

THANK the God of Heaven, for His kindness endures forever.

EVERY living soul blesses Your name, Hashem our God, and the spirit of all that lives glorifies and exalts Your every mention, our King. From eternity to eternity You are the All-Powerful, and besides You we have no King Who delivers, saves, redeems, rescues, and sustains, merciful in every time of distress and trouble. We have no King but you. God of the first and of the last, God of all creatures, Master of all events, lauded with all praise, Who directs His world kindly and His creatures mercifully.

וַיְיָ הִנֵּה לֹא יָנוּם וְלֹא יִישָׁן. הַמְעוֹרֵר יְשֵׁנִים וְהַמֵּקִיץ נִרְדָּמִים הַמֵּשִׂיחַ אִלְּמִים וְהַמַּתִּיר אֲסוּרִים וְהַסּוֹמֵךְ נוֹפְלִים וְהַזּוֹקֵף כְּפוּפִים. לְךָ לְבַדְּךָ אֲנַחְנוּ מוֹדִים. וְאִלּוּ פִינוּ מָלֵא שִׁירָה כַּיָּם וּלְשׁוֹנֵנוּ רִנָּה כַּהֲמוֹן גַּלָּיו וְשִׂפְתוֹתֵינוּ שֶׁבַח כְּמֶרְחֲבֵי רָקִיעַ וְעֵינֵינוּ מְאִירוֹת כַּשֶּׁמֶשׁ וְכַיָּרֵחַ וְיָדֵינוּ פְרוּשׂוֹת כְּנִשְׁרֵי שָׁמָיִם וְרַגְלֵינוּ קַלּוֹת כָּאַיָּלוֹת אֵין אֲנַחְנוּ מַסְפִּיקִים לְהוֹדוֹת לְךָ יְיָ אֱלֹהֵינוּ וֵאלֹהֵי אֲבוֹתֵינוּ וּלְבָרֵךְ אֶת שְׁמֶךָ עַל אַחַת מֵאָלֶף אֶלֶף אַלְפֵי אֲלָפִים וְרִבֵּי רְבָבוֹת פְּעָמִים הַטּוֹבוֹת שֶׁעָשִׂיתָ עִם אֲבוֹתֵינוּ וְעִמָּנוּ.

מִמִּצְרַיִם גְּאַלְתָּנוּ יְיָ אֱלֹהֵינוּ וּמִבֵּית עֲבָדִים פְּדִיתָנוּ. בְּרָעָב זַנְתָּנוּ. וּבְשָׂבָע כִּלְכַּלְתָּנוּ. מֵחֶרֶב הִצַּלְתָּנוּ. וּמִדֶּבֶר מִלַּטְתָּנוּ. וּמֵחֳלָיִם רָעִים וְרַבִּים וְנֶאֱמָנִים דִּלִּיתָנוּ. עַד הֵנָּה עֲזָרוּנוּ רַחֲמֶיךָ. וְלֹא עֲזָבוּנוּ חֲסָדֶיךָ יְיָ אֱלֹהֵינוּ. וְאַל תִּטְּשֵׁנוּ יְיָ אֱלֹהֵינוּ לָנֶצַח. עַל כֵּן אֵבָרִים שֶׁפִּלַּגְתָּ בָּנוּ וְרוּחַ וּנְשָׁמָה שֶׁנָּפַחְתָּ בְּאַפֵּינוּ. וְלָשׁוֹן אֲשֶׁר שַׂמְתָּ בְּפִינוּ. הֵן הֵם יוֹדוּ וִיבָרְכוּ וִישַׁבְּחוּ וִיפָאֲרוּ וִיעָרִיצוּ וְיַקְדִּישׁוּ וְיַמְלִיכוּ אֶת שִׁמְךָ מַלְכֵּנוּ תָּמִיד.

כִּי כָל פֶּה לְךָ יוֹדֶה וְכָל לָשׁוֹן לְךָ תִשָּׁבַע וְכָל בֶּרֶךְ לְךָ תִכְרַע וְכָל קוֹמָה לְפָנֶיךָ תִשְׁתַּחֲוֶה וְכָל הַלְּבָבוֹת יִירָאוּךָ וְכָל קֶרֶב וּכְלָיוֹת יְזַמְּרוּ לִשְׁמֶךָ. כַּדָּבָר שֶׁכָּתוּב כָּל עַצְמוֹתַי תֹּאמַרְנָה יְיָ מִי כָמוֹךָ. מַצִּיל עָנִי מֵחָזָק מִמֶּנּוּ וְעָנִי וְאֶבְיוֹן מִגֹּזְלוֹ. מִי יִדְמֶה לָּךְ וּמִי יִשְׁוֶה לָּךְ וּמִי יַעֲרָךְ לָךְ הָאֵל הַגָּדוֹל הַגִּבּוֹר וְהַנּוֹרָא אֵל עֶלְיוֹן קוֹנֵה שָׁמַיִם וָאָרֶץ. נְהַלֶּלְךָ וּנְשַׁבֵּחֲךָ וּנְפָאֶרְךָ וּנְבָרֵךְ אֶת שֵׁם קָדְשֶׁךָ. כָּאָמוּר, לְדָוִד, בָּרְכִי נַפְשִׁי אֶת יְיָ וְכָל קְרָבַי אֶת שֵׁם קָדְשׁוֹ:

HASHEM neither dozes nor sleeps; He arouses sleepers and awakens slumberers, gives speech to the dumb, releases prisoners, supports the failing and straightens the bent; we acknowledge You alone. If our mouths were as full of song as the sea and our tongues full of melody like the tumult of its waves, our lips as full of praise as the spacious skies, our eyes shining like the sun and moon, our arms outspread like soaring eagles, and our feet as light as gazelles, we could not thank You, Hashem our God and God of our fathers, nor could we bless Your name, for even one part out of the thousand thousand, thousands of thousands and myriad myriads of favors that You have done our fathers and us.

YOU redeemed us from Egypt, Hashem our God, delivering us from the slave house; You have nourished us in time of famine and supported us in time of plenty; You have saved us from the sword, rescued us from famine, and brought us out of dangerous and stubborn sickness. Until now Your mercy has aided us and Your kindness has not left us, and may You never abandon us, Hashem our God, for all eternity. Therefore the limbs that You have set within us, the spirit and soul that You have breathed in our nostrils, and the tongue You have placed in our mouths — all these thank, bless, praise, glorify, and exalt Your name, our King, declaring your awesomeness, holiness, and sovereignty.

FOR every mouth will thank You, every tongue will swear faith in You, every knee will bend to You, every form will bow before you; all hearts will revere You and all man's organs will sing Your name, as it says, "All my bones say, 'Hashem, who is like You?' " [Tehillim 35:10]. Who saves the poor man from those stronger than he, the poor and needy from despoilers — who is like You, who is equal to You, who is comparable to You, the great, mighty, awesome God, God most high Who possesses heaven and earth? We praise You, laud You, glorify You; we bless Your holy name, as it says, "A song of David. My soul, bless Hashem, and all my organs bless His holy name" [Tehillim 103:1].

הָאֵל בְּתַעֲצֻמוֹת עֻזֶּךָ הַגָּדוֹל בִּכְבוֹד שְׁמֶךָ הַגִּבּוֹר לָנֶצַח וְהַנּוֹרָא בְּנוֹרְאוֹתֶיךָ. הַמֶּלֶךְ הַיּוֹשֵׁב עַל כִּסֵּא רָם וְנִשָּׂא:

שׁוֹכֵן עַד מָרוֹם וְקָדוֹשׁ שְׁמוֹ. וְכָתוּב רַנְּנוּ צַדִּיקִים בַּיְיָ לַיְשָׁרִים נָאוָה תְהִלָּה: בְּפִי יְשָׁרִים תִּתְהַלָּל וּבְדִבְרֵי צַדִּיקִים תִּתְבָּרַךְ וּבִלְשׁוֹן חֲסִידִים תִּתְרוֹמָם וּבְקֶרֶב קְדוֹשִׁים תִּתְקַדָּשׁ:

וּבְמַקְהֲלוֹת רִבְבוֹת עַמְּךָ בֵּית יִשְׂרָאֵל בְּרִנָּה יִתְפָּאַר שִׁמְךָ מַלְכֵּנוּ בְּכָל דּוֹר וָדוֹר שֶׁכֵּן חוֹבַת כָּל הַיְצוּרִים לְפָנֶיךָ יְיָ אֱלֹהֵינוּ וֵאלֹהֵי אֲבוֹתֵינוּ לְהוֹדוֹת לְהַלֵּל לְשַׁבֵּחַ לְפָאֵר לְרוֹמֵם לְהַדֵּר לְבָרֵךְ לְעַלֵּה וּלְקַלֵּס עַל כָּל דִּבְרֵי שִׁירוֹת וְתִשְׁבְּחוֹת דָּוִד בֶּן יִשַׁי עַבְדְּךָ מְשִׁיחֶךָ:

יִשְׁתַּבַּח שִׁמְךָ לָעַד מַלְכֵּנוּ, הָאֵל, הַמֶּלֶךְ הַגָּדוֹל, וְהַקָּדוֹשׁ, בַּשָּׁמַיִם וּבָאָרֶץ. כִּי לְךָ נָאֶה יְיָ אֱלֹהֵינוּ וֵאלֹהֵי אֲבוֹתֵינוּ לְעוֹלָם וָעֶד. שִׁיר וּשְׁבָחָה הַלֵּל וְזִמְרָה עֹז וּמֶמְשָׁלָה נֶצַח גְּדֻלָּה וּגְבוּרָה תְּהִלָּה וְתִפְאֶרֶת קְדֻשָּׁה וּמַלְכוּת. בְּרָכוֹת וְהוֹדָאוֹת מֵעַתָּה וְעַד עוֹלָם. בָּרוּךְ אַתָּה יְיָ אֵל מֶלֶךְ גָּדוֹל וּמְהֻלָּל בַּתִּשְׁבָּחוֹת. אֵל הַהוֹדָאוֹת, אֲדוֹן הַנִּפְלָאוֹת, הַבּוֹחֵר בְּשִׁירֵי זִמְרָה, מֶלֶךְ אֵל, חֵי הָעוֹלָמִים:

Everyone drinks the entire fourth cup while reclining on the left side. Have in mind that this is the mitzvah of drinking the last of the Four Cups.

בָּרוּךְ אַתָּה יְיָ אֱלֹהֵינוּ מֶלֶךְ הָעוֹלָם בּוֹרֵא פְּרִי הַגָּפֶן:

GOD all-powerful in respect of Your tremendous strength, great in Your honored name, eternally mighty, revered in Your awesome deeds, the King Who sits on a lofty, exalted throne.

WHO dwells forever: His name is exalted and holy. And it says, "sing, *tzaddikim*, about Hashem; praise becomes the just" [Tehillim 33:1]. You are praised by the mouth of the just, blessed with the words of *tzaddikim*, exalted by the tongue of the pious, and Your holiness is shown among the holy people.

YOUR name, our King, will be glorified with song by the amassed myriads of Your people Israel throughout the generations. For that is the duty of all creatures before You, our God and God of our fathers: to thank, laud, praise, glorify, exalt, extol, bless, raise high and sing praises to You, besides all the words of song and praise said by David son of Yishai, Your anointed servant.

MAY Your name be praised forever, our King, the all-powerful, the great and holy King of heaven and earth. For these belong with You, Hashem our God and God of our fathers: song and praise, laud and hymn, strength and rule, victory, greatness, and might, holiness and kingship, blessings and thanks from now until eternity. Blessed are You, God [Who is God and King, most greatly praised: God [to Whom] all thanks [are due], God of wonders, Who chooses [to be pleased with] melodious songs: King, God, Life of all worlds.

Everyone drinks the entire fourth cup while reclining on the left side. Have in mind that this is the mitzvah of drinking the last of the Four Cups.

BLESSED are You, Hashem our God, King of the world, Who creates the fruit of the vine.

בָּרוּךְ אַתָּה יְיָ אֱלֹהֵינוּ מֶלֶךְ הָעוֹלָם עַל הַגֶּפֶן וְעַל פְּרִי הַגֶּפֶן וְעַל תְּנוּבַת הַשָּׂדֶה וְעַל אֶרֶץ חֶמְדָּה טוֹבָה וּרְחָבָה שֶׁרָצִיתָ וְהִנְחַלְתָּ לַאֲבוֹתֵינוּ לֶאֱכוֹל מִפִּרְיָהּ וְלִשְׂבּוֹעַ מִטּוּבָהּ. רַחֵם (נָא) יְיָ אֱלֹהֵינוּ עַל יִשְׂרָאֵל עַמֶּךָ וְעַל יְרוּשָׁלַיִם עִירֶךָ וְעַל צִיּוֹן מִשְׁכַּן כְּבוֹדֶךָ וְעַל מִזְבְּחֶךָ וְעַל הֵיכָלֶךָ וּבְנֵה יְרוּשָׁלַיִם עִיר הַקֹּדֶשׁ בִּמְהֵרָה בְיָמֵינוּ וְהַעֲלֵנוּ לְתוֹכָהּ וְשַׂמְּחֵנוּ בְּבִנְיָנָהּ וְנֹאכַל מִפִּרְיָהּ וְנִשְׂבַּע מִטּוּבָהּ וּנְבָרֶכְךָ עָלֶיהָ בִּקְדֻשָּׁה וּבְטָהֳרָה. (בשבת וּרְצֵה וְהַחֲלִיצֵנוּ בְּיוֹם הַשַּׁבָּת הַזֶּה). וְשַׂמְּחֵנוּ בְּיוֹם חַג הַמַּצּוֹת הַזֶּה. כִּי אַתָּה יְיָ טוֹב וּמֵטִיב לַכֹּל וְנוֹדֶה לְּךָ עַל הָאָרֶץ וְעַל פְּרִי הַגָּפֶן. בָּרוּךְ אַתָּה יְיָ עַל הָאָרֶץ וְעַל פְּרִי הַגָּפֶן:

נִרְצָה

חֲסַל סִדּוּר פֶּסַח כְּהִלְכָתוֹ. כְּכָל מִשְׁפָּטוֹ וְחֻקָּתוֹ. כַּאֲשֶׁר זָכִינוּ לְסַדֵּר אוֹתוֹ. כֵּן נִזְכֶּה לַעֲשׂוֹתוֹ. זָךְ שׁוֹכֵן מְעוֹנָה. קוֹמֵם קְהַל עֲדַת מִי מָנָה. קָרֵב נַהֵל נִטְעֵי כַנָּה. פְּדוּיִם לְצִיּוֹן בְּרִנָּה:

Three times:

לְשָׁנָה הַבָּאָה בִּירוּשָׁלָיִם:

Outside of Eretz Yisrael where two Seders are made, this song is sung on the first night.

BLESSED are You, Hashem our God, King of the world, for vines and for their fruit, for the produce of the field, and for a desirable land, good and spacious, that You gave our fathers in good will as their heritage, to eat of its fruit and be replete with its goodness. Have mercy, Hashem our God, on Your people Israel, on Your city Jerusalem, on Zion where Your glory dwells, on Your altar and Your sanctuary. Build Your holy city Jerusalem soon, in our days; take us up into it, rejoice us with it. We will eat of its fruit and be satisfied with its goodness, and bless You for it in holiness and purity. (On Shabbos add: May it be Your pleasure to deliver us with the merit of this Shabbos day,) and rejoice us with this day of the Festival of Matzos, for You, Hashem, are good and do good to all; we thank You for the Land and for the fruit of the vine. Blessed are You, Hashem, for the Land and for the fruit of the vine.

NIRTZAH

ENDED is the order of the Pesach Seder according to its laws, to all its right procedure and rules. As we merited to arrange it (the Pesach Seder), so may we merit to perform It (the Pesach offering). God of purity Who dwells on high, restore the assembly of Your innumerable community. Soon lead back the offspring of Your spiritual planting, redeemed, to Zion in joyous song.

Three times:

NEXT year in Jerusalem!

Outside of Eretz Yisrael where two Seders are made, this song is sung on the first night.

וּבְכֵן וַיְהִי בַּחֲצִי הַלַּיְלָה

אָז רֹב נִסִּים הִפְלֵאתָ בַּלַּיְלָה. בְּרֹאשׁ אַשְׁמוּרֶת זֶה הַלַּיְלָה. גֵּר צֶדֶק נִצַּחְתּוֹ כְּנֶחֱלַק לוֹ לַיְלָה. וַיְהִי בַּחֲצִי הַלַּיְלָה

דַּנְתָּ מֶלֶךְ גְּרָר בַּחֲלוֹם הַלַּיְלָה. הִפְחַדְתָּ אֲרַמִּי בְּאֶמֶשׁ לַיְלָה. וַיָּשַׁר יִשְׂרָאֵל לְמַלְאָךְ וַיּוּכַל לוֹ לַיְלָה. וַיְהִי בַּחֲצִי הַלַּיְלָה

זֶרַע בְּכוֹרֵי פַתְרוֹס מָחַצְתָּ בַּחֲצִי הַלַּיְלָה. חֵילָם לֹא מָצְאוּ בְּקוּמָם בַּלַּיְלָה. טִיסַת נְגִיד חֲרֹשֶׁת סִלִּיתָ בְכוֹכְבֵי לַיְלָה. וַיְהִי בַּחֲצִי הַלַּיְלָה

יָעַץ מְחָרֵף לְנוֹפֵף אִוּוּי הוֹבַשְׁתָּ פְגָרָיו בַּלַּיְלָה. כָּרַע בֵּל וּמַצָּבוֹ בְּאִישׁוֹן לַיְלָה. לְאִישׁ חֲמוּדוֹת נִגְלָה רָז חֲזוֹת לַיְלָה. וַיְהִי בַּחֲצִי הַלַּיְלָה

מִשְׁתַּכֵּר בִּכְלֵי קֹדֶשׁ נֶהֱרַג בּוֹ בַּלַּיְלָה. נוֹשַׁע מִבּוֹר אֲרָיוֹת פּוֹתֵר בִּעֲתוּתֵי לַיְלָה. שִׂנְאָה נָטַר אֲגָגִי וְכָתַב סְפָרִים בַּלַּיְלָה. וַיְהִי בַּחֲצִי הַלַּיְלָה

עוֹרַרְתָּ נִצְחֲךָ עָלָיו בְּנֶדֶד שְׁנַת לַיְלָה. פּוּרָה תִדְרוֹךְ לְשׁוֹמֵר מַה מִּלַּיְלָה. צָרַח כַּשּׁוֹמֵר וְשָׂח אָתָא בֹקֶר וְגַם לַיְלָה. וַיְהִי בַּחֲצִי הַלַּיְלָה

קָרֵב יוֹם אֲשֶׁר הוּא לֹא יוֹם וְלֹא לַיְלָה. רָם הוֹדַע כִּי לְךָ יוֹם אַף לְךָ לַיְלָה. שׁוֹמְרִים הַפְקֵד לְעִירְךָ כָּל הַיּוֹם וְכָל הַלַּיְלָה. תָּאִיר כְּאוֹר יוֹם חֶשְׁכַת לַיְלָה. וַיְהִי בַּחֲצִי הַלַּיְלָה

VAYEHI BA-CHATZI HA-LAYLAH

YOU did many wondrous miracles then in the night; As the second watch began in the night; You gave Avraham the victory when You split for him the night; It happened at midnight!

YOU sent the King of Gerar a dream of judgment in the night; You frightened Lavan the Aramean beforehand in the night; And Yisrael struggled with the angel and bested him in the night; It happened at midnight!

YOU struck the Egyptians firstborn in the middle of the night; They were left powerless when they arose in the night; You dispelled Sisera's army with the wheeling stars of night; It happened at midnight!

SANCHERIV shook his fist at Jerusalem; You left him stinking corpses in the night; The idol Bel and its watchmen fell down in darkest night; Secrets were revealed to Daniel in a vision in the night; It happened at midnight!

BELSHATZAR who drank from the Temple vessels was killed the same night; Daniel was saved from the lion's den, who interpreted fears in the night; The Agagite in his festering hate wrote messages in the night. It happened at midnight!

YOU aroused Your eternal faith against him as Achashverosh's sleep fled that night; You will avenge us on Edom who calls "watchman, what of the night?" God shouts like a watchman, saying "Morning comes and night." It happened at midnight!

BRING on the day which is neither day nor night! Most High, make known that Yours are both day and night. Set watchmen for Your city all the day and all the night: Make bright as day the darkness of our night. It happened at midnight!

In countries where two Seders are made, this song is sung the second night:

וּבְכֵן וַאֲמַרְתֶּם זֶבַח פֶּסַח

אֹמֶץ גְּבוּרוֹתֶיךָ הִפְלֵאתָ בַּפֶּסַח: בְּרֹאשׁ כָּל מוֹעֲדוֹת נִשֵּׂאתָ פֶּסַח: גִּלִּיתָ לְאֶזְרָחִי חֲצוֹת לֵיל פֶּסַח: וַאֲמַרְתֶּם זֶבַח פֶּסַח:

דְּלָתָיו דָּפַקְתָּ כְּחוֹם הַיּוֹם בַּפֶּסַח: הִסְעִיד נוֹצְצִים עֻגוֹת מַצּוֹת בַּפֶּסַח: וְאֶל הַבָּקָר רָץ זֵכֶר לְשׁוֹר עֵרֶךְ פֶּסַח: וַאֲמַרְתֶּם זֶבַח פֶּסַח:

זוֹעֲמוּ סְדוֹמִים וְלוֹהֲטוּ בָּאֵשׁ בַּפֶּסַח: חֻלַּץ לוֹט מֵהֶם וּמַצּוֹת אָפָה בְּקֵץ פֶּסַח: טִאטֵאתָ אַדְמַת מוֹף וְנוֹף בְּעָבְרְךָ בַּפֶּסַח: וַאֲמַרְתֶּם זֶבַח פֶּסַח:

יָהּ רֹאשׁ כָּל הוֹן מָחַצְתָּ בְּלֵיל שִׁמּוּר פֶּסַח: כַּבִּיר עַל בֵּן בְּכוֹר פָּסַחְתָּ בְּדַם פֶּסַח: לְבִלְתִּי תֵּת מַשְׁחִית לָבֹא בִּפְתָחַי בַּפֶּסַח: וַאֲמַרְתֶּם זֶבַח פֶּסַח:

מְסֻגֶּרֶת סֻגָּרָה בְּעִתּוֹתֵי פֶּסַח: נִשְׁמְדָה מִדְיָן בִּצְלִיל שְׂעוֹרֵי עֹמֶר פֶּסַח: שׂוֹרְפוּ מִשְׁמַנֵּי פּוּל וְלוּד בִּיקַד יְקוֹד פֶּסַח: וַאֲמַרְתֶּם זֶבַח פֶּסַח:

עוֹד הַיּוֹם בְּנֹב לַעֲמוֹד עַד גָּעָה עוֹנַת פֶּסַח: פַּס יַד כָּתְבָה לְקַעֲקֵעַ צוּל בַּפֶּסַח: צָפֹה הַצָּפִית עָרוֹךְ הַשֻּׁלְחָן בַּפֶּסַח: וַאֲמַרְתֶּם זֶבַח פֶּסַח:

קָהָל כִּנְּסָה הֲדַסָּה צוֹם לְשַׁלֵּשׁ בַּפֶּסַח: רֹאשׁ מִבֵּית רָשָׁע מָחַצְתָּ בְּעֵץ חֲמִשִּׁים בַּפֶּסַח: שְׁתֵּי אֵלֶּה רֶגַע תָּבִיא לְעוּצִית בַּפֶּסַח: תָּעֹז יָדְךָ תָּרוּם יְמִינְךָ כְּלֵיל הִתְקַדֵּשׁ חַג פֶּסַח: וַאֲמַרְתֶּם זֶבַח פֶּסַח:

In countries where two Seders are made, this song is sung the second night:

VA'AMARTEM ZEVACH PESACH

YOU showed the wonder of Your might on Pesach. You placed at the head of all festivals Pesach. You revealed to Avraham the split night of Pesach. You shall say, "A Pesach sacrifice."

YOU knocked at his door in the heat of the day on Pesach; He fed fiery angels matzah cakes on Pesach, And ran to the herd in token of the steer that comes with the Pesach. You shall say, "A Pesach sacrifice."

THE people of Sodom were punished, burned with fire on Pesach. Lot was rescued from them, for he baked matzos on Pesach. You swept clean the cities of Egypt as You passed through on Pesach. You shall say, "A Pesach sacrifice."

HASHEM, You struck down the firstborn on the guarded night of Pesach. Mighty One, You skipped firstborn because of the blood of the Pesach, Not letting the Destroyer enter our doors on Pesach. You shall say, "A Pesach sacrifice."

JERICHO was thrown down at the time of Pesach. Midian was destroyed by Gidon's Omer sacrifice at Pesach. Sancheriv's men were burned in the blazing fire of Pesach. You shall say, "A Pesach sacrifice."

"THIS day at Nov will arise" retribution when comes the time of Pesach. The hand wrote on the wall that Bavel's end comes on Pesach. Belshatzar's watchmen told him to lay his table on Pesach. You shall say, "A Pesach sacrifice."

ESTHER gathered the people to fast three days on Pesach. The heir of Amalek was hung on the gallows on Pesach. Bring death and sudden bereavement to Edom on Pesach! May Your strength and victory be revealed with song like the night that we celebrate Pesach. You shall say, "A Pesach sacrifice."

כִּי לוֹ נָאֶה כִּי לוֹ יָאֶה

אַדִּיר בִּמְלוּכָה בָּחוּר כַּהֲלָכָה. גְּדוּדָיו יֹאמְרוּ לוֹ לְךָ וּלְךָ. לְךָ כִּי לְךָ. לְךָ אַף לְךָ. לְךָ יְיָ הַמַּמְלָכָה. כִּי לוֹ נָאֶה כִּי לוֹ יָאֶה:

דָּגוּל בִּמְלוּכָה הָדוּר כַּהֲלָכָה. וָתִיקָיו יֹאמְרוּ לוֹ לְךָ וּלְךָ. לְךָ כִּי לְךָ. לְךָ אַף לְךָ. לְךָ יְיָ הַמַּמְלָכָה. כִּי לוֹ נָאֶה. כִּי לוֹ יָאֶה:

זַכַּאי בִּמְלוּכָה חָסִין כַּהֲלָכָה. טַפְסְרָיו יֹאמְרוּ לוֹ לְךָ וּלְךָ. לְךָ כִּי לְךָ. לְךָ אַף לְךָ. לְךָ יְיָ הַמַּמְלָכָה. כִּי לוֹ נָאֶה. כִּי לוֹ יָאֶה:

יָחִיד בִּמְלוּכָה כַּבִּיר כַּהֲלָכָה. לִמּוּדָיו יֹאמְרוּ לוֹ לְךָ וּלְךָ. לְךָ כִּי לְךָ. לְךָ אַף לְךָ. לְךָ יְיָ הַמַּמְלָכָה. כִּי לוֹ נָאֶה. כִּי לוֹ יָאֶה:

מוֹשֵׁל בִּמְלוּכָה נוֹרָא כַּהֲלָכָה. סְבִיבָיו יֹאמְרוּ לוֹ לְךָ וּלְךָ. לְךָ כִּי לְךָ. לְךָ אַף לְךָ. לְךָ יְיָ הַמַּמְלָכָה. כִּי לוֹ נָאֶה. כִּי לוֹ יָאֶה:

עָנָיו בִּמְלוּכָה פּוֹדֶה כַּהֲלָכָה. צְבָאָיו יֹאמְרוּ לוֹ לְךָ וּלְךָ. לְךָ כִּי לְךָ. לְךָ אַף לְךָ. לְךָ יְיָ הַמַּמְלָכָה. כִּי לוֹ נָאֶה. כִּי לוֹ יָאֶה:

קָדוֹשׁ בִּמְלוּכָה רַחוּם כַּהֲלָכָה. שִׁנְאַנָּיו יֹאמְרוּ לוֹ לְךָ וּלְךָ. לְךָ כִּי לְךָ. לְךָ אַף לְךָ. לְךָ יְיָ הַמַּמְלָכָה. כִּי לוֹ נָאֶה. כִּי לוֹ יָאֶה:

תַּקִּיף בִּמְלוּכָה תּוֹמֵךְ כַּהֲלָכָה. תְּמִימָיו יֹאמְרוּ לוֹ לְךָ וּלְךָ. לְךָ כִּי לְךָ. לְךָ אַף לְךָ. לְךָ יְיָ הַמַּמְלָכָה. כִּי לוֹ נָאֶה. כִּי לוֹ יָאֶה:

KI LO NA'EH KI LO Y'AEH

MIGHTY in majesty, truly supreme, His companies [of angels] say to Him: To You, again to You; to You, for to You; to You, indeed to You; to You, Hashem, belongs all sovereignty. For to Him it is becoming; for to Him it is fitting.

EXCELLING in majesty, truly resplendent, His faithful [in Jewry] say to Him: To You etc.

PRISTINE in majesty, truly powerful, His [angelic] princes say to Him: To You etc.

UNIQUE in majesty, truly omnipotent, His disciples [in Jewry] say to Him: To You etc.

RULING in majesty, truly held in awe, His surrounding [Heavenly] companions say to Him: To You etc.

HUMBLE in majesty, truly a Redeemer, His righteous ones [in Jewry] say to Him: To You etc.

HOLY in majesty, truly compassionate, His chorus of angels say to Him: To You etc.

FORCEFUL in majesty, truly all-sustaining. His perfect ones say to Him: To You etc.

אַדִּיר הוּא

אַדִּיר הוּא יִבְנֶה בֵיתוֹ בְּקָרוֹב. בִּמְהֵרָה בִּמְהֵרָה בְּיָמֵינוּ בְּקָרוֹב. אֵל בְּנֵה. אֵל בְּנֵה. בְּנֵה בֵיתְךָ בְּקָרוֹב:

בָּחוּר הוּא. גָּדוֹל הוּא. דָּגוּל הוּא. יִבְנֶה בֵיתוֹ בְּקָרוֹב. בִּמְהֵרָה בִּמְהֵרָה בְּיָמֵינוּ בְּקָרוֹב: אֵל בְּנֵה אֵל בְּנֵה. בְּנֵה בֵיתְךָ בְּקָרוֹב:

הָדוּר הוּא. וָתִיק הוּא. זַכַּאי הוּא. חָסִיד הוּא. יִבְנֶה בֵיתוֹ בְּקָרוֹב. בִּמְהֵרָה בִּמְהֵרָה בְּיָמֵינוּ בְּקָרוֹב: אֵל בְּנֵה אֵל בְּנֵה. בְּנֵה בֵיתְךָ בְּקָרוֹב:

טָהוֹר הוּא. יָחִיד הוּא. כַּבִּיר הוּא. לָמוּד הוּא. מֶלֶךְ הוּא. נוֹרָא הוּא. סַגִּיב הוּא. עִזּוּז הוּא. פּוֹדֶה הוּא. צַדִּיק הוּא. יִבְנֶה בֵיתוֹ בְּקָרוֹב. בִּמְהֵרָה בִּמְהֵרָה בְּיָמֵינוּ בְּקָרוֹב: אֵל בְּנֵה אֵל בְּנֵה. בְּנֵה בֵיתְךָ בְּקָרוֹב:

קָדוֹשׁ הוּא. רַחוּם הוּא. שַׁדַּי הוּא. תַּקִּיף הוּא. יִבְנֶה בֵיתוֹ בְּקָרוֹב. בִּמְהֵרָה בִּמְהֵרָה בְּיָמֵינוּ בְּקָרוֹב: אֵל בְּנֵה אֵל בְּנֵה. בְּנֵה בֵיתְךָ בְּקָרוֹב:

אֶחָד מִי יוֹדֵעַ

אֶחָד מִי יוֹדֵעַ. אֶחָד אֲנִי יוֹדֵעַ. אֶחָד אֱלֹהֵינוּ שֶׁבַּשָּׁמַיִם וּבָאָרֶץ:

שְׁנַיִם מִי יוֹדֵעַ. שְׁנַיִם אֲנִי יוֹדֵעַ. שְׁנֵי לוּחוֹת הַבְּרִית. אֶחָד אֱלֹהֵינוּ שֶׁבַּשָּׁמַיִם וּבָאָרֶץ:

שְׁלֹשָׁה מִי יוֹדֵעַ. שְׁלֹשָׁה אֲנִי יוֹדֵעַ. שְׁלֹשָׁה אָבוֹת. שְׁנֵי לוּחוֹת הַבְּרִית. אֶחָד אֱלֹהֵינוּ שֶׁבַּשָּׁמַיִם וּבָאָרֶץ:

ADIR HU

HE is mighty; may He build His house soon, speedily, speedily, in our days, soon. Build, O God: build, O God! Build Your house soon.

HE is victorious; may He build His house soon, speedily, speedily, in our days, soon. Build, O God: build, O God! Build Your house soon. He is great, He is renowned; may he Build His house soon, speedily, speedily, in our days, soon. Build O God, build O God; Build Your house soon.

HE is splendid, He is noble, He is just, He is generous: may He build His house soon, speedily, speedily, in our days, soon. Build, O God: build, O God! Build Your house soon.

HE is pure, He is One, He is above all, He is all-including, He is King, He is full of light, He is exalted, He is stern, He is a redeemer, He is righteous; may he build His house soon, speedily, speedily, in our days, soon. Build, O God; build, O God! Build Your house soon.

HE is holy, He is merciful, He is Shaddai, He is powerful; may He build His house soon, speedily, speedily, in our days, soon. Build O God; build, O God! Build Your house soon.

ECHAD MI YODE'A

WHO knows one? I know One: One is our God Who is in heaven and earth.

WHO knows two? I know two: two tablets of the covenant; One is our God Who is in heaven and earth.

WHO knows three? I know three: three Fathers, two tablets of the covenant; One is our God Who is in heaven and earth.

אַרְבַּע מִי יוֹדֵעַ. אַרְבַּע אֲנִי יוֹדֵעַ. אַרְבַּע אִמָּהוֹת. שְׁלֹשָׁה אָבוֹת. שְׁנֵי לוּחוֹת הַבְּרִית. אֶחָד אֱלֹהֵינוּ שֶׁבַּשָּׁמַיִם וּבָאָרֶץ:

חֲמִשָּׁה מִי יוֹדֵעַ. חֲמִשָּׁה אֲנִי יוֹדֵעַ. חֲמִשָּׁה חוּמְשֵׁי תוֹרָה. אַרְבַּע אִמָּהוֹת. שְׁלֹשָׁה אָבוֹת. שְׁנֵי לוּחוֹת הַבְּרִית. אֶחָד אֱלֹהֵינוּ שֶׁבַּשָּׁמַיִם וּבָאָרֶץ:

שִׁשָּׁה מִי יוֹדֵעַ. שִׁשָּׁה אֲנִי יוֹדֵעַ. שִׁשָּׁה סִדְרֵי מִשְׁנָה. חֲמִשָּׁה חוּמְשֵׁי תוֹרָה. אַרְבַּע אִמָּהוֹת. שְׁלֹשָׁה אָבוֹת. שְׁנֵי לוּחוֹת הַבְּרִית. אֶחָד אֱלֹהֵינוּ שֶׁבַּשָּׁמַיִם וּבָאָרֶץ:

שִׁבְעָה מִי יוֹדֵעַ. שִׁבְעָה אֲנִי יוֹדֵעַ. שִׁבְעָה יְמֵי שַׁבַּתָּא. שִׁשָּׁה סִדְרֵי מִשְׁנָה. חֲמִשָּׁה חוּמְשֵׁי תוֹרָה. אַרְבַּע אִמָּהוֹת. שְׁלֹשָׁה אָבוֹת. שְׁנֵי לוּחוֹת הַבְּרִית. אֶחָד אֱלֹהֵינוּ שֶׁבַּשָּׁמַיִם וּבָאָרֶץ:

שְׁמוֹנָה מִי יוֹדֵעַ. שְׁמוֹנָה אֲנִי יוֹדֵעַ. שְׁמוֹנָה יְמֵי מִילָה. שִׁבְעָה יְמֵי שַׁבַּתָּא. שִׁשָּׁה סִדְרֵי מִשְׁנָה. חֲמִשָּׁה חוּמְשֵׁי תוֹרָה. אַרְבַּע אִמָּהוֹת. שְׁלֹשָׁה אָבוֹת. שְׁנֵי לוּחוֹת הַבְּרִית. אֶחָד אֱלֹהֵינוּ שֶׁבַּשָּׁמַיִם וּבָאָרֶץ:

תִּשְׁעָה מִי יוֹדֵעַ. תִּשְׁעָה אֲנִי יוֹדֵעַ. תִּשְׁעָה יַרְחֵי לֵידָה. שְׁמוֹנָה יְמֵי מִילָה. שִׁבְעָה יְמֵי שַׁבַּתָּא. שִׁשָּׁה סִדְרֵי מִשְׁנָה. חֲמִשָּׁה חוּמְשֵׁי תוֹרָה. אַרְבַּע אִמָּהוֹת. שְׁלֹשָׁה אָבוֹת. שְׁנֵי לוּחוֹת הַבְּרִית. אֶחָד אֱלֹהֵינוּ שֶׁבַּשָּׁמַיִם וּבָאָרֶץ:

עֲשָׂרָה מִי יוֹדֵעַ. עֲשָׂרָה אֲנִי יוֹדֵעַ. עֲשָׂרָה דִּבְּרַיָּא. תִּשְׁעָה יַרְחֵי לֵידָה. שְׁמוֹנָה יְמֵי מִילָה. שִׁבְעָה יְמֵי שַׁבַּתָּא. שִׁשָּׁה סִדְרֵי מִשְׁנָה. חֲמִשָּׁה חוּמְשֵׁי תוֹרָה. אַרְבַּע אִמָּהוֹת. שְׁלֹשָׁה אָבוֹת. שְׁנֵי לוּחוֹת הַבְּרִית. אֶחָד אֱלֹהֵינוּ שֶׁבַּשָּׁמַיִם וּבָאָרֶץ:

אַחַד עָשָׂר מִי יוֹדֵעַ. אַחַד עָשָׂר אֲנִי יוֹדֵעַ. אַחַד עָשָׂר כּוֹכְבַיָּא. עֲשָׂרָה דִּבְּרַיָּא. תִּשְׁעָה יַרְחֵי לֵידָה. שְׁמוֹנָה יְמֵי מִילָה. שִׁבְעָה יְמֵי שַׁבַּתָּא. שִׁשָּׁה סִדְרֵי מִשְׁנָה. חֲמִשָּׁה חוּמְשֵׁי תוֹרָה. אַרְבַּע אִמָּהוֹת. שְׁלֹשָׁה אָבוֹת. שְׁנֵי לוּחוֹת הַבְּרִית. אֶחָד אֱלֹהֵינוּ שֶׁבַּשָּׁמַיִם וּבָאָרֶץ:

WHO knows four? I know four: four Mothers, three Fathers, two tablets of the covenant; One is our God Who is in heaven and earth.

WHO knows five? I know five: five books of the Torah, four Mothers, three Fathers, two tablets of the covenant; One is our God Who is in heaven and earth.

WHO knows six? I know six: six orders of the Mishnah, five books of the Torah, four Mothers, three Fathers, two tablets of the covenant; One is our God Who is in heaven and earth.

WHO knows seven? I know seven: seven days in a week, six orders of the Mishnah, five books of the Torah, four Mothers, three Fathers, two tablets of the covenant: One is our God Who is in heaven and earth.

WHO knows eight? I know eight: eight days until a circumcision, seven days in a week, six orders of the Mishnah, five books of the Torah, four Mothers, three Fathers, two tablets of the covenant: One is our God who is in heaven and earth.

WHO knows nine? I know nine: nine months until a birth, eight days until a circumcision, seven days in a week, six orders of the Mishnah, five books of the Torah, four Mothers, three Fathers, two tablets of the covenant; One is our God Who is in heaven and earth.

WHO knows ten? I know ten: Ten Commandments, nine months until a birth, eight days until a circumcision, seven days in a week, six orders of the Mishnah, five books of the Torah, four Mothers, three Fathers, two tablets of the covenant: One is our God Who is in heaven and earth.

WHO knows eleven? I know eleven: eleven stars, Ten Commandments, nine months until a birth, eight days until a circumcision, seven days in a week, six orders of the Mishnah, five books of the Torah, four Mothers, three Fathers, two tablets of the covenant; One is our God Who is in heaven and earth.

שְׁנֵים עָשָׂר מִי יוֹדֵעַ. שְׁנֵים עָשָׂר אֲנִי יוֹדֵעַ. שְׁנֵים עָשָׂר שִׁבְטַיָּא. אַחַד עָשָׂר כּוֹכְבַיָּא. עֲשָׂרָה דִבְּרַיָּא. תִּשְׁעָה יַרְחֵי לֵידָה. שְׁמוֹנָה יְמֵי מִילָה. שִׁבְעָה יְמֵי שַׁבַּתָּא. שִׁשָּׁה סִדְרֵי מִשְׁנָה. חֲמִשָּׁה חוּמְשֵׁי תוֹרָה. אַרְבַּע אִמָּהוֹת. שְׁלשָׁה אָבוֹת. שְׁנֵי לֻחוֹת הַבְּרִית. אֶחָד אֱלֹהֵינוּ שֶׁבַּשָּׁמַיִם וּבָאָרֶץ:

שְׁלשָׁה עָשָׂר מִי יוֹדֵעַ. שְׁלשָׁה עָשָׂר אֲנִי יוֹדֵעַ. שְׁלשָׁה עָשָׂר מִדַּיָּא. שְׁנֵים עָשָׂר שִׁבְטַיָּא. אַחַד עָשָׂר כּוֹכְבַיָּא. עֲשָׂרָה דִבְּרַיָּא. תִּשְׁעָה יַרְחֵי לֵידָה. שְׁמוֹנָה יְמֵי מִילָה. שִׁבְעָה יְמֵי שַׁבַּתָּא. שִׁשָּׁה סִדְרֵי מִשְׁנָה. חֲמִשָּׁה חוּמְשֵׁי תוֹרָה. אַרְבַּע אִמָּהוֹת. שְׁלשָׁה אָבוֹת. שְׁנֵי לֻחוֹת הַבְּרִית. אֶחָד אֱלֹהֵינוּ שֶׁבַּשָּׁמַיִם וּבָאָרֶץ:

חַד גַּדְיָא

חַד גַּדְיָא. חַד גַּדְיָא. דְּזַבִּין אַבָּא בִּתְרֵי זוּזֵי. חַד גַּדְיָא. חַד גַּדְיָא:

וְאָתָא שׁוּנְרָא. וְאָכְלָה לְגַדְיָא. דְּזַבִּין אַבָּא בִּתְרֵי זוּזֵי. חַד גַּדְיָא. חַד גַּדְיָא:

וְאָתָא כַלְבָּא. וְנָשַׁךְ לְשׁוּנְרָא. דְּאָכְלָה לְגַדְיָא. דְּזַבִּין אַבָּא בִּתְרֵי זוּזֵי. חַד גַּדְיָא חַד גַּדְיָא:

וְאָתָא חוּטְרָא. וְהִכָּה לְכַלְבָּא. דְּנָשַׁךְ לְשׁוּנְרָא. דְּאָכְלָה לְגַדְיָא. דְּזַבִּין אַבָּא בִּתְרֵי זוּזֵי. חַד גַּדְיָא. חַד גַּדְיָא:

וְאָתָא נוּרָא. וְשָׂרַף לְחוּטְרָא. דְּהִכָּה לְכַלְבָּא. דְּנָשַׁךְ לְשׁוּנְרָא. דְּאָכְלָה לְגַדְיָא. דְּזַבִּין אַבָּא בִּתְרֵי זוּזֵי. חַד גַּדְיָא. חַד גַּדְיָא:

וְאָתָא מַיָּא. וְכָבָה לְנוּרָא. דְּשָׂרַף לְחוּטְרָא. דְּהִכָּה לְכַלְבָּא. דְּנָשַׁךְ לְשׁוּנְרָא. דְּאָכְלָה לְגַדְיָא. דְּזַבִּין אַבָּא בִּתְרֵי זוּזֵי. חַד גַּדְיָא. חַד גַּדְיָא:

WHO knows twelve? I know twelve: twelve tribes, eleven stars, Ten Commandments, nine months until a birth, eight days until a circumcision, seven days in a week, six orders of the Mishnah, five books of the Torah, four Mothers, three Fathers. two tablets of the covenant; One is our God Who is in heaven and earth.

WHO knows thirteen? I know thirteen: thirteen Divine Attributes, twelve tribes, eleven stars, Ten Commandments, nine months until birth, eight days until a circumcision, seven days in a week, six orders of the Mishnah, five books of the Torah, four Mothers, three Fathers, two tablets of the covenant; One is our God Who is in heaven and earth.

CHAD GADYA

ONE kid, one kid, that my father bought for two dinars. One kid, one kid.

THEN a cat came and ate the kid my father bought for two dinars. One kid, one kid.

THEN a dog came and bit the cat that ate the kid my father bought or two dinars. One kid, one kid.

THEN a stick came and hit the dog that bit the cat that ate the kid my father bought for two dinars. One kid, one kid.

THEN fire came and burned the stick that hit the dog that bit the cat that ate the kid my father bought for two dinars. One kid, one kid.

THEN water came and put out the fire that burned the stick that hit the dog that bit the cat that ate the kid my father bought for two dinars. One kid, one kid.

וְאָתָא תּוֹרָא. וְשָׁתָה לְמַיָּא. דְּכָבָה לְנוּרָא. דְּשָׂרַף לְחוּטְרָא. דְּהִכָּה לְכַלְבָּא. דְּנָשַׁךְ לְשׁוּנְרָא. דְּאָכְלָה לְגַדְיָא. דְּזַבִּין אַבָּא בִּתְרֵי זוּזֵי. חַד גַּדְיָא. חַד גַּדְיָא:

וְאָתָא הַשּׁוֹחֵט. וְשָׁחַט לְתוֹרָא. דְּשָׁתָה לְמַיָּא. דְּכָבָה לְנוּרָא. דְּשָׂרַף לְחוּטְרָא. דְּהִכָּה לְכַלְבָּא. דְּנָשַׁךְ לְשׁוּנְרָא. דְּאָכְלָה לְגַדְיָא. דְּזַבִּין אַבָּא בִּתְרֵי זוּזֵי. חַד גַּדְיָא. חַד גַּדְיָא:

וְאָתָא מַלְאַךְ הַמָּוֶת. וְשָׁחַט לְשׁוֹחֵט. דְּשָׁחַט לְתוֹרָא. דְּשָׁתָה לְמַיָּא. דְּכָבָה לְנוּרָא. דְּשָׂרַף לְחוּטְרָא. דְּהִכָּה לְכַלְבָּא. דְּנָשַׁךְ לְשׁוּנְרָא. דְּאָכְלָא לְגַדְיָא. דְּזַבִּין אַבָּא בִּתְרֵי זוּזֵי. חַד גַּדְיָא. חַד גַּדְיָא:

וְאָתָא הַקָּדוֹשׁ בָּרוּךְ הוּא. וְשָׁחַט לְמַלְאַךְ הַמָּוֶת. דְּשָׁחַט לְשׁוֹחֵט. דְּשָׁחַט לְתוֹרָא. דְּשָׁתָה לְמַיָּא. דְּכָבָה לְנוּרָא. דְּשָׂרַף לְחוּטְרָא. דְּהִכָּה לְכַלְבָּא. דְּנָשַׁךְ לְשׁוּנְרָא. דְּאָכְלָא לְגַדְיָא. דְּזַבִּין אַבָּא בִּתְרֵי זוּזֵי. חַד גַּדְיָא. חַד גַּדְיָא:

Now is the time for everyone to settle down to learn the halachos of Pesach talking about the Exodus and other miracles that the Holy One, Blessed be He, did for our fathers, until sleep overcomes him. Some people have the custom to read Shir HaShirim out loud — slowly and with the melody.

THEN a bull came and drank the water that put out the fire that burned the stick that hit the dog that bit the cat that ate the kid my father bought for two dinars. One kid, one kid.

THEN the *shochet* came and slaughtered the bull that drank the water that put out the fire that burned the stick that hit the dog that bit the cat that ate the kid my father bought for two dinars. One kid, one kid.

THEN the Angel of Death came and slaughtered the *shochet* who slaughtered the bull that drank the water that put out the fire that burned the stick that hit the dog that bit the cat that ate the kid my father bought for two dinars. One kid, one kid.

THEN the Holy One, Blessed be He, came and slaughtered the Angel of Death that slaughtered the *shochet* who slaughtered the bull that drank the water that put out the fire that burned the stick that hit the dog that bit the cat that ate the kid my father bought for two dinars. One kid, one kid.

Now is the time for everyone to settle down to learn the halachos of Pesach talking about the Exodus and other miracles that the Holy One, Blessed be He, did for our fathers, until sleep overcomes him. Some people have the custom to read Shir HaShirim out loud — slowly and with the melody.